SQUEEZE THE TRIGGER GENTLY

Robert Arthur Balfour
The Right Honourable The Lord Riverdale of Sheffield, Deputy Lieutenant
Born September 1st, 1901

Printed in Great Britain by
Edward Fox & Son Ltd.,
Greenhill Street,
Stratford-upon-Avon,
Warwickshire, CV37 6LB

A CIP catalogue record for this book
is available from the British Library.

ISBN 0-9518055-09

Published by Lord Riverdale
Ropes
Grindleford
Sheffield
S30 1HX.

FOREWORD

The ideas that led to this book started quite accidentally in the autumn of 1987, a talk to Christopher Borthern at the Game Fair resulted in a request from him that I write an article for ''Stalking'', a magazine he was starting in January 1988. That was a challenge which I accepted without any conception of the developments that might follow. In February/March 1988, Christian and I were on holiday for 6 weeks in Martinique. It was my practice on such occasions to take a task of some sort to supplement the vegetation under the influence of sand, sun and sea; this time I intended to write a few articles ahead for ''Stalking''. The result was incredible, I still find it difficult to account for, but I found myself unlocking memories, and enjoying the process. I returned from that holiday with about 50 articles; admittedly some of them might not be applicable to ''Stalking'', but I now had a new task.

When I had read and redictated the bulk of that material in almost unreadable writing, it was only then, when I had a typed version, that I started to regard it as other than an exercise and wondered if perhaps I had the basis of a ''Stalking'' book. A possible title came up in my mind, and so we arrived at Xmas 1989 with more articles published in ''Stalking'', and after recovery from a motor accident, we found ourselves on a world voyage in a ship, and the task this time was to edit the material and try to lick it into shape.

I am grateful to Christopher Borthern, not only for the initial idea, but also for encouragement, and finally for the ready permission to use what had been published in ''Stalking'', now an established and successful monthly magazine. My grateful thanks also are extended to Christian for forbearance during this process and added encouragement and also with the editing.

So at last we have a book. I hope it may give pleasure to others who may share the memories and experiences and some of the rewards, mental, physical and spiritual that have built up as I have tried to ''*Squeeze the Trigger Gently*'' for more than 80 years.

I cannot close this foreword without a tribute to all the splendid people who have shared my exploits, so many of them becoming friends, who have enriched my life for many years, and added breadth and depth to my knowledge and experience.

At last the rifle speaks,
The bullet streaks
At supersonic speed upon its way,
The arbiter of life or death this day.
At best the end as by some lightning stroke,
Too swift and deadly ever to evoke,
An apprehension, fear or any pain,
So, Squeeze the Trigger Gently, or refrain.

INDEX

Early Days ... 1
Were Those the Days? ... 3
First Time Lucky – Hooked for Life ... 5
Sixty Years a Rifle ... 7
Shikar in India ... 9
Tiger! ... 13
Hand Guns and Howdah Pistols ... 15
Man is a Dangerous Animal ... 17
More Farce than Firearms ... 19
Why "Skips"? ... 21
It can all go wrong ... 23
A Trophy by Accident ... 25
Do not Drown Yourself ... 27
Even Bad Weather Can Help ... 29
Recoil is an Enemy ... 31
In Darkest Africa ... 35
Fever of Unknown Origin ... 39
Joining an Exclusive Club ... 41
A Very Odd Shot ... 43
Seamanship in a Forest ... 44
The Problems of "Sighting In" ... 45
Botswana ... 47
Kalahari ... 51
Okavango ... 53
The River Camp in the Okavango ... 55
Lion ... 57
Fear and Danger ... 59
Roe Deer at Last ... 61
A Medal Head ... 63
Golden Orioles ... 65
Hill Sticks ... 67
Australia and New Zealand ... 69
Which Rifle? ... 71
Triumph or Disaster ... 73
My Forests in Scotland ... 77
The Master Buck of Fingland Hill ... 79
Mechanisation ... 83
A Peep into the Future ... 85
Another Angle on Hind Stalking ... 87
Freak Conditions ... 89
Is it a Miracle? ... 91
An Adventure in Norfolk ... 93
Rock to Rifle ... 95
The Wheel-Lock ... 97
The Flintlock ... 99
The Percussion Lock ... 101
Breech Loading and Cartridge ... 103
Chamois ... 105
A Very Beautiful Rifle ... 107
Rifles for the World ... 109
Is there Something Different? ... 111
Inventions and Original Ideas ... 113
Was it a V.C. Rifle? ... 115
Tints and Hips ... 117
A MacNab at 90 ... 119
Went the Day Badly ... 121
Two Days on the Hill without a Rifle ... 123
The "Noo" ... 125
Addenda ... (i)-(vii)

EARLY DAYS

Many thousands of years ago our remote ancestors — some ancient Britons — lived and died by their prowess in hunting with their very primitive weapons. This has left us with atavistic instincts for the chase. This tendency has missed some of us entirely, with some it is dim, with others it is strong, and with a few it becomes an overriding influence throughout a lifetime; I put myself in that category.

The start of a new magazine ''Stalking'' appropriately turns my mind back. We must all start somewhere some time. How then did I start?

My tale might well be prefixed ''Once upon a time, long, long ago''. My first memory must have been when I was about six years old when my father took me out one evening from the Isaac Walton Hotel in Dovedale, across the fields at the back and up the hill with the limestone rocks. Of course in those days there were rabbits everywhere and in profusion. My father waited behind a boulder with his ·22 rifle enjoying the silence, I played with empty cartridges at his feet. Eventually the shot, and I ran out to grapple the rabbit, still kicking and in those days seeming to me as big and strong as a roe deer would be today.

My father had learned his love of shooting as a young man in Canada, going out with a friend in the woods, shooting with rifles such small game as squirrel and woodchuck. He was dedicated to the rifle, a good shot, and I particularly remember as I accompanied him one evening, six rabbits, five of them shot in the eye. His weapon was then a Stevens Rolling Block Under Lever Single Shot Rifle, heavy and clumsy as it then seemed to me and with a telescope mounted in exterior rings with three adjusting screws, rather fragile but effective.

Pleasant summer days with the keepers on an adjacent pheasant rearing field as we stayed on a farm in the Derbyshire countryside gave me more insight. It was not long before I was allowed to have a shot, and a year or two later at school I was shooting regularly on the target range at 25 and 50 yards with a B.S.A. Martini-Henry, and from the start acquitting myself quite well, but the big break through was when my parents bought a property in Sussex, and at the age of 12 I found myself living in the country, with a wide range of new experiences and opportunities before me. Another telling point was my discovery that Jack Hope, a boy a little older than myself, living next door, had a double ·410 gun which he showed to me at our first meeting. By then I had a Marlin Pump Action Repeater, which my father had given me on my 10th birthday. We went forth together on our first expedition. He shot a rabbit running with the ·410, a new marvel to me, and I killed a rabbit at about 60 yards with the rifle, an equal marvel to him. From then on we were inseparable, and always dedicated to the hunt, in a friendship that lasted until he was killed flying over France in the Second World War.

This photograph was taken in 1914 and shows Lord Riverdale (left) as a thirteen-year-old, with his brother Francis who was four years younger. The opportunity of becoming accustomed to the wide variety of weapons in his possession at that age — impossible for a youngster to-day — gave Lord Riverdale the groundings in a fascination for sporting rifles which has remained with him all his life.

My mother, busy with a young family, backed me up in all adventures. My father intensely occupied at the outset of the 1914/18 war did not supply any restraint that might have applied if he had been more at hand. We had about 15 acres with three little paddocks and a stream, we had permission to shoot on an adjoining farm with about 600 acres. Our legitimate quarry was rabbits, pigeon, water hen, an occasional rat and various birds such as jay or magpie, a taboo, of course, on song birds. We might see a fox. I do not remember seeing roe deer or hearing them mentioned, but with growing ambition there were long discussions on ballistics and on shooting methods. We were not to be contained and started roving over a wide area. Times were not normal, all formal shooting was at an end. One old keeper whom we knew, a kindly character, kept a watching brief over an enormous area. My mother wisely laid down a guideline. ''I am not going to have any mess in the house, anything you shoot you prepare yourself outside, and if you bring it in properly prepared it will be cooked'', and indeed as the 1914/18 War developed towards starvation in Britain, any extra was welcome to a large family, so we learned to skin, pluck and dress our quarry.

So to our weapons, Jack had his double ·410 gun, I had my Marlin rifle, I also had the use of my father's Stevens rifle, I bought a ·22 revolver from a pawnbroker in Sheffield for 3/6d. Catapults never left our pockets. I found a bullet mould of suitable size for lead pellets in an old pistol case. We learned the skills of melting and casting lead, but lead was scarce, and much of our practice was done with lead shot from cartridges encased in baked clay. I think we were more effective with catapults than we were with the revolver, but we learned to handle it, and it was a lovely feeling to go abroad with a real revolver hidden on one's person. We went out together whenever we could and learned the delights of early mornings and late evenings. We learned observation of the countryside, the ways of birds and beasts, patience, silence, an ability to move unobtrusively and to stalk. One remembers highlights. I had developed a technique of making a face shield with string and elastic. I would make a shield of the actual herbage in which I was stalking. This was called a ''green as grass''. One day out by myself I spotted a hare feeding out in the middle of a big meadow about 150 yards away. Testing the wind and with my ''green as grass'', I started my stalk with the grass only about 6 inches high. It must have taken at least an hour, moving absolutely flat and only when the hare had its head down feeding, to close in at 50 yards. Then the unbelievable, the hare, for no reason, stopped feeding, sniffed the wind and ambled gently towards me, stopping about 12 yards away, to resume its feed. I was absolutely pinned down, unable to move a muscle, hardly daring to breathe, and in a state of excitement impossible to describe. What could I do? With one hand under the barrel of the rifle half underneath me, I got my eye down, squinting up the side of the barrel, so aligning the rifle as best I could, I pulled the trigger. Before I could raise my head, the hare in a flat out gallop went lickety split and disappeared through the nearest hedge into woodland. I think it is significant that at moments such as that, our instinct was to rush home and find each other. So on this occasion I found Jack, we went out together, followed the line and there was the hare, stone dead just inside the fence, shot through the heart with a solid bullet that had not expanded.

To match this, one day Jack sought me out with the unbelievable. He had shot a pheasant flying with his catapult in a wood a mile away. Appalled by the magnificence of the shot, a crime and not daring to bring it home, he in turn had sought me out. I had the solution, returning to the spot where he had hidden the bird, we plucked it, cleaned it, carefully removed all evidence and buried it, we then cut the bird into its component parts, stowed them in our pockets, and hurried home in a state of euphoria and exultation.

There were quite a few such highlights, but they must be set against days and hours in profusion when nothing happened. On another occasion Jack winged a partridge and it disappeared, until our combined search eventually found it down a rabbit hole. Again I shot a hare with the rifle, running at 100 yards; my first shot a puff of dust just behind it, my second shot broke its back.

Against such highlights must be set many days and many hours roaming over a wide range with nothing happening at all. Imagine the thrill, lying in the herbage as the keeper walked past us on a 'ride' gun in hand. I wonder how much he knew about our activities? But in truth we did so little harm, he probably thought it wiser not to start anything. I do find it strange that we never had an accident, though we did have incidents, but I don't remember any neighbouring landowner or farmer coming to my father with complaints about our depredations.

We were lucky enough to have a den of our own which was a combination of hide out, workshop and gun room. The armoury had extended, I had bought for a few shillings of my pocket money, a double-barrelled 12 bore gun. I had overhauled this with what skills I had, and I think it was safe unless dropped or struck. This extended our range considerably. My father perhaps thinking that this gun was unsafe, then let me use a double-barrelled 12 bore Belgian gun that had been given to him in Belgium. This was short barrelled, designed I think for rabbit shooting and much better than my pawnbroker's gun. I remember my father talking about rabbit shooting in Belgium. ''You should wear very strong boots and strong leggings, they may be good shots, but they will shoot a rabbit right off your toenails''.

Jack and I had many adventures, many other incidents, some of them quite enterprising, but the hunting and the weapons were at the head of the list in our minds and our activities. Older than I, he disappeared into the Royal Naval Air Service, and became what I called ''A man who smashed aeroplanes'', as was quite common in the flying training of those days. I had an illicit flight with him, first time in the air at the age of 16; it may have been canvas, sticks and string, but what a thrill! And then I was in the Royal Flying Corps, due to start flying training, but imagine the outlook of those days at school. In the Army on the Western Front, mud, blood, rats, trenches and all the horrors with an expectation of life of from 3 to 6 months average. Not for me, I managed to get into the Royal Flying Corps. There if, and I think the 'IF' should be in capitals, you survived flying training, and reached the Western Front, the expectation of life might be 3 weeks, but you lived decently, a clean fight in the air, and the end was usually swift.

So this chapter comes to an end, the foundation of an education to stalking, shooting and weapons was firmly laid, and as the serials of those days used to say ''to be continued in our next''.

WERE THOSE THE DAYS?

We now take a quantum leap from the early memories through the years of the 1914/18 War and into the much changed times of the 1920's. What changes in those years! But the object of this recall is rather to show how different the sporting world was in the 1920's as compared with the present day.

I was working in a Sheffield steel works and I had shooting in Sussex, but with an occasional chance to stalk red deer in Scotland. As far as roe deer were concerned in Sussex, usually landowners appeared to take no notice of them, they were regarded as a sort of vermin, left to the keepers. Perhaps once a year at the end of the season, there would be a sort of 'free for all' day, when anybody brought a gun and great sweeps were made across the territory. Any deer encountered would be shot at regardless of age, sex or type with any gun, any cartridge, and alas, all too often, at excessive range. Altogether a beastly business with many woundings. I never took part in such 'battues' but I heard about them.

My occasional opportunity in Scotland was by invitation; I made my first stalk, I shot my first stag, and I got my first rifle; all of which I might well mention again. Stalking was predominantly on private estates by invitation of the owner and staying in the house. There may have been hotels where stalking was possible, I didn't know any. The Forestry Commission was inaugurated with the generally praiseworthy idea of carrying out the replacement planting necessary owing to the heavy felling of timber in the 1914/18 War, but it was not a force and was rarely mentioned.

A typical foray might be to an estate where there were perhaps 6 or 8 guests in the house, 3 or 4 rifles including the owner, and a whole area, sometimes including grouse areas and frequently with some, but not too many, sheep. There would be typically one stalker and usually also a ghillie if there was salmon water, and usually a general factotum on the estate. There would certainly be trout fishing in either river or loch, and the whole area might well provide four separate beats for stalking. Only 2 rifles a day would go out and an extra stalker would be brought in for perhaps a month. Your stalking was often on an every other day basis, the intervening days being occupied by excursions with the ladies, picnics, walks and fishing. The attitude to rifles was very casual. If you had not got a rifle, there would be one that you could borrow and use. It might be old, it might be an odd calibre special to the maker, such as Purdey, Holland, Rigby Henry and so forth; I remember one fellow guest with a much prized Ross ·280 rifle. Ammunition could still be bought for an astonishing range of calibres. There would be rifles based on the American 30/06 military cartridge, the European 7 × 57 mm. cartridge, sometimes a British ·303, which, although it killed a great amount of game around the world, never became one of the really favourite or great game cartridges. The ·222's, ·22/250, ·243, Winchester ·270 and most of the Magnums such as Weatherby lay far in the future for their popularity. Telescopes were almost unknown; if you had such you might be greeted with the attitude, "Have you weak eyes or something"? The rifles you borrowed were assumed to be 'sighted-in' and probably were. If you took your own rifle the same assumption was made. Some but by no means all estates had an iron stag, and you were invited to have a shot, the stalker usually being far more concerned with whether you knew where to put the bullet on the stag than the actual performance of the rifle. Failing this on your insistence it might be, "Take a shot at yon staine in the burrn". Having sorted out with difficulty which 'staine' out of about 50 was intended, there would be no knowledge of the distance, you might be shooting down-hill, the stone relatively small or large. If the stalker said you hit it that was good enough. You might go up a hill road in the morning to a take-off point, after that there was of course no mechanisation. Beasts would be recovered by a pony with no communication between ponyman and stalker after the initial directions, so that a beast killed might entail a wait of well over an hour before the stalker brought the ponyman, and with a long walk out this much inhibited the stalks possible in the day and to kill 2 beasts would be an embarrassment. Leaving a beast out on the hill overnight would spoil the plans for the morrow and a late walk out stretching into the dark could be very unpleasant. Loading the stag on to the pony usually meant the rifle holding the pony's head with a jacket over it and keeping it quiet, but the ponies themselves were good and sagacious on the hill avoiding bogs and dangerous places. It was a lovely life, it gripped my imagination and aroused an enthusiasm that I have never lost. I was even impelled to attempt a description in verse:—

At last the rifle speaks,
The bullet streaks at supersonic speed upon its way.
Arbiter of life and death that day,
Whether swift kill, like sudden lightning shock,
A miss; worse, wounding, no notch on the stock. . .

and so on.

There were, of course, very grand establishments. Imagine the noble earl with many thousands of acres, the castle, large numbers of distinguished, titled and other guests. I am tempted to tell a tale for which I cannot remember the date or origin, but it seems to me to give a picture of the attitude in those days. At such an establishment the noble earl was in the gun room, discussing with Dougal the head stalker, the plans for the coming week, but among the guests there was a young man, Mr. John Smithers, kindly and thoughtfully invited by the earl. He was perhaps in the category then known as a 'poor relation'. Maybe the offspring of some girl in the family who had in the past married 'beneath her'. Smithers much out of his element and wandering by chance, found himself outside the door of the gunroom to overhear the conversation. 4 or 5 beats, rifles and stalkers arranged with no difficulty for the morrow, Lord so and so, colonel so and so, a naval captain and so on, mainly guests who had been there before. A few tentative words about rifles for the following day after and the business almost concluded, Dougal came up with ''er hmm, my Lord, there's this man John Smithers''. ''Oh yes'', said the earl, ''I was forgetting him, he had better make a start''. Dougal, ''We-el he could tek the old Purdey rifle, young Duncan could tak him oot along the Eastern March we-ere he'd no be likely to interfere with the other beats''. The earl, ''That would be splendid Dougal''. A second er-hmm my Lord, and what would I be telling Duncan, ''Wad he show him a beast, wad he try to get him a beast, or wad he just walk him oot''?

FIRST TIME LUCKY — HOOKED FOR LIFE!

The great day arrives when you are to go out for your first foray after the red deer stags. The preliminaries are all behind you and with the stalker, ponyman and pony, you are at the head of the glen. You probably feel more anxiety than anything else, not knowing what is expected of you, feeling that there is a test before you, but also a feeling of elation and excitement. This is soon tempered by a long slog uphill. You may be quite fit, but you don't spend your life doing this and it takes its toll. The stalker may adjust his pace somewhat for your benefit, and give you a chance to catch your breath if he senses distress. With a few words of instruction the ponyman is left behind to make his way to a predetermined spot, while you continue the climb.

It is not a brilliant day but at least you can see, the light is not bad and there is no fog. When well up there is a pause and the stalker goes forward alone to peer cautiously over a rise, nothing ensues and on again. After two such incidents you sense that there is something afoot. Very slowly and carefully the stalker proceeds, favouring the ground and making use of small depressions. A motion and it is hands and knees, but peering over a knoll the stalker makes a sign and you sink down and wait, not knowing why (he is probably waiting for a wayward hind to move on). After a time you walk further and crawl again. Before doing so he has taken the rifle out of its case and loaded it. So far, you have seen no beast but the pattern of the nails in his boots are imprinted on your mind, as your nose has been close to them while crawling. Slowly and carefully, this time flat, only the stalker can see over the heather.

"They're awa!"

"They're awa!" The disappointment is evident and you don't know whether the beasts have seen you, or just departed on their own business.

Tension relaxes, the stalker unloads the rifle and you march on for quite a time with an occasional spy. You have not realized that three hours have passed when the stalker says, "We will take our piece", and in a sheltered spot out of the wind you undo the lunch that you have brought with you. In those days it was unlikely that there would be a thermos flask. If your lunch was in a satchel you would carry that and the stalker would carry your rifle. If thirsty, it would be a drink from the burn. You don't eat much, partly excitement and partly the feeling that you will travel better without too much load on your stomach. You are high, there is a marvellous view, sky and hills and the muted colours with little sign of life. You proceed further, a crest and the stalker settles down with his long telescope for a careful examination of a new stretch of country. At last he speaks "There are two beasts over on the other face across the valley. It will be difficult

to get down''. You realize what he means as the ground on your side of the valley is fairly open and in view of the beasts halfway up the hill beyond. ''Keep close'', he says and using every bit of ground, slowly and carefully you work your way down the hill, occasionally crawling over an open piece until at last, with relief, you are in the valley bottom, out of sight of the beasts and you can tell from his attitude that all is well.

Once again a real stalk, this time with mounting excitement until at last, the ritual loading of the rifle, discard satchel and stick, crawl forward, a final wriggle, and the stalker motions you to come up beside him, at the same time indicating with his hand to keep your head down. Carefully you peer through the tops of the heather, and yes, there are two stags about a hundred and twenty yards away, lying placidly twelve yards apart, more or less broadside; they are at peace and not alerted. The stalker has put the rifle in your hand and you wriggle carefully until you are settled, legs apart, toes in to avoid slipping back, both elbows down and the rifle, with iron sights, your eye close to the bore can cover the beasts without intervening heather. Unasked the stalker puts his telescope case forward under your left hand. You are not breathing too hard as the stalk has been easy, but the intensity of the moment grips you. Very carefully you say ''Which beast?'' The reply comes ''Prefair left, either will do'' and after waiting on a little longer, another whisper, ''W'll a pit'm up?'' You don't really know what he means and you certainly don't know what is going to happen, but it is a question and you do know that you don't shoot them lying down, so a safe reply seems to be ''Aye''. Very cautiously the stalker fishes around and produces a once white handkerchief. This he slowly raises with one arm, pauses a moment, slowly lowers it. Nothing happens. When this has been repeated at the third show, one of the beasts is alerted, turns its head, stares and gets to its feet; it is the left hand beast. You take your sight without delay and squeeze the trigger. Your beast falls, dead with hardly a kick, and the other beast disappears. ''Good'' says the stalker, but you must reload and put your rifle on safe. It is, at this moment of thrills, all too easy to forget your rifle drill and be careless. You walk forward and as you come up to the dead beast, you have a sudden intense feeling of regret, a sorrow that you have taken the life of this lovely animal. It is a good, heavy stag, not old, with a quite large eight-point head but rather lopsided and badly shaped, I have it yet. You watch the gralloch which you have never seen before. The stalker goes to one side to find some water to wash his hands and arms, and a thrill of satisfaction and relief takes over.

The stalker departs briskly over the hill to find the ponyman, and you lie down close to the stag, your rifle by your side, occasionally spying with your fieldglasses, to see if you can see more beasts. It may well be an hour or more before the stalker comes back with the ponyman. You are initiated into loading the stag, your part being to hold the pony's head with a coat over it to keep it calm and quiet while the job is done, and the stag is secured with leather straps. The long march home, mostly down hill, and again a chance to appreciate the beauty and peace of the hills. You sense that you have passed the test, there is a subtle change in the stalker's attitude and you chat a little by the way. Into the larder and again initiation into the final treatment of the beast.

And so to the house, a welcome cup of tea, a good hot bath, a good dram, a quiet evening after dinner, and as you review the day in your mind, tremendous satisfaction. You have been very lucky. Your first day has been not too easy, not too difficult; you have had a straightforward shot at a fair range, without the agony of being further than your confidence approves, with no chance of getting any closer, you have been spared a fruitless day when mist descends; you have been spared a day when two or three stalks all go wrong; you little know all the variations and possibilities. Since then I have known many people go out for the first time. Usually it does not take long, some feel they never want to shoot a beast again, with others — ''it is all very well and I quite enjoyed it, but it is not my thing'' — and a few, like myself on that day, for of course it was I who experienced this, are hooked for life.

SIXTY YEARS A RIFLE

In the 1920's I had had little experience of stalking and big game rifles other than the use of the Military Long Lee Enfield ·303 and one or two borrowed rifles in Scotland. I felt that both status and satisfaction demanded my own rifle. Setting out my requirements, the main objective would be red deer stalking in Scotland, I had not started on roe deer. It must of course be legal in England and Scotland, and I had the background thought that I might take it abroad on business travel if I saw the opportunity for big game hunting overseas, though obviously the big bore rifles for dangerous game were ruled out for Scotland.

After considerable search I found a secondhand Rigby ·275 high velocity at a London gun dealers. I think I was lucky that with so slight an experience I settled on this, and I could not have done better. Based on the old Spanish military cartridge 7 × 57 mm, this had been developed by Rigby in 1912 with 142 grain bullet in place of the 175 military. There was a story from the 1914/18 war that a Rigby had been hit on the head by a German sniper and the pointed bullet had glanced off and been deflected on his skull so that he lived, with a fixed belief that a round nosed bullet would be superior for his game rifles.

It is easy to fill an article with statistics and figures, but you do not shoot deer with either figures or ballistics and they can all be looked up in any reference books and tables, so the one effective figure is 2700 ft. a second...? and an energy of 2200 ft.lbs...? at 100 yards.

Now back to my rifle. From a label on the case it appeared that it had been in Africa, but definitely not used by Karamojo Bell for elephant! It was in almost pristine condition — a 26″ barrel and weighing 7½ lbs...? in a long green canvas case with full equipment including a cranked funnel for the still obligatory ritual of cleaning with boiling water to offset the deadly effects of corrosive primers used in the early days, but wait for it! It even had a telescope. This was a long, thin job by Aldis, magnification 2¼, field of view very small indeed, no bloomed lenses, primitive range adjustment and mounted on the rifle by quick detachable 2 claw feet (similar to the excellent continental 4 foot mounts which were perhaps superior). This mount was quite effective, but there was a tunnel underneath the telescope, surely reflecting the lack of faith in telescopes in those days, so that you could use the open sights with the telescope mounted. This alas meant that the telescope was so high above the bore that your head was floating about above the stock when you used the scope, and a pad to correct this would have been dead wrong for the open sights. Completing this set up with Rigby's patent Peep Sight mounted on the end of the bolt you had the lot. My memory is a cost of £20. How little that sounds today, but it was a lot to me in those days and if one applies the correct multiplier for the value of money it would be expensive on the market today.

The author with his modernised 1920s Rigby ·275.

Playing with this outfit, first on the range and then in the field, I soon found myself completely convinced that the telescope was near useless (though I did shoot one or two beasts with it), and I could shoot better with the iron sights, again, and I am sure my own fault, I never acquired sufficient faith in the Peep Sight. We are told that it is true that the eye will always look through the middle of a hole, but I never acquired sufficient faith and was happier with the 'V' sight. Of course my eyes in those days were quite equal to focussing on the rear sight at 8/9″ 28″? for sight bead and at the same time perfect definition of the scene and the beast at 100 yards or more.

Once established and settled down with this and the standard English factory ammunition, I used this rifle for 40 years, moving also on to roe deer in due course. Alas, I didn't take it abroad because I found that on a business journey the details and bureaucracy involved in moving a rifle from country to country were too difficult.

We come now to the middle sixties; my eyes much older, I am still killing my beasts, I am not having trouble with wounded beasts, but I have to admit that the foresight bead no longer seems to be large enough and is dim, while the rear sight has become distinctly fuzzy. Telescopes are very different now, so do I go back to a telescope? Consult Rigby.

A mount on the side of the receiver, and a modern telescope mounted lower than before, but still not low enough owing to the turnover Mauser safety, but Oh dear! the price, £75 for the job plus the telescope. A long, hard think resulted in my finding a really excellent rifle which with telescope included and fitted that was within £100. I may have more to say about this later, but meanwhile I sadly put the dear old Rigby on one side in retirement. I did not sell it, it had too many happy memories.

Move on another 10 years — 75 — I now had a commodity that had been in short supply all my life, I was retired and I had time. I also had a workshop, and I had skilled hands (both of them as I am ambidextrous). A visit to Rigby gave me a sight of the Rigby ·275 rifles in for a check-up from Balmoral where they were used by the Royal Family. This triggered the thought; ammunition will always be available while the Royal Family are using these rifles, and if they are still acceptable for royalty, I must have another look. So I undertook the overhaul and modification of the old rifle myself; the barrel was shortened by 2″; I altered the safe to enable the telescope to be mounted acceptably low down and I devised and made a mounting bar marrying the modern scope to the original claw mounts on the rifle. Quite a job in all, and all done by hand. Imagine the thrill of the great day, when I took the trusted old rifle out in the field, and again shot my beasts, this time with a modern nilkel 4 × telescope, the reticle a slightly tapered flat topped post with cross wire, a complete success, and more good news! Ammunition now made by Norma could be had with the Nosler bullet in which I had great faith and was using with my own loaded cartridges in other rifles.

A final and rather lovely thought, I gave the rifle to my grandson. He shot his first beast with it, and he and my son use it still. I should guess that if thoroughly bench tested it would still put 5 bullets inside 2″ at 100 yards. What is the final assessment? With experience now of many rifles, many calibres, and many requirements, you can forget the ballistics, you can forget the apparent attractions of high velocity Magnums, in my experience, nothing, but nothing, puts red deer to sleep more effectively than the dear old Rigby.

SHIKAR IN INDIA

It was in 1930 when travel weary after a long day and night in the train with meagre effects, the bedding roll and the Indian bearer without which one never moved in India, I stepped out one morning into the bright sunshine at little more than a wayside halt by a village in northern India, on a vague assignment and little knowing what to expect. What greeted me I count as one of the most delightful memories of a lifetime. There was 'B' who was in the service of the Raj as a policeman, but behind him no less than two elephants. Just imagine it, he had come in to greet me using the occasion to take stores and requirements out to the forest bungalow where he was located.

It was my first experience of travel by elephant. We were on 'Pads', no howdah, the pad being a grass-filled mattress strapped to the elephant, there was a rope to hang on to. The motion was a lurch of considerable range, difficult to describe, and our journey out took about three hours, first on a definite track, then a less definite track, and then no track at all until we came to a primitive bungalow and a couple of tents. A catering for 'shikar' in the midst of a forest block, and far from even a small Indian village.

There is so much in the memory, how I came to be in India, how I came to know 'B', how this had been arranged, what was happening in the Indian Raj with the rising troubles from Mahatma Ghandi and his followers, but none of this is relative to a hunting tale.

'B' whom I only knew quite slightly was an austere man about my own age, slim and fit, difficult to know well, and we lived happily together for three weeks or so. I shall always be grateful to him, not only for the opportunity of hunting in the Indian jungle, but also for his wide knowledge of India, and particularly for a facet of it I should not otherwise have encountered with his career as a policeman.

For the remainder of that day we rested. I absorbed the atmosphere and the set up, and made acquaintance with the small team, a shikari, a skinner, a cook, B's bearer, 2 mahouts and the three elephants loaned by courtesy of a neighbouring Rajah. Next morning after a delicious cool night on a bed which was my bedding roll on a charpoy*, it was luxury after the train, my first sight from my window was of some beautiful little birds in irridescent colours, about the size of finches, flirting and making love in the sunshine. 'B' had been there a few days; there were one or two skins pegged out; panther and tiger were confirmed in the area. A couple of buffalo calves had been purchased and staked out in suitable areas, each with a machan but no kill as yet to these, or one or two evenings spent sitting up over a bleating goat, after a marauding panther. We were in the area known as the 'Terai', which in my mind signifies the area in the north where the vast plains of India begin to breathe gently and heave slightly as they rise to the foothills of the mountains ascending to Nepal and the Himalayas.

There were one or two skins pegged out: panther and tiger were confirmed in the area. . .

By day we might set out on the elephants and do a circuit within the elephants' day marching range, allowing time for rest and feeding. So doing we would traverse a varied terrain, there was 'Sal' jungle (a teak related tree), some denser jungle, some scrubby jungle, clearings, quite a lot of 'tiger' grass 6 feet high. Nullahs, dry river beds at this time of year, numerous jheels surrounded by reeds and containing 'muggers' — the Indian crocodile, (I shot one small specimen). Mounted on the pads on our elephants we would lurch gently through the varied rolling countryside. I was amazed at the dexterity with which the elephant could negotiate any sort of country and the control of the mahout with his ankus. We would patrol depending on the conditions, either in file or preferably 30 to 60 yards apart, and to me this was pure delight, observing the varied jungle in the beautiful weather, and such birds and beasts as we might encounter, and with the delicious feeling that we might put up anything from a tiger to a porcupine. It was easy to imagine such stories as a right and left on peacock and panther.

So to our weapons; I had not got my own Rigby and my shotgun, as I had found it impossible to deal with the regulations covering these in different countries on business travel around the world, but 'B' was well armed. I had the use of his older rifle, a well-worn, sturdy, good English make, double ·500, while he used a

*Charpoy: *Primitive wooden bed frame with cords across.*

Holland ·375 Magnum, both adequate for anything we might encounter, especially when backed up for both of us with a sturdy shotgun, a second weapon carried by an Indian behind us on the pad. I spent some time each day trying to talk to the mahouts, and making friends with the elephants. I wanted to be sure that they would recognise me and be on my side if anything went wrong in the jungle.

With the guns we had the choice of bird shot, heavy slugs and solid ball, in the latter case an old type known as "Manton's retractile ball", Manton of course being the well established gunmakers of Calcutta, of original English origin from the famous Mantons, and the retractile ball was designed to pass without causing damage through the choke of any shotgun. As a rule I had bird shot in one barrel and ball in the other,

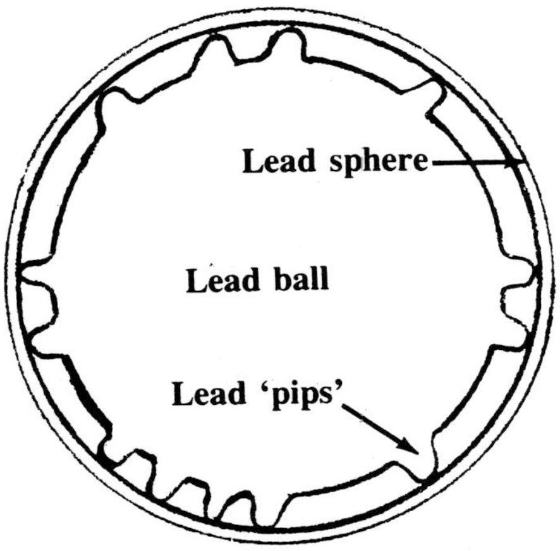

Manton's retractile ball.

Lord Riverdale, Mahouts and three friendly elephants.

'B' usually preferred bird shot and slugs. The motion of the elephant and the mahout a little lower on the elephant's neck in front of one did not make shooting any easier. I have already referred to the Paradox, ideal for some of the jungle hunting in India. I now wonder whether Colonel Forsyth, when he developed this weapon in 1885 had any thought that it might be equally effective against a mob. The idea of course was simple, it was a rugged shotgun, but the barrels were rifled about 4″ at the muzzle giving a stabilizing spin to a special bullet, and Holland and Holland could show some impressive targets at 150 yards. When the patent ran out Westley Richards a competitor, came out with their version, an "Explora" and whereas the Hollands were side-lock, Westley Richards was box-lock, but to compete with the detachable side-lock they developed a delightful detachable box-lock mechanism. So successful was the 12 bore Magnum that some customers asked for 10 bore, and even 8 bore, and these were used in Africa, but of course, they departed from the dual purpose, you would not go out to shoot guinea fowl for your supper with an 8 bore Paradox which indeed was comparable to the heavy bore, slow velocity weapons of an earlier age. Westley Richards, on the other hand, came out with a 16 bore and even a delightful little 20 bore called the "Fawnetta". This, however, was judged far too light for serious use, for example after a wounded leopard. My mentor Sir Samuel Baker, I think wrote about these weapons, "I should not go to Africa again without a Paradox". I have a 12 bore Super Magnum Explora with the detachable side-locks. It is a delightful weapon as the photograph will show. Just the job for the mob.

I can only give a few outstanding incidents to build up an impression of the days. One morning in some rather swampy country I saw a large snake disappearing into the reeds. With an extremely lucky shot from the heavy rifle I broke its neck just behind the head, and as it was still thrashing vigorously a second extremely lucky shot broke its backbone some 6 feet further aft. After more thrashing all movement ceased. I then learned an Indian belief that no python, for such it was, dies until sundown, and to counteract this a charge of shot into its tail proved to them that it was really dead. Have you ever tried to load a 17 ft. 6 inch python on to the back of an elephant? Quite a feat and an incredible weight, but it was done and secured by ropes. This was a large python by Indian standards; it had a bulge well down its middle which proved to be the remains of a fair sized deer, and there were 14 eggs, well developed and almost ready to hatch (how else do you determine a male or female python by casual inspection?). I have the remains of its skin in my study to this day.

Another incident when I shot a duck at the edge of a jheel. It fell some way off, and for sure it would be good eating, but we hesitated to send an Indian in to retrieve it because of the muggers. While we pondered, there suddenly developed a noise like a naval shell overhead; before there was time to think an eagle swooping at incredible speed came into view below the brim of my Bombay bowler (a pith sun helmet). Checking its speed and flattening out with a roar of wind through every strained feather of its wings, one claw descended, grasped the duck and with relatively little wing beat, the eagle ascended and departed with its prize. Just imagine the visual picture of that episode fixed in my mind, so that I can see it with all its vivid detail as if it was yesterday.

Again we put up a pig and it ran across a nullah before us and diagonally up a sandy track on the other side. I took a shot and saw the strike just behind it, but before I could shoot again, thinking to myself, 'I'll get it this time', a sharp call in rebuke from 'B', ''Don't waste cartridges on pig''.

Early one morning, awake and restless, I got up and went out into the jungle. It was just before dawn, and though the light would come very swiftly, I could not yet see in the trees. Suddenly I got a feeling, an instinct only, but I froze in my tracks, and remained totally still, so remaining as the light grew, and there in front of me only 10 paces away was an enormous boar, its glistening white tusks ready for action. We regarded each other with mutual suspicion until it decided, turned and trotted away into the jungle. If I had walked another 10 paces forward who knows what might have happened; it could have been fatal.

One evening it was my turn; we observed a sort of rota for this. I sat up over a pathetically bleating goat in the hope that a panther would come. You probably know the noise that can be made by amorous cats at night. Enlarge this in volume and pitch to that emitted by amorous panthers, too concerned in those affairs that night to bother about my goat they ranged around me in the jungle sometimes as close as 30 or 40 yards away, though I never saw them, giving me no chance of a shot, but yet another unforgettable experience.

We saw chital, sambhur, pig, brown bear, monkeys, and even, quite rare, wild cat and wild dog. I didn't see nilghai, though possible, or black buck, I think more a creature of the plains. Birds innumerable, including the lovely little jungle fowl, a character with some resemblance to an English fighting game cock. It was a gorgeous life, time passing all too swiftly, until one day news came in, ''The tiger has killed''. One of our buffalo calves had been taken. Perhaps this is a good moment of tension in which to pause.

TIGER!

Can you imagine the excitement with which we received the news that a tiger had killed one of our buffalo calves? To my delight it was my turn on our roster. Preparations were made; my command of the language, though increasing and useful, was still not adequate, and I had to depend on B's complete knowledge of the language and communication. At last I set out at a time set, with the two elephants, shikari, gun bearers and mahouts. I walked most of the time and it took us nearly three hours to reach the edge of the jungle where the kill had been made, and this is where a mistake had been made, as I had expected it to be between 2 and 2½ hours not 3. Leaving retinue and the elephants in the open outside the jungle, the shikari led me in. There was no track though they had been in and out to seek out the buffalo calf, build the machan and do a daily inspection. After a distance of no more than 250 yards, we came to a small clearing. The shikari pointed, there was the dead buffalo calf in the middle of the clearing. Beyond on the other side a machan — a little platform built up in a tree. No word was spoken, he pointed to the machan and departed, perhaps glad to be away. I walked slowly across the clearing past the buffalo calf. On my left as I approached the machan there was high grass. Suddenly a sound I had never heard before, it was that made by an angry tiger, and for a moment I could see his face at the edge of the grass 15 yards away. Hungry, he had arrived a little early for his dinner. Without an accurate estimate of the distance I had arrived a little late, and I was standing between him and his intended meal. Remember at this point that my knowledge and experience of the Indian jungle rested on Kipling, which in those days of the Raj and with a member of almost every English family serving in India, was inevitably in the upbringing of any English boy. I had perhaps read one or two books on 'shikar' in India, but nothing had really prepared me for this situation. A thought flashed through my mind like lightning. If I fire I am likely to wound as I have no clear view of the tiger. In that case he would be on me whatever I did next. If the tiger decided on attack I should have one shot with the heavy ·500, but even if mortally hit the tiger would virtually fall on me at that range. If I retreated would it not provoke attack? The upshot was to stand still, rigid, but ready with the double ·500. It was probably the best decision; time passed very slowly, beyond a faint movement of the grass I saw nothing more, but after an estimated 10 minutes, I assumed that the tiger had decided to retreat. I then slowly completed my journey to the tree and up into the machan where I settled myself, hoping that the hungry tiger might return to claim his dinner.

The late afternoon progressed, the noise of the Indian jungle seemed to accelerate as the light declined. There might be an insect crawling down the back of your neck, but you could not move, and then in the dusk a movement, something was coming into the clearing from the left. Gradually it came into my line of vision, it was a brown bear. I decided not to take this with the rifle, still hoping that the tiger might return, so the bear, unconscious of my presence went on its way. The light failing, again a very slight sound of movement, this time behind me. I dared not move or turn, could it be the tiger, slowly and hesitantly approaching? After a minute or two squinting downwards, there below I saw a jungle fowl cock, leisurely picking its way across the clearing for a last bite before going to roost. Time went on, the light declined, it became almost dark. I had no powerful flashlight to lash to the rifle, so even if the tiger came, I should be almost helpless now. Perhaps another hour passed and my nerves had been at full stretch for a very considerable period. Within the rather limited language exchange I had provided to some extent, if I made the call of a chital stag, repeated regularly at about 2 seconds interval, the shikari was to come in with the elephants to take me out. I had not arranged a signal like rifle shot thinking this dangerous. With one shot they would not know whether I had killed or missed or wounded, with two shots it would be similarly uncertain, with three shots it could be that I was in bad trouble. I judged the moment had come and I started making my rehearsed call of a chital stag, but we had not allowed for the fact that there was a tiger in the area, nor that every chital stag was making its alarm call frequently and mine was lost in their volume. So after perhaps another hour, I can only explain it by saying that my overstretched nerves had reached their limit, and I did what was probably a very foolish thing. I descended from my tree and started to walk out of the jungle in the night, relying on a memory sense and a usually pretty good ability in maintaining direction. Perhaps I didn't deserve it, I don't know what would have happened if I had lost myself, but imagine my relief when the trees thinning I found myself almost touching the welcoming trunk of my friendly elephant, and so back to the bungalow in the night, turning over the possibilities in my mind, wondering what else if anything I might have done, hoping that we might perhaps tomorrow still raise that tiger.

Many years later this tale became legendary and was on demand by the grandchildren as a bedtime story under the title, ''How Skips did not get a tiger''.

HAND GUNS AND HOWDAH PISTOLS

I have never been without a hand gun of some sort, I have never been dedicated to them, and they have never turned me on in the same way as a rifle. Thank heaven I never thought of collecting them as they have become increasingly unpopular with the Police over the years and the number of types, forms and patents seems limitless. I have always regarded them as dangerous, too easily turned against oneself in any struggle at close quarters, and long ago J. B. Priestley wrote articles in "Punch" which as well as being witty and ingenious, left one with the conviction that to use them to defend yourself on such occasions as a burglary would be quite disastrous. Enlarging somewhat on Priestley, if your house was broken into, some priceless possessions removed, your wife threatened with rape, malicious damage done, and you yourself beaten up, only then on the verge of consciousness, if you managed to put a bullet into the attacker, would you escape being arraigned yourself for manslaughter or murder? Often the law is aligned in favour of the intruder so that even with a scatter gun, it is better in words from an old comic turn featuring a pawnbroker, who exhorts you: "Shoot him in the trousers, the coat and vest are mine". A brief experiment with hand guns will also convince you that any ideas you may have picked up from the telly where the felons are mown down at incredible range without fail and apparently without any need to reload the weapon, are just not true. I also ignore the cult in America to go hunting with them, apparently for anything up to an Alaskan grizzly bear, but they have their uses, they are interesting to handle, they can give a lot of pleasure in practice at a target, or even better perhaps on a well arranged assault course.

Considering only the basic forms, there is the revolver, the automatic, small and large calibres, short and long barrels. I have always preferred the automatic, the revolver seems to have so many unconnected bits and pieces in the open. Early forms look as if they would bust open in the middle when fired, and to me it always seemed bad engineering to have the line of recoil so far above the hand grip. Larger calibres jerk your arm up, not conducive to accurate shooting with repeating shots from your six-shooter. The automatic on the other hand is neater, I like the easy loading of a clip, the possibility of a reserve clip of cartridges, the safety unless the weapon is correctly and firmly gripped, the neat accessible thumb safety, the quick insertion of a cartridge by one motion of the slide. A marked reduction in recoil, and the recoil itself more nearly aligned with the resistance of hand and arm, the longer sighting plane. I had a ·45 Colt automatic, U.S. Naval pattern with a 4" barrel in the Second World War and found this a splendid weapon with no argument but that it was a real man stopper. I had a lot of fun with this, as in my 'dirty tricks' department, I could lead on Flying Officers who fancied themselves somewhat, until I had worked them into the position where I could say: "Cor! I could take you on left-handed". Only then, too late, did they discover that I was ambidextrous and could score just as well with either hand. Long barrels make for accuracy, short barrels for neatness. I even have my own idea which might be an invention. Why not redesign the revolver with the barrel firing at the bottom instead of the top of the cylinder? I have never worked this up to the point of constructing a weapon, so it remains a possibility in the category of "Useless inventions".

Leaving all this behind us let us now turn to a very special department, the "Howdah" pistol. This has always attracted me intensely as it was allied to the high powered rifle. I have never seen any useful purpose in going stalking with a hand gun (additional to the rifle). Even in Africa I would rather have a stout hunting knife of adequate length against the odd chance that one might tangle with a leopard, but the Howdah pistol is quite different. This is the scenario:—

Back in the 1870's as guest of an Indian Rajah you are invited to take part in a great tiger hunt. Alas, one of your neighbours on his elephant has wounded a tiger. The beast, maddened and intent on mayhem is trying to climb up the side of your elephant. Bad luck for the mahout at a lower level, sitting on the elephant's neck with an unprotected leg each side. You are not on a pad but in a Howdah with a gun bearer. If you work it out carefully, you suddenly realize that your high powered rifle is useless. What to do? If properly equipped, you pass the rifle swiftly to the bearer, pick up your Howdah pistol from its holder at hand on the inside of the Howdah, lean over to right or left as required, place the muzzle of the Howdah pistol neatly behind the right or the left ear of the tiger as the case may be, and so bring the episode to a successful conclusion with all reasonable dispatch. Interesting to say the least, exciting without a doubt, hardly in the category of "an enjoyable time was had by all" (particularly the poor old mahout), but what is your elephant doing meanwhile? It might be departing to pastures new at its maximum rate of revolutions, it might be imitating a Victorian lady trying to climb on a chair with a mouse up her voluminous skirts, or if experienced and staunch, executing a ballet intended to shake off the tiger while saying to itself. "If only I could get this damn thing on the ground, I could either stamp on it or kneel on it". All in all and even with a Howdah pistol, the cool, calm character, well practised with a hand gun, is required, and it is no bad thing if he is also ambidextrous.

What is the form or forms of the Howdah pistol? It could be an old heavy calibre revolver, say ·455, the old ·476, I have even encountered a six shot ·577, but there were also specialized weapons such as a beautiful double barrel 20 bore with pistol grip, barrels about 10" long, of high quality and beautifully engraved (the tiger will not notice this). It might occur to you at this point, that this lovely weapon is a refined first cousin of a shot gun with sawn off barrels favoured by those intent on bank robbery or wages snatchery, but there is one weapon which I think beats them all, the Lancaster Patent 4 barrel pistol. The beautiful thing about this is that you simply pick it up, press the trigger firmly, and for quite a long travel, 4 times in succession, and you have four absolutely certain shots. Calibre? — I think a ·476 for this; the barrels, Lancaster smooth oval bore, increasing velocity and reducing recoil as against close rifling in that the bullet rarely requires any spin at such short range. Come to think of it, what better weapon could you have at your hand at night in India if dacoits are prevalent? Am I talking through the back of my neck? No, I have one of these weapons (see photograph), I think it is quite beautiful, a favourite and treasured possession.

A Lancaster patent 4 barrel Howdah pistol ·476, circa 1880.

MAN IS A DANGEROUS ANIMAL

There was, and is another side of life in India, call it the phenomenon of a dangerous mob. Many many times in the history of India this has surfaced, the best known and well documented being the Mutiny of 1856, with its reprisals, perhaps the most widespread and bloody. There were family memories on this as Christian's grandfather as a boy, 8 years old, was smuggled out of the siege of Meerut by a faithful amah, and came home in a sailing ship round the Cape of Good Hope in the care of the captain. When I was young almost every family one knew had some member serving in India. England and Scotland were full of men and women retired after a lifetime in India, and everywhere you found children sent home for health or education in the care of grandparents, an aunt or a sister. All right minded children were brought up on Kipling, and an older generation read Blackwood's Magazine, most of its articles relating to India.

I spent a year in India about 1930 going about my business and covering the country from Colombo in what is now Sri Lanka to the Khyber Pass on the North West Frontier, and from Bombay to Calcutta, not forgetting an excursion into Assam and another almost up to the Chinese border in Burma.

Nobody at that time I think admitted the possibility of the end of the British Raj, but under the influence of Ghandi a mounting pressure was building up. Ghandi did not himself intend to ferment violence, and believed in peaceful pressure for change, but as usually happens, not all his disciples were under control and violence was increasing.

This is far from a treatise on India, but some survey is necessary to build a mental background, of a life long since gone, before I can tell my tale. A mob in full frenzy is possibly the most dangerous thing on earth, Hydraheaded and composed of great numbers of human beings, capable of being fermented, organised and directed, there can come a moment when it is no longer human, it is a mass of malevolence, unpredictable, uncontrollable and evil. Like a prison, it has its own smell, it is bent on death, and may only be checked or broken by death. As I went about my business I had seen disturbances, an attack on a train and other incidents. Abnormal gatherings of people could be encountered anywhere, rumours were rife, but I had no thought that I might be involved.

From Madras I made my way up-country to the Kolar Goldfields in Mysore, a native state. My visit had been advised, I was received and housed in a guest bungalow, soon to present myself to the General Manager. ''You have come here at a bad time'' he said, ''and may not have heard as it was only last week that there was mob violence, some bungalows were sacked, men, women and children lost their lives. All workers are on strike, but I feel that most of this is the work of trained agitators from outside''. I came to understand that a fine character, much involved with his people, was trying to persuade himself that they were not to blame; deeply saddened, he hoped that it was all due to outside influence. I must say that I found nothing later that would prove him wrong. He continued: ''There appears to have been a reaction after this violence, things are now calm, but no doubt agitators are hard at work behind the scenes, you never know what may develop. Now to your visit, we have had some drilling trouble reported, particularly by the End Mine; the rock is hard in that region, and they may have run into a bad patch. We shall be very grateful if you can help. You can have free access and all facilities to investigate. Meanwhile I hope you are comfortable in the bungalow. You have your bearer of course, come and dine with me tonight about 8.00, it's only a short walk''. This was all pretty disturbing, but what a nice reception by a man I liked at once and came to admire as he struggled with his personal grief over the loss of life.

A pleasant evening ensued, trying hard not to talk about the troubles, and as he said Goodnight, ''I have been thinking what is the best thing you can do. Take my car in the morning and drive yourself to the End Mine, it is about 25 miles out, on that road you cannot get lost, the Manager will expect you and I hope you have good luck''.

So at 8.00 a.m. before the heat of the day had struck up, I was on my way in the General Manager's very nice six cylinder Buick Tourer, my bearer left behind at the bungalow, I was on my own. A beautiful morning, a lovely run and the prospect of an interesting day before me. Then there were people, then there were more people, and they were converging on the road. It was soon obvious that they were all going one way and that was my way, I was slowed down and gradually reduced to a walking pace: I was thinking furiously, I cannot stop, I cannot turn, I cannot go back. The road was closed up ahead before and behind. This was a mob but it was still a collection of people rather than an uncontrollable instrument. They have no doubt been directed to assemble at some time and place, where could it be? I had travelled about half the distance, the objective must be the mine to which I was bound, out on its own at the end of the road. Now I must proceed carefully, no horn, no pressure, not even an aggressive engine burst; above all look as if this was normal, as if I was just one of the crowd, accompanying them and enjoying myself, a cheery wave if a group stopped to let me pass, and the occasional greeting of a man alongside in my halting Hindustani. Was I frightened? Yes, definitely, but not so much as when I thought about it afterwards. Of course I knew that around me were included people who had murdered the week before. I was in the General Manager's motor which many must know. Less danger perhaps from those close enough to see that I was a stranger, and not the known Mine Manager. More menace perhaps from those further away who knew the car but could not recognize the occupant. What was the reaction of the normal men in the crowd to the General Manager, was it good or bad? Probably good enough I thought, but it only needed one 'agent provocateur' seeing a chance with a white man on his own to score a goal and whip up the frenzy necessary to overrun the mine to which they were bound. It only needed one unutterably bad man who might pick up a stone, give a yell and start an attack that would have had but one end, messy and nasty. If it started could I put my foot down regardless of casualties and hope that the power of the car might get me through? No, no hope that way. One stick or one stone could disable me and the mass of people was too great. It didn't occur to me at that time but if the worst had happened the resultant fury might have escalated the whole trouble and sealed the fate of much of the mine management. So, ran my thoughts, and did I drive carefully! It went on so long, perhaps for 45 minutes. Was the press a little thinner? Yes, imperceptibly I had worked my way towards the front. I was improving my speed slightly, I was nearly clear, finally I was clear. Faster now I urged the Buick, and the remaining few miles were passed at speed. I pulled up at the mine office, little more than a large bungalow, the mine buildings behind, and a Maidan, a large, open, grassy space in front. I alerted the Mine Manager. ''How many he asked''? Difficult to estimate but I thought perhaps 2,000 men. ''I don't know how you got through'', he said, but there was no time for discussion, telephone quick. He was able to get through to Headquarters, indicate the scale and prospects and request assistance, before the line was cut. Had I not reached them the line would have been cut before they knew what was happening or what threatened.

''BESEIGED BY THE MOB''

Mysore, as I have said, was a native state, and this meant that military intervention had to be requested from and provided by the Rajah. A force large enough to deal with such a situation might have a long way to come from its headquarters. We could expect no quick relief from such a force. Meanwhile the 8 or 10 white men did a little rather futile barricading and assembled weapons. There was not much, something like one rifle, 3 scatter guns, and 4 or 5 revolvers, being carried after last week's mayhem, insufficient cartridges, rather a feeble and pathetic defence.

By 10.30 the mob had arrived, surrounded the area and mustered its principal core on the Maidan. The Mine Manager, another courageous and decisive man, guessed the type of demand and marched out, perhaps 10 yards, with a clerk, a table and pay books, and asked for four representatives to come forward from the mob, massed about 40 yards away. After an obvious argument in the crowd, most of them saying ''not me!'' 4 men eventually came forward. It seemed that the plot was for the men on strike to demand their 'week in hand', pay to which they were, of course, in no way entitled, but the agitators working on this had no doubt guided the idea and spread the word, ''If you don't get it, go in and take it'', but far more men were involved than those actually concerned with this mine. An attractive idea to the striker, if he could get some money, he could return to his village in triumph with money in his pocket and await events. I think this was the most dangerous moment, there was a lot of movement in the crowd as the Manager came back and the 4 men went back into the mob with the refusal. We could only wait, but without being aggressive, we passed our few pathetic weapons around to try and give the impression that we were better armed against attack. That was all that stood between us and the mob if they were now to be whipped up into the frenzy of the previous week, which could only end in another incident for the history, nasty and messy.

Time was passing, perhaps the heat of the midday had helped, and the movement in the mob seemed to have settled somewhat into a sun-soaked indecision. At no point could we identify agitators if indeed they were at work from behind. With less stress for the moment, it was then that my mind wanting something useful to do, started off on a definite track. I thought of incidents like General Dwyer at Amritza, past and to come. He was backed by disciplined armed troops, and he ordered them to fire into the mob and continue until it broke and fled. Disgraced of course and his career in ruins under the influence of politicians far away. Was his decision with the horrendous casualties correct, did it serve as an example, and did it in fact save lives by preventing far more and far more widespread violence? Nobody will ever know, but we were about 10 men, virtually unarmed with no disciplined force. My mind turned to weapons and I pondered long and hard before I came up with a solution. It ran like this: Give me a Paradox, or an Explora, give me plenty of cartridges; both the bullet and heavy shot; give me a stout man at my right hand to speed the loading of those cartridges. The greater accuracy of such a weapon would give a chance to pick off any leaders up to about 125 yards, but below 75 yards, the heavy shot would come into play aimed at belly button level which would make most effective use of the pattern vertically and horizontally. About 15 aimed shots a minute might be possible, your hand would have to be wrapped against the heated barrels of the gun, but in a couple of minutes you might put 100 men out of action, and with luck, the mob would break and run. (I have tried a dummy run test with an Explora achieving 12 shots a minute). If under pressure from behind they closed in to 20 yards, it would not matter which cartridge, every shot would be a kill, possibly two. I think the odds would be on the defence and it would not reach the messy and nasty, but back to our situation. At about 4.30 p.m. a splendid force of native cavalry arrived, armed with lances, tulwars and carbines. About 100 strong, they were hot, tired and thirsty, both horse and man as they had travelled at speed for 40 miles. Were we glad to see them! As soon as they deployed in front of the mob, it was all over, and the crowd just melted away as we went into the late afternoon and the swift darkness fell.

I stayed the night at the mine, feeling one of the team as we all relaxed after the tension and stress of that day. A very welcome shower, a quiet drink, speculating whether the agitators had failed, whether they had drawn back, whether they had really tried, or whether there was a feeling of revulsion in the crowd after the murders of the previous week.

I eventually returned to headquarters, this time in convoy, the Manager's car undamaged, two days later my business completed satisfactorily, I returned to Madras, enriched by an experience etched deeply into the memory and never to be forgotten. I had also built up a considerable admiration for the white men, quietly doing their jobs often in lonely outposts all over India, armed only by tradition, fortitude and courage.

MORE FARCE THAN FIREARMS

You might think that the traumatic experience at the Kolar Gold Fields was enough contact with the mobs in India, but no, there was more to come. Back in Madras going about my business by day, I encountered small, sporadic assemblies and had little difficulty in avoiding them. I had a friend, one Dick, working with an oil company. He was a bachelor and living in a chummery about 8 miles down the coast south of Madras. There I was a guest by invitation while I was in the area. Joining up one day in the late afternoon as arranged, to drive out of Madras to our base, Dick had a delightful little Triumph car, an open 2 seater about 10 horse power, I remember the emblem at the front on the top of the radiator was a globe, well executed and shining.

We set out and came to the front, turning right past an old fort, on our left there was nothing but a fairly wide beach and the sea. Oh no, not again! Before us between the old fort and the sea was an enormous mob, there might well have been 5 or 6 thousand people. Dick was not surprised, a 'salt making' demonstration had been staged at that spot more than once before. With deliberate publicity the leaders would light fires, boil sea water, symbolically make a little salt and address the crowd. The demonstration was a protest against authority and the salt tax. I cannot tell you much about the salt tax and its origin, it was probably a silly little bit of bureaucracy picked upon by the Ghandi disciples to make an effective protest and the maximum possible demonstration. It was now broadcast fairly widely throughout India. As long as it was peaceful the authorities did not usually oppose it in a heavy handed way, which would have resulted in violence. Compared with my other experience as we were gradually hemmed in and came to a halt in an embrasure in the old fort, the atmosphere was quite relaxed, and most people had simply come out as spectators to see the fun, rather than to join in with serious intent. Along came a smart native Police Sergeant with a squad of six native constables, armed with lathis. Seeing the sahibs immobilized in their car he saw a chance to make an impression. He came and spoke to us asking where we had come from, and where we were bound, and finding that we were in no distress and quite prepared to wait until the roadway cleared, he determined to assist us. He paraded his squad of men in front of the car, brought them to attention and gave them this magnificent order. ''Squad prepare to surround mob by numbers''. ''About turn, quick march''. Off they went along the road, clearing a path as they did so, the lathis a threat without violence and motioning us to follow. We did so at walking pace, and so in the protective shadow of the Raj, we cleared the mob and went upon our way. How charming, how different an atmosphere of farce and frolic; no frenzy and no firearms.

WHY "SKIPS"?

Some of those who may have read previous chapters quite possibly wondered casually the significance of "Skips", and then sharing memories of adventures, weapons and travels put it out of their minds, and those to whom this is all new may have the same thought. It certainly has nothing to do with 'Stalking', indeed its origin can be said to have developed from one of my other lives. It so happens that I have done considerable cruising and voyaging in yachts, that I have designed myself and of my own type, and sailed something over 100,000 miles as far as New Zealand and around the Pacific Islands — "half this our world". My son Mark as a young man did quite a lot of sailing with me, from this developed a habit of calling me "Skipper". In due course he married, and in due time there were three grandchildren growing up. It was they who picked up "Skipper" from their father and it became "Skips".

We rather encouraged this as "Skips" and "Christian" were a quite convenient differentiation for their other Grandma and Grandpa. "Skips" became proprietary with the young and I valued this. I remember No. 1 granddaughter "Nancy" explaining to her friends "*My* "Skips" has a nobbly nose, no-one in the whole world has a more nobbly nose than my "Skips". This was rewarded by a verse:—

The nose you see is not the one that Nature did intend,
A brutal game of rugby squashed it flat with nobbly end.

I have had other nicknames, and I was told that at my christening, my mother was determined to enthrone "Edmund". I think this derived from a cousin who may have been much admired when she was 17. My father, however, marched firmly to the font and announced "Robert Arthur". My mother staged a slight comeback. "He will be known in the family as Robin". With the family name 'Balfour' I was known as 'Bally' all through my school career, only in my industrial life was I 'Meister Robert', elevated to the 'Mr.' as I progressed in seniority and rank. In the 1939/45 war I was invariably "Balf" while in the Navy. The Black Brothers in Botswana later applied "Buffalo", I cannot remember any special variation in India or Australia, or elsewhere around the world, but back to "Skips", I have had 7 labradors extending over about 50 years. All these had short, single syllable names such as "Jet" or "Lark", easy to apply from a whisper to a shout; I cannot see myself marching across a grouse moor calling out "Ermyntrude where art thou?", and it was from this base that I encouraged the use of "Skips" when stalking. I have never used a title unless it was necessary, and a stalker wishing to draw my attention saying perhaps "Lord. . .er. . .Riverdale, will you please keep your bottom down", was far better produced by "Keep flat Skips".

So the word spread from one life to another, and gradually became common parlance, surely better than having no nickname, and not a bad one.

—::—

In America things are apt to be very different, and it is said to be a mistake to assume that we speak the same language. In 1918 on my first trip to America, I was introduced to the habit of Christian names. There is indeed a saying: "You have got to know a man awfully well in America before you know his surname", and so to my astonishment I was even addressed and introduced as 'Barb', i.e. 'Bob'. Once in circumstances that really made my flesh creep "Barb meet my son Hank, I guess you two boys will just love one another". I am sure that his thoughts were absolutely pure, but not surprisingly I took an instant dislike to both Hank Sr. and Hank Jr. In later years there was a question of titles, alien to the American scene, and much misunderstood. Happily they tend to use the words 'Lord, Earl, Duke and King' as normal Christian names (forenames) to them. I now let it be assumed, and indeed encourage this to save a good deal of difficulty and misunderstanding. In this idiom I am introduced as "Mr. Lord Riverdale".

IT CAN ALL GO WRONG

When I read fishing stories I often find myself in slight disbelief. However well written and enjoyable they may be, why? Because nearly every time incredibly wily fish are inevitably brought to the net in the end by the wonderful skill, artistry and knowledge of the man with the rod. Sure, a good, skilled fisherman will catch more than the unskilled but equally, surely there are many many days when the fish will just not take at all. No skill can make a fish that is not feeding take some artificial fly on a hook. Many a blank day have I had myself, the entry in the diary might be: 'Beat so and so, weather excellent, fish not taking, caught nothing'! But this does not make for an attractive tale in a magazine. Happily it is a wellknown characteristic to remember the good and forget the bad, to talk about the winners but not the losers. You may well wonder what I am leading up to. Is there not a risk of the same thing in stalking? A tendency to talk about the skilled stalker and the good shot bringing home the beasts with a regularity beyond reason and beyond experience. If it were like this it might well become boring, and lose its zest. There are days when the stalker greets you perhaps thus: "I saw a young stag in the plantation by the road, the foresters don't want them in there, I don't want them crossing the road, we had better try and get him". You may then walk down the road to the corner of the trees, which are perhaps 5 or 6 years old, you see the stag, you stalk him 50 yards through the trees, you shoot him and walk back to the house where the stalker's wife gives you a cup of coffee, all within an hour. If that is an extreme example of easy stalking how difficult can it be. Somehow every stalk is a little different, you are always learning and the entry in the diary might well be: "4 beasts this week, weather mainly bad, spying difficult, saw many beautiful beasts. Several stalks failed, 3 blank days".

So, to put things into perspective, let us look at some of the times when 'It all went wrong'.

The weather of course dictates the score; fog is hopeless. If you blunder about you merely move beasts out of an area, they always see you before you see them and you are doing no good at all. If spying is so bad that you cannot see the beasts you cannot stalk them. Blizzard conditions get beasts down and how often they tend to be just below the snowline, and when the cold winds are hard enough, the area where they will not be is obvious and it is easier to pinpoint the sheltered corners where they are likely to be lying. You may see no deer without any reason, you may see deer but none that you can take. Stalks may go wrong for so many reasons or no reason at all. The beasts may simply move, there may be an impossible situation, pinned down far from a shot, unable to move. Very frequently an unseen hind and calf will appear just at the wrong moment and do the damage; an old cock grouse may rise with his familiar cackle at the very moment when it is fatal. The deer may get you before you get them. Sky lights, shadows, reflected light, movement or noise, may all give the game away. Failure to crawl flat enough, a rifle barrel hooked up in the air. Once I remember I was struggling to extract something from a pocket and in doing so my elbow went up and that was sufficient; and with the rifle, I suppose in my time I have made every mistake in the book. You can leave cartridges behind, you can fail to have a cartridge in the breech, you can squeeze the trigger with the safe still on. Things can happen with the scope. A low sun may be shining straight towards you. The scope lens may be obscured by rain before you can take your shot. A bad shot you cannot help is possible when a beast moves just as you touch off the trigger; better then a miss than a bullet 12″ back. You may still get the beast, but it is a wounding memory. You can fail to reload quickly enough, you can take the wrong beast, you can take a beast not knowing that there is another beast behind it. Surprisingly, on several occasions when I have done this, both beasts have been cleanly killed, but the second one may have been, of course, a beast that you should not have taken. Waiting on for a lying down beast may be trying, and can easily lead with stiffening muscles to a bad shot. You can "crease" a beast with a bullet through the neck muscle; cold, wet fingers can be responsible for a miss or a fumble in the reload. I have shot a hind instead of a stag confused by movements of the beasts, I have shot a staggie instead of a hind, and I am pretty sure that most stalkers would admit this themselves. Many a time I have missed the chance of a second beast not knowing it was there. I have shot a doe instead of a buck, the buck walked behind 3 or 4 trees and waiting for it to emerge into a gap before more trees, I touched off when it appeared, but it was not the same beast, a doe had taken its place. In the doe cull it is, of course, all too easy to take a buck with no horns by mistake; rare it may be but you can have a misfire. You can cause a misfire by having the bolt lever of the repeater not firmly down, or the lever of a single shot falling block rifle not firmly up. We all know the ethics of the game, never take a shot unless you are certain. Should certain be 90% or 99% in practice this ideal may be impossible, but the range of human reactions and the complications of the unknown that can happen to confound intention make it an ideal and an objective rather than a certainty.

I have surely said enough to explain quite a lot of those blank days, but let us close with the human reactions. It takes courage, particularly when out with a strange stalker, but if you are unhappy with a shot, say so. It may be that you are too far out, the visibility may not be good enough. Then the stalker may say, "I will try to get you in a bit closer, but I doubt it will be no good". He is likely to be right, but better to lose the shot than risk a wounded beast. Equally, it takes courage for the stalker to say in the firing position at the end of a long hard stalk: "Hold it, the beast is too good to take". Disappointment must be overcome, better to control yourself and say: "Lovely to see such a good beast, let us watch him awhile before we crawl back out.

A TROPHY BY ACCIDENT

For several years in the 1950s I used to go with my wife Christian, to stay in September at a hotel 'not a thousand miles from Loch Ness'. They had the stalking on three or four forests, and the proprietors stalked themselves and were keen, knowledgeable, and helpful. It was a good holiday from housekeeping for Christian, she liked the place and the people and enjoyed ranging the countryside. I stalked and gained experience from different areas, and different stalkers, and from these experiences I remember special occasions that imprinted special memories.

One such was on a fairly small forest area not far away. I had met the stalker one evening at the hotel before I went out with him, and the proprietors had given me a run down. He was young, tall and good looking with a delightful personality, I took to him at once and always enjoyed being out with him. My first day with him was in most unusually fine and pleasant weather. I had been warned that he was very fast, and that was almost another British understatement. We had covered quite a lot of country before we spied a beast way out, and his telescope confirmed that it was a stag that would do. We looked at each other; two minds with but a single thought. There was just no possibility of approach from where we stood. The stalker's knowledge of the ground was necessary, we should have to walk round the back of a young mountain, perhaps two and a half miles, to come in from an entirely different angle, offering a better approach and correct for the wind. Off we went, fast again, and we had covered perhaps half the distance, when suddenly, a motion of the hand, a whisper ''Down'', as the tips of antlers appeared before us. The stalker's decision was like lightning. ''The wind is wrong, he will get us any minute, go in quickly by yourself and get him if you can''. It was only about fifty yards, first walking, then stooping, then hands and knees, then flat crawling, always watching the tops of the antlers and ensuring that the top of my head would never get into the beast's eye level. A fast shot, no delay, almost without thought, and the beast was down. The stalker came up, ''Well done, good shot, but just look at that'', then only had he and I realised that the head was a good royal, not enormous but beautifully shaped and symmetrical. ''I have never seen him before, he must have travelled in for the approaching rut''. No more was said, and when the necessary rites were done, we resumed our trek, and in due course came up to the beast that we had originally spotted afar off. Our approach was successful, and at last I had my rifle on this beast. He was exactly facing me. This presents a pretty small target but is quite deadly and I don't mind this shot to the base of the throat. I don't like it at all if the beast is facing me but is not truly end on, as a very small deviation, one way or the other, can be nasty with the shoulder on the one side and the risk of hitting too far back in the ribs on the other.

There we were, all very satisfactory, two beasts down into the afternoon, but we were far out, and by the time we had both beasts brought into the larder, it had been a long, hard day. I was feeling exceptionally well used; my goodness, that man was fast. I should have insisted on slowing down, but I tried to keep up with him. I paid the penalty, that night, when overstretched muscles reacted with excruciating cramp and I was back to the days of similar agony after a hard game of rugby football.

So that is how I took my first really good trophy head. I shall never know whether that splendid stalker would have allowed me to take the beast if it had been sighted normally beforehand. Since then, through the years, I have shot one or two good beasts, one or two larger perhaps, but never one that I considered so beautiful.

DO NOT DROWN YOURSELF

Operating from the same hotel but on a very different forest ''not a thousand miles from Ben Nevis'', I was out again. The stalker here had been a head stalker on a large and famous forest, but getting older and with his sight deteriorating he had retired, but came out of retirement occasionally to help the hotel in the stalking season. To deal with the sight problem he had a young nephew with eyes like a hawk to accompany him, and as a team with the old man's experience they made a splendid job of it. On this particular day, it was already raining with a bad forecast. Not for nothing was Fort William credited with the highest annual rainfall in the British Isles. A long, slow, steep approach by Land Rover on a very rough track; on the way up we had a splendid view of a wild cat, a memorable sight. We stopped at last, still below the highest point over which the Land Rover would go, up to and over a crest and down to a bothy where, presumably, we should eventually meet up again and where the pony was maintained. Meanwhile we set off to our left, down a piece, across a burn, up a shoulder, over a crest and so on to an area spread before us to cover and to spy.

Nothing showed at first, but we worked out further, trending down and to our right, but the day was deteriorating by the hour, the rain now far beyond ''A bit showery the day'', had developed to ''pissing doon'', but much more important, the cloud base was coming down and we were soon in visibility down to 100 yards. Useless to try and stalk in these conditions, inevitably beasts will get you before you get them and you move them and clear areas without sight and to no purpose. Nothing to do but 'wait on', and pretty miserable it was. Perhaps a slow soaking hour had passed, and then glancing up, a momentary slant through the cloud showed a cleft perhaps 250 yards above and to our left, and out of it were walking two stags. A moment later they were gone from sight, but their course if continued would take them diagonally across our front and perhaps 200 yards away. Using another phrase, ''with all reasonable dispatch'', we covered about 125 yards forward and lay down, in a good position 'waiting on'. Yes, just visible, the two stags walked by, a whistle, they checked, the right hand one the better. The shot and against all the odds and all probability, we had taken a beast right out of the clouds, but now we had problems, the young nephew went off into the mist to make his way to the bothy to fetch the pony. He was away a long time, I was worried that he might have lost his way, not so the old stalker who had complete faith in his knowledge of the ground. Eventually he returned, we loaded the stag, but he had alarming news. ''The burn is up, it was bad crossing and it may be impossible by the time we make it''. Make it we did, but in those conditions, a slow, rough journey. The burn between us and the bothy was now a river in spate, rushing past out of its banks, and no doubt with the rocks beginning to roll on the bed below. The alternatives were all unpleasant: to cross somehow taking risks, to wait and in this weather there might be no end to that, or to make our way upstream until we at last reached the head waters where we could cross safely and then all the way back down. A daunting task all unknown length and distance, and so reluctantly we decided we would have a go. It would have been unthinkable had there not been a man across with the Land Rover, and we could indeed get a rope across. As I remember it, it was shoulder deep and the power and pressure of the water tremendous, with no firm footing below. If carried away from the rope you would have been in real danger, one blow on the head from a rock, and curtains. The good pony, the stag unloaded, gallantly made it with two men encouraging it, and holding to the rope. The stag had been placed at the margin with the rope attached, the young nephew the last man across, then all hands, pull like hell, the stag into the burn to be taken floating down and pulled diagonally across and hauled up far below on the other side. We had made it, a triumph against odds, but pretty disspirited and not a dry stitch amongst us, all we had to do was to get off that mountain, but easier said than done. The track that had been bad coming up was now much worse and at

We loaded the stag but he had alarming news.

points almost like a river. Back at last to the larder where we could relax, wring out some wet clothes, have a welcome dram and a bite. A proper dry-out would have to wait as we had no change of clothes, but that was not the end of a memorable day. Attending to the beast in the larder, the old stalker was talking to his mate who had driven the Land Rover. I happened to hear as I passed the open door. *''The Leddy, Baroness she calls hersen'' — pause — ''Weel she can aye put a bullet into a beast, but only the Good Lord His sen would ken chust whaur that bullet wed be''. — another long pause — ''but yon chentleman noo, he kens fine hoo tae haundle his musket''. What restraint and dignity in expressing disapproval. You can imagine the feelings of euphoria at this statement, we are only human are we not? This hit me so high up in the stratosphere that we need something to bring us down to earth again to be reminded that overhearing things about ourselves is not always thus. In one of my other lives, I had a yacht at Beaumaris in Anglesey, kept at a yard run by Morris and Leavett, known to the fraternity, though quite affectionately as 'Muckit and Leave it'. One fitting out weekend, we went unusually for us, to a pub to get some supplies. There propping the bar were two yachtsmen. One asked, ''Have you seen that queer craft up at Gallows Point?'' ''Yes'', said the other, ''very odd, have you seen the owner''? Back came the reply. ''I saw him go ashore in the dinghy, he looks like a broken down bruiser''. So you can take your choice.

***N.B.** For two years at the hotel our visit had coincided with a Belgian couple, Baron and Baroness. He did not stalk, but enjoyed fishing, she was keen and they came over to Scotland every year. They were delightful people and good company.

EVEN BAD WEATHER CAN HELP

It was on the third forest from this hotel that we had a useful experience. One day the weather was bad, spying was difficult, and half the day had gone without a stalk. We had our piece and the stalker considered the problems, thinking aloud. ''I ken where beasts may be the day, but its a bad place. We are doing no good else, we med as well look and see what we can mek of it''. And so we went over the hill and down to an open, really large, almost flat area, heather covered with peat below, but it was not broken up into peat hags, which might have helped an approach. The only possibility looked like a very long, flat, difficult crawl because, and due to his local knowledge, there were beasts right in the middle of the flat. It was as if two old hinds had got together that morning and had a conference. ''This is just the sort of day those damn stalkers might come out, I am fed-up with them, what can we do''? and where do we go to have a little peace''? The other hind might have said, ''I agree with you, lets go right into the middle of that great flat, I have never known a rifle doing any good out there''. We were looking pretty glum, neither of us keen on trying to crawl in, the distance was too great and the going too bad, but as we stood, preparing to excuse ourselves and without much hope, I was looking around and about. ''See over there, the sky is almost black, that is windward and its a snow shower or I am a Dutchman''. It was and the worst of it missed us, but where there is one there may be another. We waited on and sure enough, another snow shower came on and straight towards us and passed over, and as it did so we walked out briskly and completely hidden over the flat towards the deer for a carefully judged distance. We found ourselves a likely spot to wait on again. Cold, but no longer in despair, the sky began to clear, the snowflakes less thick, light showing at last until we could see again. We had got it just right, there were our beasts, calm and peaceful, the nearest about 100 yards away, upwind and a useful stag at about 120 yards. All we had to do was to wriggle into a better firing position and wait on a wee while until the stag turned. No difficulty, we had our beast, though it was quite a job dragging him out off the flat and completely dark when we eventually got down, soaked to the skin of course, tired but triumphant, having turned the very horrible aspects of the day to our advantage.

RECOIL IS AN ENEMY

On one occasion in the 1939/45 war, I was in the forward gun turret of the battle cruiser 'Renown' when she was firing fifteen inch guns in the Atlantic; it was an unforgettable experience. The actual guns were much muffled by the heavy armoured turret, but there was an almighty 'whoomph' as the massive charge of cordite sent a shell weighing about one and a half tons to a range of fifteen miles. In the turret one was conscious of a hundred and fifty tons of gun sliding back at one, to stop inches from one's face, squeezed into inadequate space at the rear of the turret. You may say, "what on earth is all this about?" But I think it was that experience, an extreme example of recoil, that started me thinking seriously on this subject. The lower deck guns in the 'Victory' with Nelson at Trafalgar, would throw an iron ball about two miles, the gun nine feet long and weighing three tons would leap back, this was on eight feet restrained by massive hemp breech tackles. Mental arithmetic began to play with the relation between projectile weight and gun weight.

To take another approach; about 1855 in Ceylon, Sir Samuel Baker was slaying elephants in great numbers, often to save villagers from starvation, their crops ravaged by the herds of elephants. He used weapons of his own specification for this purpose, strong, heavy double ten bores, smooth bore to increase velocity, and slightly reduce recoil as no long range accuracy was required. He used a lead ball or a bullet carefully controlled in hardness by an antimony inclusion, propelled from the muzzle loaders by twice the customary charge of black powder. He would have three of these weapons, two in the hands of gun bearers for reloading, and in his own words: "I was seldom, if ever, without a loaded rifle in my hand".

His carry-about rifle was a single barrel rifle eight bore, this time with a rifled bullet which would penetrate a buffalo from end to end — it was accurate to a considerable range. Though heavy, both examples of weapon would have had a massive recoil. Baker appears to have been immune to recoil and in his works hardly ever mentions it. Again from information on the velocities achieved by his massive powder loads some interesting correlations might result, but I doubt that they would help us much. What are our requirements? We want a light handy weapon, easy to carry about; we want a calibre, a velocity and a trajectory and bullet to do a satisfactory job on a red deer stag up to two hundred yards, and our ideal would be, no recoil. We are, of course, asking for the impossible. We know that for target accuracy, the heavy rifle with a so-called 'Bull' barrel is better, but this will not do on the hill. We know that smaller calibres tend in practice to be more accurate than larger bore weapons. Why? I can see no intrinsic reasons in the weapons themselves. I suspect that this trend is mainly due to the lesser recoil having a beneficial effect on the man behind the rifle. Look around today, every military weapon from the Kalashnikov type of quick firing hand held weapons to a tank gun has some sort of contraption at the muzzle end. Being hand held weapons this may help to prevent your bullets climbing steadily up the wall as you fire a burst. In the tank gun it may be intended to reduce flash and flip as well as recoil. We also know that auto-loading, whether automatic pistols, FN type reloading shot guns or auto-loading rifles tend to reduce recoil. Is there anything we can do to benefit our hunting rifles?

My first start in this problem was a BSA Majestic ·30/06 with a BSA Patent muzzle brake. I have checked up on the patent and it tallies. This was a very light rifle, only six and a half pounds without a telescope, very handy to carry about the hill, would have had a quite unacceptable recoil without the muzzle brake, its light weight, however, did cause it to wobble easily in a strong wind. BSA supplied a sleeve which eliminated the muzzle brake so the difference in recoil was easily tested. After one try I never used the sleeve again. Satisfied that this set-up did a useful job, and that it did not affect accuracy, trajectory or bullet performance, I was on my way.

I studied what was available finding most gadgets in America, and many of them useless here, as they involved sending your weapon to the factory in America for actual machining work on the barrel. One example of these, the 'Magnaport' using spark erosion techniques to form an integral muzzle brake. The next step was to make my own muzzle brakes. I have now done five of them; they all work and I do not think any of them would prevent your selling the rifle, but if there is any doubt about this, or if you have a very beautiful weapon that you do not want to impair, then you must use a form of muzzle brake which is an attachment not an integral alteration to the barrel. On all muzzle brakes, mine included, work on the principle of deflecting gas behind the bullet at right angles and reducing the rocket like effect when the gas in a normal rifle explodes from the muzzle. A logical development is to increase its suppression of recoil by some degree of reverse travel of the gas (see sketch).

In general terms the reduction in recoil depends on many factors, at the maximum with the lightest weapon, larger calibre and high velocity Magnum type ballistics and at its minimum with heavier rifles, smaller calibres, modest velocity cartridges. My range from 5% to 30% would naturally be less effective on automatics and self-loaders.

What are the objectives to muzzle brakes? Unpleasant, of course, to your neighbours in a target competition shoot, and apt to promote remarks such as, "I don't like the look of the thing," or "too much noise and blast." My comeback on this. "Yes, certainly, firing in cold blood on the range, though you probably are, and certainly should, then be wearing some form of ear protection." You can of course eliminate the muzzle brake by applying layers of tape if you have not got a sleeve, and it is interesting to find the number of layers of tape necessary to eliminate the effect, which also indicates a rough measure of effectiveness, but on the hill, firing the odd shot at a beast with the adrenalin flowing, you are unlikely to notice anything at all. Some might say, "Don't the contraptions easily get made up with dirt, mud or snow?" The answer is, "Not more than a normal muzzle, easier to see, and this can be eliminated by a single layer of sellotape that disappears on firing." I am still satisfied that accuracy is improved by the fact that a reduction in recoil is beneficial to your own reactions. There might even be an increase in the inherrent accuracy of the rifle, I can illustrate the theory behind this by a simple experiment. If you put, for example, a garden cane in a vice horizontally, tap it with a hammer, observe the speed and amplitude of movement at the end of the cane, and repeat with similar hammer blows, but with a weight at the end of the cane you will be astonished at the difference in the amplitude and speed of movement, so the small mass of the muzzle brake added to the muzzle end of the rifle may modify the vibrations that occur on firing. Are there other advantages? I have found on the hill that beasts do not so easily pinpoint the origin of a shot, as the sound comes out in different directions and rebounds over a wider range of obstructions, one can imagine that if a shot is missed, the reaction of the beast is, "Well that was a funny sort of thunder", rather than an instantaneous swing of the head and location of the source of the noise.

Another advantage, more important with roe deer than red deer, perhaps, is that the reduced blast and flip, may enable you to see the beast and the effect of the strike of bullet instead of a momentary black-out, during which the beast may have disappeared, leaving you uncertain whether it has moved behind cover, or, if struck, has dropped into a ditch.

Turning again to an attempt to put some of this into figures, I have always intended to construct a rig to enable me to measure recoil. It would be nice to be able to take velocities and note bullet behaviour at the same time; a really interesting project ahead. However, if we say that we are concerned with recoil in the range from ten ft., lbs., to fifty ft., lbs., that should cover it. At ten ft., lbs., maybe we can forget it anyway, and the higher you go from there the more important it becomes. In Africa, when I fired a great number of rounds from a Weatherby ·300 Magnum, I developed a bruise on the bone of my second finger, which took weeks to disappear, it hurt, and it certainly didn't improve my pleasure or my performance. Roy Weatherby, when I had a discussion with him on this, told me that he preferred to fit the Pendelton type muzzle brake to his weapons and reckoned the effect at about twelve and a half per cent recoil reduction, preferring a more modest recoil reduction in conjunction with a slightly rifle and integral barrel effect, but remember again that if you sell a rifle, the purchaser may have a 'scunner' on muzzle brakes of any sort and refuse to purchase unless he can remove it.

Have we finished? Not quite, there is another factor. I came across the Edwards patent butt recoil reducer in America, used, I think, mainly by the clay bird gun shooting fraternity — shooting hundreds of shells, but surely, the theory is equally applicable to rifles? The analogy is that it does to a small degree what the massive hydraulics do to the fifteen inch guns. Why, my thought ran, do we not apply this in conjunction with the muzzle brake? Particularly in the case of the large bore magnum rifles. I consulted Edwards on this, and he recommended two of his gadgets in such a case; with a less powerful rifle in conjunction with the muzzle brake, one might be enough and effective. After allowing for the removal of the wood weight, the Edwards recoil reducer adds four to five ounces to the weight of the weapon, and so with the ounce or two of the muzzle brake (if additional) at the muzzle, the balance of the rifle is unaffected. Does this modification work? As I have not yet got my rig I cannot give figures, but subjectively, the effect can be described as taking 'one on the chin' from Mohamed Ali, and the much pleasanter effect if this were done with a much thicker and softer glove, converting, as it were, a bang to some extent into a push. So we now have a means of taming that great, big, bellowing magnum. Are we now satisfied? I think so, but there are always fresh fields to conquer. I remember that I first fired a Double ·500 Nitro Express from a weapon weighing about ten pounds. My goodness, what an enormous blessing a muzzle brake would have been with this type of weapon, had it ever been done? To my knowledge, No! Why not? Had nobody thought of it, or was it too difficult? The obvious answer, have a go, I retired to the workshop, and before long I had a wooden model, I then made a metal model, followed by a Mark II, I then had a project that I could take and manufacture in a sophisticated way with machinery. To what weapon should I apply this? There was an easy answer, I happened to have a lovely Rigby double ·470. I remember a white hunter in Africa saying to me. "If I was finally up against it with a client who had made a total mess of things, it had all gone wrong and I had but one chance of saving life, what weapon would I choose? A double ·470! If you ever come across a good one short of a King's ransom, buy it for me". An additional advantage with my double ·470 was that it had been rebarrelled with slightly shorter barrels than originally and slightly lesser weight. When it was ready — the first try on the range. My goodness, I thought I had it solidly attached, but after the first shot that double muzzle brake, was well on its way to the target; pure engineering and easily dealt with. I can now report success. Is this an invention? It is at least original thought. If only I had been around in 1890 and produced this and patented it, my name might have been enthroned in the Weapons' Halls of Fame alongside Colonel Forsyth and his Paradox. Only about a hundred years too late, but here is the ultimate, 'The Riverdale Double Muzzle Recoil Reducer' (see sketch).

In the old days, the big double rifles often had a hard rubber pad on the butt. This used to get so hard that I think it did little good. Modern ventilated rubber types are much better. Before the muzzle brake era I used to put a stocking over my rifle shoulder under my jacket, and this was helpful. Now we have the energy absorbing synthetic rubber, on its specification it must be good, but before I rush out and apply it to the butt of my rifles, I shall go back to the over the shoulder idea with a strip of this new formula and I am certain that I shall approve.

DIAGRAMS OF MUZZLE BRAKES

NOT TO SCALE

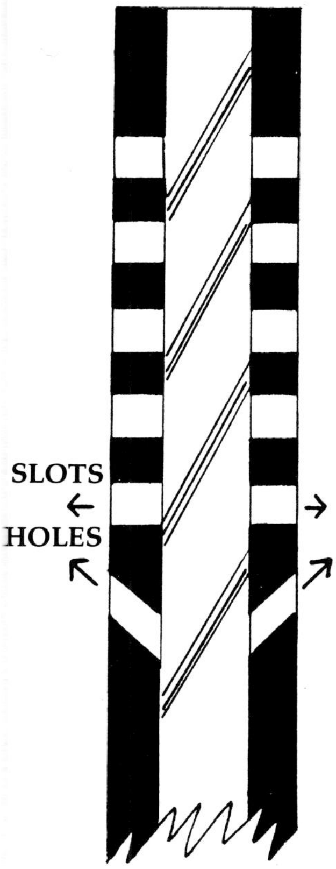

BSA PATENT
INTEGRAL
NEAT AND GOOD

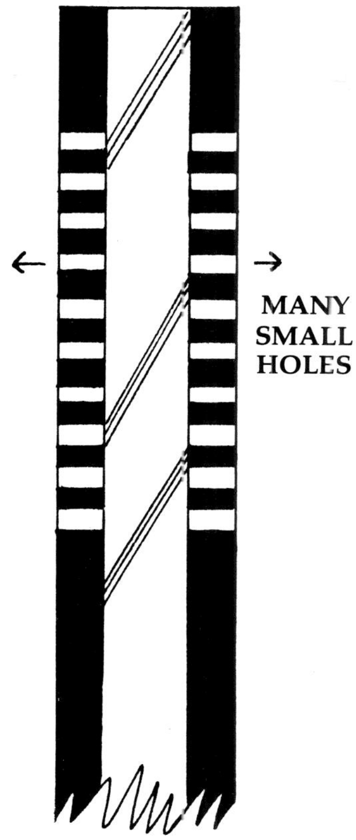

PENDLETON
USA
INTEGRAL

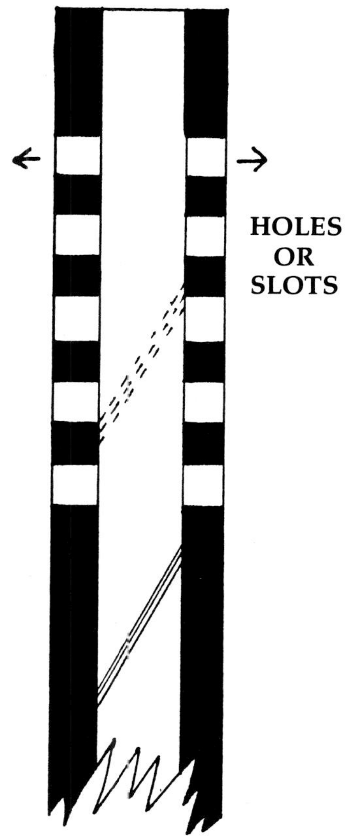

RIVERDALE
HOME MADE
INTEGRAL OR ATTACHED

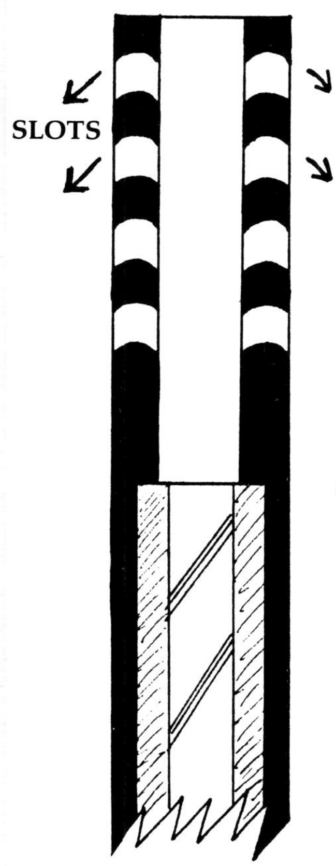

RIVERDALE
ATTACHED
REVERSE GAS FLOW

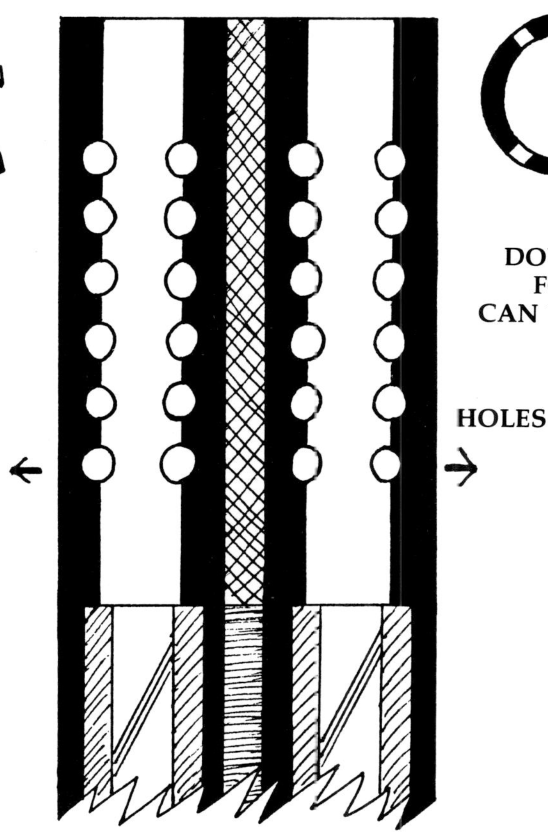

RIVERDALE
DOUBLE MUZZLE BRAKE
FOR DOUBLE RIFLES
CAN BE REVERSE GAS FLOW

IN DARKEST AFRICA

In the early 1930's I had occasion to make a business voyage which was unusual and turned out to be a fascinating set of adventures and experiences in many countries. It deserves a chapter in its own right, but here we are only concerned with the sections that relate to hunting and the rifle.

I had met Smith when he was on leave in England, his parents living close by my home. From then I kept contact hoping for a chance to join him in Africa if an opportunity offered, so there I was flying up to Khartoum in an old Hannibal, an aircraft in which it was said they never lost a life, and if a forced landing was inevitable, they came down slowly and landed in a short distance, more like an old hen than an aeroplane. This time it was a hen but in a different context, a stork came through the fuselage and there was a shower of blood and feathers in the passenger area. No great harm done and in those days there was no pressurization anyway.

Khartoum, we still had an empire, so in the atmosphere of 'the sun never sets on Government House', and relics and memories of Kitchener and Gordon, the old Nile steamer still there and remains of battle and strife, of Omderman; Churchill, as a young man, had a part in these operations. With retrospect, the whole affair was probably a ghastly mixture of mistakes in high places, massive mismanagement, resulting in an unnecessary tragedy. Somehow this mess has been turned into a sort of heroic memory.

Baggage Express: Any distance or destination.

The water supply.

In Khartoum a message from Smith caught up with me; in essence it was 'come' so again airborne, this time in a twelve seater monoplane, I was bumping along in the turbulance, slow, tiring and sick making, through the southern Sudan with Dinkas, tall, thin men standing on one leg at airports where we landed to refuel. Uganda, the lake, Myanza and at last we reached my destination in 'Darkest Africa' Dodoma. This had been a German fort in German East Africa in the 1914/18 war. It was now a district headquarters in Tanganyika. I found that Smith was out in the country but expected back in a day or two. I was hospitably received at the Administrative Headquarters, made welcome and a member of their Mess provided me with sleeping quarters and told me to make myself at home, all very British and very pleasant. Smith came back in three days, only to make plans for and prepare in the next two days a new tour of almost six weeks on which I was welcome to accompany him. I left a suitcase containing business kit at Dodoma and kitted myself up with the items advised by Smith, in the local bazaar. I asked Headquarters to keep an eye open for a way to get out again in about six weeks' time, made my farewells and off we went into 'darkest Africa'. Smith was a veterinary officer and it will save time if I give some picture of his work. A large part of this was the innoculation for prevention of 'rinderpest' a particularly nasty and damaging cattle disease, very detrimental to the standard of life of the native population. There was a new plan afoot. The considerable Indian population were addicted to 'ghi', a fermented milk product like rancid butter. It was necessary to import much of this expensively from India. Somebody had the bright idea that if they could persuade the native population to raise the quality of their cattle, produce milk and cream, they could turn it into ghi, and this would not only improve the economy as a whole, but would give the native population some actual income with which they

The old Chief reviews his cattle.

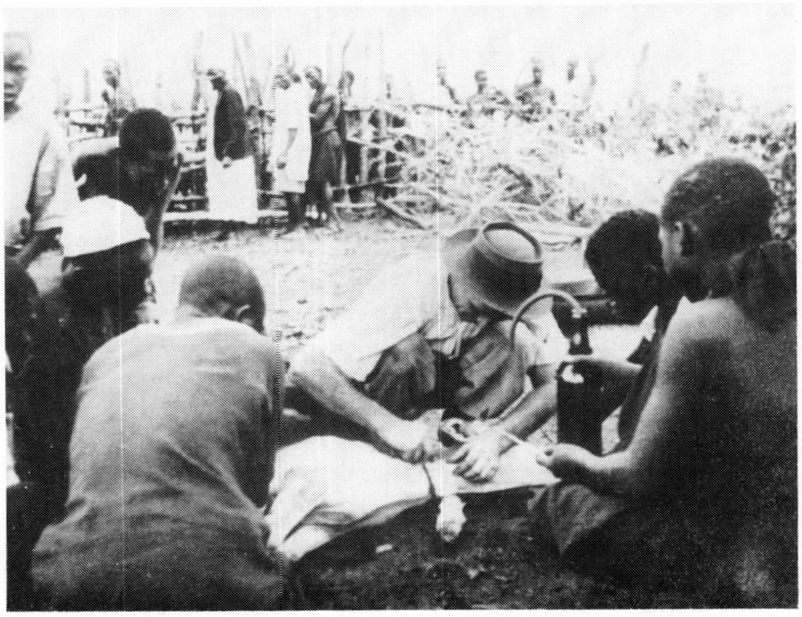

Inoculation against rinderpest.

Dr. Corson with tame eland: tsetse fly research.

could buy products such as cloth and tool supplies for themselves. Good thinking, nothing wrong with the idea, but as usual trying to graft some of this upon the native population was so difficult that it was almost a non-starter, as it would involve reducing the numbers of cattle and raising their quality, whereas the wat of life was 'to hell with the quality', wealth in cattle was simply numbers, and this equated with wives in particular, but the furtherance of this scheme was part of the objective of our tour.

The outfit was Smith, myself, a native Askari who spoke English, a cook and an odd-job man. Our transport was a battered Model 'A' Ford pick-up, a tent for the two white men, a few stores, the veterinary requirements, a small ration quantity of whisky, but a full load for the Ford pick-up. We were in roadless country, much of it not bad going as long as it was dry. If rain came down, movement became virtually impossible, and you camped where you were until it dried out. If the sturdy Ford 'A' pick-up were to pack up irretrievably, there was one simple option, sort the gear, cut down our loads to the bare essentials that we could carry and walk. It would take longer, but in Africa's vast spaces time seemed insignificant and almost infinite. I soon fell into the routine as we made our way from village to village, sometimes camping out in between and spending a day or two at each village inocculating cattle, investigating complaints, interviewing chiefs and explaining the ghi project. Smith had little time for stalking in his job, but I endeavoured to shoot enough to provide food for the outfit, and an occasional gift to the villagers. The weapon was a sturdy, English made, double ·500 rifle; of course with iron sights, and because it was rather light for its power, it had a truly ferocious kick. There was also a rare, battered but serviceable, side by side 12 bore top lever, box lock, non-ejector shot gun. With our route and our job we might almost be said to be avoiding the best game country, but there were plenty of ordinary species, such as Tommy gazelle, impala, wildebeest, zebra and so forth. We encountered no elephant or rhino, then much more abundant than they are today, plenty of buffalo if we had had time to go and look for them. The villagers were delightful, simple people, welcoming and helpful. They would see to our water supply, give us a hut if required, and perhaps put on a dance. My part in the plot was, very shortly, to help in any way I could, lighten Smith's load, and one way of doing this was to take over the stalking and ensure a supply of meat. At one point in our travels we encountered an area where an attractive grass seed must have been ripe. Large numbers of quail in that part of Africa had homed in on this bounty. A party of guns with the right cartridges could have bagged hundreds, but we, short of cartridges and none with small shot, just took enough for a delicious supper that night. We deviated from what would have been our normal track for a whole day to visit a Dr. Corson who was running a dedicated, rather shoestring and self sacrificing research into tsetse fly and sleepy sickness, fascinating, but very inconclusive at this stage.

At night that wonderful sound of Africa! Lions roaring, an occasional hyena, with vultures giving away the location of any kill. I could not have enjoyed myself more. Acquiring the feeling that I was bearing my part of the white man's burden, and helping to maintain a beautiful and satisfactory way of life in Darkest Africa. One night in heavy rain the team requested permission to crowd into our tent for shelter. We had mosquito nets, they did not, and in the morning the colour of the tent had changed as the interior was almost covered with the mosquitoes, resting after their feed on the black bodies. Going out at dawn from the slightly smelly scrum in the tent, it was fine, the rain had ceased, and there 100 yards away, a few beautiful giraffe feeding on the tops of the thorn trees. After a few hours we could resume our progress without too much struggle through the Mbuga, the native word for mud. The natives in this area were known as Basacuma Wanuweze (phonetic), and the basic language a brand of Swahili. Unfortunately I only had a pretty primitive camera, and in those days no long range lens; and then suddenly it all went wrong. Smith went sick, suddenly and seriously. My simple medical knowledge decided that it was not malaria.

Old warthog tusks.

FEVER OF UNKNOWN ORIGIN

Smith had gone sick suddenly and serious, I had problems. It was not typhoid and it was not pneumonia, but in 36 hours he was dehydrated with a fantastic temperature, practically unconscious and on the verge of coma. Primitive nursing, get some liquid into him somehow, sponging him down very frequently to the same end and hopefully reduce the temperature, massive doses of quinine, the only medication we had; no antibiotics in those days. Nothing dramatic came up from a conference with a helpful native witch doctor. It did not occur to me at the time but this was bad news, if the witch doctor had decided that it was simply malaria, what would have been better for his kudos and reputation than a little incantation, a mauseous draught, and a prediction of a dramatic cure, confirmed in three or four days, but wait! If the b'wana was going to die it would not be clever to put himself in the position where the white b'wanas might be asking questions: ''and just what treatment did you give him before he died''? So the witch doctor retired, no doubt thinking up his Swahili equivalent for 'PUO', apt no doubt to puzzle any doctor, particularly in Africa where 'pyrexia of unknown origin' was always possible with so many sources of infection from man or beast, air, soil, water, food, drink or injury. But what was I thinking as the days went on, faced by this time with all options gone? I was terrified of septicaemia, in that case and in those days with no antibiotics, it would have been certain death; I was a very worried man; I had to make an important decision. Did we try to get Smith back to civilization, a long and arduous trek? He was in no condition to stand this and I decided it would kill him. The other grim alternative was to sit tight, do the best we could for him, and hope that he didn't die which seemed quite likely. A message to Dodoma was unlikely to help as it would take too long, and even if relief was sent out it would be too late. Meanwhile I had my occupations. The Askari was good and helpful so we could share a watch and nurse Smith round the clock, though there was little that we could do. I went out hunting and kept the camp in meat. I continued to do Smith's job inocculating cattle against rinderpest, talking to the chiefs, sitting in on the ceremonial stool and with the assistance of the Askari as translator and adviser, administering justice as best I could, I even took the opportunity of having a go at the lion. To this end I would shoot a beast, perhaps a zebra, drag it in a wide circle to lay a trail of scent, leaving it for the coming night in what I hoped was a suitable location, have a hollow dug out in which I would sit awaiting lion. They might follow the trail and come to the kill. It did strike me that the lions might equally get the scent of the kill from down wind, in which case as they came to the scent, they would arrive as it were on the back of my neck. But this was a tiring performance, as it yielded no results after a couple of nights I gave it up. Time passed and on the day when I decided that Smith was likely to die tomorrow, the fever broke, and he started to recover. He was young, he was tough and he fought his way back, but we could not move him for several more days. I managed to shoot kanga (guinea fowl) and the little partridge like birds, both of which, first in soup, then solid, were good fodder for Smith. You seldom got a sporting shot at kanga, and only saw them in the air briefly when they flipped over some scrub. Going out with the gun of an evening, your usual view of kanga was a family party of five or six, in line running swiftly away from you along a path. The treatment then was to drop to one knee and ''ground sluice'' them, an American phrase. Aiming a little high and with a little bit of luck, you would get one or two clean killed, with a bullet in the head or neck, and there was your dinner without damage done to the rest of the family. Ensuring good relations with the village and preventing our becoming a burden to them, I was able to bring them in occasionally, some very welcome meat. Then one day a native trotted out of the bush with a message on a forked stick. How he had found us was, of course, an African mystery, presumably by bush telegraph village by village, he had learned that we might be at 'X'. The message was that if I could be at a given location about 250 miles from our present position in 14 days time, there was likely to be a light aircraft coming through. It would take me to Uganda and the lake, from which I might be able to return to Khartoum as I had come. Again it was a balance, would Smith be fit enough? I ought to take this chance of getting out as I was becoming overdue on my general journey. It was decided that we should attempt this. Meanwhile with this worry and stress, the fantastic memories, our bath water arriving in the morning, carried on the heads of a line of women. The useful knowledge acquired that although the ·500 rifle had great power, it was still necessary to put the bullet in the right place. One fantastic experience, I hit a wildebeest too far back, incredibly, two of its companions ranged up, one on each side, holding it up with their shoulders and urging it forward. This left me quite helpless as a tail end shot into three beasts would be almost certain to produce a worse situation with wounded beasts. The difficult takes a little longer! One day after the

Remedy for mbuga (mud).

message in the forked stick, another native trotted out of the bush, and yes, he had my suitcase on his head, the stout composite globe-trotter with a permanent head dint had completed its long safari through the bush.

We made our farewells of the village, of the nice old chief, and started out for a more or less day and night run to the appointed spot. Another lovely picture and memory. We were stuck in a river bed with no hope of extricating ourselves. Out into the night went our team to find villagers to help. A village they found, but all the strong and healthy had gone to a beer drink and dance at another village a long way away. Never give up, we mobilized the inhabitants, old men, young women, pregnant women and totos (children). There they were in the light of our headlamps, being organised on to ropes with which they finally succeeded in pulling us bodily out of the muddy bottom of the river bed; what a picture! Of course, I was now doing almost all the driving. With little time to spare we arrived at the designated airstrip. In came the little aircraft; yes, the pilot would take me out. I was on my way after six weeks in Darkest Africa.

Smith was now well enough to complete his tour and eventually return to Dodoma. I parted with him with African experiences shared, and mutual thankfulness that we had escaped worse disaster. What words would be appropriate in such a parting? As I remember it, we had none, a steady look, a very heartfelt handshake, and I climbed into the little biplane, while Smith turned back into the vast spaces of Africa.

There was one more experience in the little aircraft; we came down at a very primitive little strip in the middle of nowhere. A white man walked out to us carrying something heavy. A few words and he handed this to the pilot, who heaved it in and stuck it down by my feet. We took off, but when we had gained altitude, I tapped him on the shoulder and said, "Don't want to worry you chum, but whatever it is you put down by my feet is bouncing up and down and gives me the impression that it might go through the floor". "My God!" he replied, "It has come off the beam. Heave it back until you feel it on the solid spar". "What is it"? I said. "Only six months' supply of gold from a little isolated gold mine", he replied, and that night I was in a hotel with a bath, a bed, all pretty primitive, but even so, how far removed from the experiences of Darkest Africa.

Meat for camp.

JOINING AN EXCLUSIVE CLUB

There came a time much later in my stalking memories when I was staying with a friend on an estate I knew well and with a stalker who had also become a valued friend. The best laid plans can 'gang aft agley', and one day suddenly with no warning, no stalker was available. We talk about the British habit of understatement, and perhaps we tend to cultivate this almost as a form of ''stiff upper lip''. Why not a dash of overstatement for a change? In this vein if I say that we were ''not a thousand miles from Inverness'', you can draw your own conclusions. I cannot say that I had been waiting for an opportunity but I saw my chance. ''Could I go out by myself today''? I asked my host. He thought a moment, ''I don't see why not''. Discussion followed. ''It would be best to go to the small beat at the right hand side of the loch, not many beasts but almost certain to be a few, and after all you only need one suitable cull stag''. I could see his thinking, if anything went wrong it was not far out, and would limit the area and make it easier to find me. If I got a beast it could be brought in quickly next morning and be less likely to spoil the next day's stalking if the stalkers were again available. Here I utter a caution which I have not always obeyed myself as may appear later. Never walk off by yourself into the 'wild blue yonder' without letting someone know. If necessary leave a note, indicate an area and an expected time of return. Accident or injury may both be very remote, illness perhaps more so, though one shudders to think nowadays of the number of people who have heart attacks without warning and occurring apparently at any age over 30. The weather is the more likely enemy, particularly fog in which you can lose yourself or be immobilised. I once spent four hours on top of the Cuillins in Skye, walking not stalking, and not daring to move as you could easily walk over a precipice.

With everything settled for this venture, I kitted myself up and set out. No rifle case as it was fine, a rope, a hill stick and a whistle. No compass as I knew the area well and there was no threat of fog. I intended to go to the head of the loch, across the stream leading into it, and climb to the highest point in that area; that would put me generally able to work upwind along the highest ridges, stretching out towards my right and tending to reduce my distance to my base. I should also be likely to be above any beasts, an important advantage. After a long, long slog I achieved this objective, and I could start spying. Visibility was good, though it was mainly overcast. Off I went until about half way on my intended route I at last spied beasts, half left and below me, 2 or 3, possibly there could, of course, be more hidden, and yes my glasses revealed what looked like a suitable cull beast. As I had no high powered telescope to be sure of this and the head, I should have to close in quite a distance to make certain of my quarry. There was no difficulty at this stage, how pleasant it is to be above your beasts, the ground was sufficiently broken to make the initial approach no problem. When I did close in sufficiently, I could confirm that the stag would do. More care now, but little crawling needed until the final approach to a possible firing point. Almost copybook stuff, and there was my beast some 100 yards away, undisturbed, not alerted, and standing almost broadside. I still had my trusty old rifle with the iron sights which gave the advantage that your head could probably be 1½″ lower than with a telescope, and you are less likely to have grass or heather in the path of the bullet without realizing it, and in this case also, no need to get a beast to its feet with all the risks that involved, no need for an agonizing wait until the beast turned to give a suitable bullet placement. With no delay a final sight, a squeeze on the trigger, the bullet away, and the unmistakeable thud of a strike, the hunch of the beast and it was down within a few yards. Careful now with the drill, relief, no need to move, why further alarm the other beasts, and above all before moving, be quite sure that your beast might not get to its feet again. The other beasts have moved away, walk in, rifle reloaded and still ready, all well. The accustomed feeling of regret, now take the cartridge out of the chamber and proceed with the gralloch. This done and the hands cleaned it was time to think again. I examined the situation. My course had brought me quite a short distance from the edge where the ground fell away steeply through stunted birch trees and rock to the foot of the loch. Could I make the drag myself? The ground almost level and slightly downhill rather than up, not very broken, I could try. If it was too much for me there would be nothing lost, I could take my time and rest when necessary, the beast was not a monster and should be manageable. After a series of muscle stretching and heart and lung testing sessions I found myself at the edge. Careful now! All too easy for the stag to get jammed on the way down, steep ground and if freed incautiously with yourself below, there might

My glasses revealed what looked like a suitable cull beast.

be the 'stag's revenge', but all went well, the edge of the loch and a short distance on a level path to the road by the bridge. There leave the beast just waiting to be picked up by the Land Rover. This would be easy and popular saving an excursion in the morning. The walk up to the house, the report, congratulations. I can hardly describe the feeling of satisfaction and achievement. Surely the splendid stalkers might think nothing of it, all in the accustomed day's work for them, but more frequently with hinds, but on the other hand I have never done this before, it might be long before I ever did it again. I wonder how many amateur rifles visiting the Highlands had in fact gone out on their own, planned their own operation, found their own beast, shot it, gralloched it, and brought it home? With a feeling of general euphoria, I had the illogical thought that it might be analogous to being elected unexpectedly to membership of an exclusive club.

A VERY ODD SHOT

In the 1950's a friend of mine invited me to stalk on an estate in the centre of the Highlands where, in my now familiar idiom, we were not a thousand miles from Fannich. From a narrow road you entered the estate through a locked gate, which was necessary to prevent tourists galloping over the estate and blocking the one way road which was about 12 miles up the glen along the lower part of a loch to the house. There was a very small community here, and my friend used to talk about "My people", it was indeed no larger in numbers than a large family. I expect like families there were tensions and life might not always be sweetness and light, but he had identified himself with the little community and did everything he could for the welfare of his "people".

The loch about 12 miles long, an average of a mile wide, had been harnessed for hydro-electric power, so that the level varied considerably and this had affected the stalking by at times eliminating what had been a track along the edge of the loch to its higher end where there was a bothy. Behind the house there was a great bowl in the hills, perhaps 3 miles wide, and its rim rising 1,000 feet or more above the level of the loch. There were obvious difficulties in stalking in the bowl, and probably the best way was, go down the road a mile or two, or up the loch a mile or two, and climb up to the top of the rim so that one could stalk down into the bowl, depending on the wind, but with the advantage of height and able to spy the bowl from above, but this involved a hell of a trek.

Coming off the hill with pony and stag.

One day the stalker, doubtless thinking of my welfare, attacked the bowl from below. Three hours later we had reached the rim, about a mile and a half from the upper end of the loch. On the way we had found beasts, we had stalked beasts, but we had been defeated every time with a tendency to move others out of the bowl. We had our piece and the weather then shut down, the cloud came down, and the ground being precarious in places, it was not safe, and quite ineffective to blunder about, and we had to stay where we were getting colder and stiffened until about 4 o'clock. Before the evening dusk the weather, however, improved, the cloud lifted. "My hands are so cauld I couldna' use a rifle the noo", said the stalker, blowing on his fingers. We were now able to examine the ground over the lip with the basin behind us and the valley descending to our left to the head of the loch. Below us on our right the glen narrowed to a cleft beyond which it opened out again, and this area was a sanctuary in the middle of the property. In the old days before any mechanisation, many areas had sanctuaries formed accidentally by the great difficulty in extracting beasts because they had to be dragged a considerable distance uphill, but some areas, as in this case, deliberately created sanctuaries in the interest of the beasts, and to keep them on the territory.

The stalker said that he now expected beasts to start moving down out of the sanctuary before long. He was right, a few hinds showed, working to the left out of the cleft and moving across, then a good stag, pitch black after rolling and wallowing in a peat hag. He was a suitable beast, we could take him, but instead of following the hinds as might have been expected, and which would have given us a shot at 150 yards 45° downhill, he came closer until he was invisible below us. He might, of course, reappear, but he might cross our front only to reappear out of shot on our left, and if we moved we could just as easily be wrong as right. Immediately before us the ground was so steep that we could not go down, but I had an idea. Taking our rope I made a bowline, tested it, I put it round my chest. We went forward as far as possible, and then the stalker under my direction took a round turn and wound it round a suitable rock so that he could control my weight. I inched down on my back, working down to the edge of an almost vertical cliff. My foot went over, my bottom was on the edge. I was held only by the rope, I sat up slightly, and then I could see the stag, 100 yards away, and below me at about 80°. I crossed my feet, put the rifle barrel between them, and sitting up slightly I could get my sights on to the stag. He leapt at the shot, the strike was definite, but he remained on his feet without moving. Where do you place your bullet when you are shooting down almost vertically on a stag from above? The next shot a clean miss, another finished the business. With some relief and not without difficulty I was recovered by the stalker hauling on the rope and my own efforts. Now we could work along to our left to a place where we could get down to the stag, see where my bullets had gone and complete the gralloch. We were on our way, the day was spent, but we were in luck as there was a good path back to base and the pony was not far away. The scene was beautiful and very like the lovely painting on the cover of the February 1988 issue of ''Stalking'', but here the floor of the valley was the loch. Home just before dark, we had our beast, and it had been an interesting day. I had taken a very odd shot indeed. I hope never to have to repeat this, I think I was scared and perhaps I had taken a chance.

SEAMANSHIP IN A FOREST

There is another special day in my memories of my times at Fannich. As I have said before, the rise and fall of the loch in the hydro-electric dams had destroyed the path from the house to the head of the loch, and the bothy where a pony could be kept. There was a good, sturdy boat about 20 feet long with an adequate outboard engine which was used to go up or down the loch 8 miles to the bothy. There had been some accident in the past in bad weather, I never discovered what had happened, but it had left everybody nervous, and permission to take the boat out was firmly in the hands of the host. This day the weather was uncertain, the wind was high, there was a considerable sea running on the loch, and permission was refused, so we faced a rough walk of 8 miles before we could start the day's stalking, with the prospect of another 8 miles home at the end of the day.

Out we went and after a brief rest we took to the hill, up and out there was an unexpected chance of a stag showing away above us and I made a clean miss of this. On and up and over the top to stalk down into a valley running down to our left to the river at the head of the loch. There were beasts below us, we stalked down a burn which brought us into touch with them and a successful shot. No mistake this time, but it was about 4.30 before we had the stag down to the bothy. The prospect of that 8 miles home was not inviting, but the weather had taken up slightly and our host had mercifully released the boat to come and fetch us. Were we glad to see it! Loading ourselves, our gear and the stag, I had them all stowed well down in the middle of the boat, and took the helm without demur for the passage home.

I was, I suppose the most experienced in boat handling and seamanship. Rugged squalls swept down on the loch, it could be dangerous and it was an uncertain decision to sail or stay. I plotted a course that I thought best with wind and sea to gain the far shore where there were bays which reduced the sea and gave some slight shelter. This attained we worked down until we were almost opposite the home jetty where I again plotted the best course running to make the home bay and the jetty; not good, but we made it thankfully, glad to be home, wet to the skin and cold. That is perhaps the second way in which you can drown yourself while stalking, the other being the flooded river; I don't know which is the least inviting.

THE PROBLEMS OF "SIGHTING IN"

Whether you have just bought a new rifle, or whether it was your old faithful 'Betsy', (does that word conjure up an American friend with his trusty Winchester "thutty thutty"?) you must check and sight in your rifle before taking it to the hill. There are, of course, excellent rifle books on this, but if I run through my own practice and experiences, it might be a fresh approach.

First let us assume that your home is far from a 100 or 200 yard range; it may be such an expedition, leading to the attractive thought, 'oh well, I can do it when I get up to Scotland before going out'. I have found that this will not do. I have managed, however, to rig up an absolutely safe 25 yard range, and with cooperative neighbours, and a warning to one whose dog doesn't like it, I have the priceless advantage that sighting in at 25 yards in theory approximates the results at 100, probably uses less cartridges, and is more accurate in that in your concentration on the rifle, there is less likely to be human error at 25 yards than at 100. You should have checked that all the relevant screws are tight; there may be one screw on an old rifle that obstinately tends to slack back in use. If so damp its ardour with a spot of 'lock tight'.

Then to the firing position, and the target. I find that firing over a car roof with two soft cushions, one can get a steady position leaning over the car with both elbows down, the rifle supported fore and aft, and still with an approximation to an actual shot on the hill with one hold on the rifle. Be sure to achieve the correct eye relief and concentricity with the telescope. Off we go with the old accustomed rifle, you know how it was shooting the last time you used it, and you may have adopted my idea of making a note of this on a little strip of paper and sellotaping this under the fore end of the rifle. With this set-up, a couple of shots may well confirm "no change and all's well". If in any doubt, three shots, and at 25 yards, the bullet holes should be touching or making a group of not more than 3/8″.

With a new rifle, the dealer will have mounted the telescope, all the better if the rifle has integral mounts, it is all too easy for mounting blocks added to the rifle to be just not good enough. Nowadays the dealer will almost certainly have adjusted the telescope with a collimator, what an invaluable asset that instrument is to a gunsmith or dealer.

However, you may well find that your shots at 25 yards are grouping an inch away from central or vertical, or both. You can adjust the telescope, of course, the principle, at 25 yards you need four times the adjustment that would apply for one inch off at 100 yards. You should know from your telescope literature what the adjustment clicks may be. For example, 4 clicks to an inch at 100 yards, or perhaps with a continental scope, 3 clicks to a centimetre. So you may perhaps require 25 clicks before you are satisfied with your group and its position at 25 yards.

Yes, you can now go out on the hill, but don't. If your scope is the old-fashioned sort where the reticule moves in your field of view, it will now be well to one side of centre; with a modern sight you will not see this, but the effect is the same, you may be near the limit of adjustment of your scope. I prefer now to stop, put the adjustment of the scope back to zero, bore sight the rifle and carefully move the mounting screws of the telescope until on a fresh test, you are within say 10 clicks of adjustment, that is far better. Are you finished, no, you should check again at 100 yards before you go out on the hill. In theory, and the reference books will no doubt tell you, the rifle will shoot to the same point at 100 yards as at 25. Don't accept this, it may not be true. My faithful and excellent old BSA Majestic ·30/06 for example, shoots 2″ high at 100 yards if it is dead on centre at 25. Decide on your objective and adjust accordingly. Let us say that with 1½″ high at 100 yards, good medicine this for most rifles for red deer. Therefore, my BSA must be sighted ½″ low at 25 yards to achieve this point of strike at 100. Keep a careful note of the correlation of your rifle in this respect against adjustments in the future.

There is yet another caution, check with any change of cartridge, or even a fresh batch. Rifles are very individual, the good old BSA holds itself down for a day, a month or a year and swallows almost any fodder with little need for adjustment, even between factory ammunition and my home loaded ammunition with my favourite Nosler bullet. There is a slight change as the home loaded groups ½″ left and ½″ low as against the factory loaded at 100 yards. Why? I simply don't know, I wish I did! I have had other rifles which are apt to move an inch or more from their setting when laid aside for a month or two.

Remember you are always testing the rifle, not yourself, and I have found a good target to assist you in taking exactly the same aim every time, is an ½″ black square at 25 yards with two 1/8″ black lines horizontal and vertical (see sketch).

The cross wires on the reticule of your telescope should subtend exactly to match the thickness of the lines on your target. At 100 yards this becomes a 2″ square and the horizontal and vertical lines ½″ thick. A handy way of doing this is to mount two such targets, one on the side, and one on the end, of a grocery carton in which you can put all your ammunition and equipment when setting out in the car. The carton is easily mounted in some safe spot on the hill,

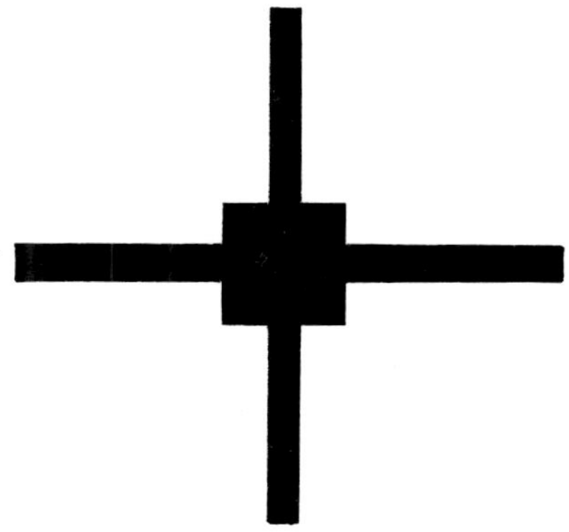

This target will assist in taking exactly the same aim every time.

and anchored, if necessary, with a little earth or turf (not stones). Shoot at this lying down over a rock with a suitable soft rest. If everything is perfect, you may be happy after one shot, but take 3 shots before you make any adjustment. Now, at last, you are ready for the hill. If all this sounds complicated, it is only because I have tried to cover most possibilities. Let us hope that most of them will not occur. With the BSA for example, one or two shots at 25 yards, and one or two at 100, usually do the trick, with no adjustment at all. When you are doing this it is as well to have a piece of paper and a target diagram, and write down every shot, it is surprisingly easy to get into a muddle. If things go wrong, and you find yourself having fired perhaps nine shots, and you are still not satisfied, better stop, you will be getting shaky yourself. Drop it and start completely fresh again another day. Whether you bother or not on the hill, it is as well to wear ear defenders when you are firing in cold blood.

It is a lovely feeling if you can achieve complete confidence, and provided you do so, the rifle will be an extension of your mind and hand.

Odd things can happen, I remember an occasion taking a young friend up for his first red deer stalking. I had kitted him up with a rifle and telescope and he had done the right things. There we were doing the 100 yard check before starting up the hill for the first day's stalk. Oh dear! He put 3 shots, each about 3″ off at 120°. A hopeless situation, unable to adjust without 3 more shots, and if they failed to give a firm indication, real problems, the worst feature being lack of confidence for the young man, So I came up, ''Let me have a go''. I took the rifle and 2 shots came up about 1″ high and 1″ apart. ''Fear not'', I said, ''you were probably just over anxious, concentrate like hell on the spot on the beast where you intend your bullet to strike, squeeze gently, and it will make a clean kill'', and so he did, acquitting himself well.

BOTSWANA

Ventures and new challenges can start in the most unexpected ways. Who would have thought that an accidental contact at a shooting weekend in Norfolk would lead to a hunting safari in Botswana? It is true that I had a gap in my yacht voyaging and I had been thinking that if I was to go hunting in Africa I had better get on with it as time was passing by. It was 1967 and when I found that I could work in a business visit to South Africa before the safari, plans began to fall into place. Introduced to and correspondence with Tony firmed up the arrangements. I assembled and sent off my weapons and looked forward to the day.

The real start was one morning in Pretoria when I joined a little private aircraft on charter. We took off heading eastward to Botswana and the Kalahari. "Have you flown aircraft"? said the pilot. "Yes", I replied confidently, "I was in the Fleet Air Arm in the 39/46 war". He was not to know that they then considered me too old and would not allow me to go and learn to fly. He was not to know that kindly pilots used to let me fly their aircraft, and so I was a rather rare individual who had flown quite a lot of aircraft, quite a lot of hours, though with a minimum of circuits and bumps without ever having an official lesson, far from achieving a licence. What fun it was to fly this nice responsive little aircraft out into the Kalahari, and eventually land at a very minimal strip in the desert, and there was Tony, our first meeting after the correspondence. I formed an instant liking for this splendid young man which rapidly ripened into a satisfying mixture of respect, companionship and friendship. Game was in sight and in a four wheel drive we made our way into camp. I had some idea what to expect from my memories of Tanganyika in 1930, but this was the middle sixties and a very different set up in a very different terrain.

Now to my weapons; in California by chance, returning from a voyage to Australia, I had taken occasion to go and see Roy Weatherby, and have a session with him. Primed up with the information from his stalking experience, I came away with a specially selected Weatherby ·300 Magnum. It had a satisfying test target and was fitted with a Weatherby 2x 7x scope. This was to be my all purpose carry in the hand weapon in Africa. I had designed and had made two leather ammunition pouches, one to contain soft nosed expanding bullets, the other the solid nosed that I might require. The ammunition was 180 grain Nosler partition bullets, and the rifle was sighted an 1½″ high at 100 yards. To comply with regulations, and to provide heavy metal, I bought a second-hand BSA Majestic in Winchester ·458 calibre. It was virtually new and had probably done one safari in Africa. No doubt available now because after one trip its owner felt: "Present owner having no further use for same". To my regret this was not fitted with the BSA patent muzzle brake, it should have been, it was not a heavy rifle and the kick was severe, but I reasoned that it would fire but few shots and that when the adrenalin was flowing freely. I didn't want a telescope on this weapon, likely to be used at fairly close range, though my eyes could no longer cope with the standard express sights. I solved this problem by designing, making and fitting my own sights; a larger front bead of 1/12″ diameter that I could see and a rear sight best shown by a sketch. I had adjusted this and tested it at 50 yards range. This worked so well that I have no hesitation in recommending it to anyone for a heavy rifle if they don't want a telescope and their eyes can no longer cope with the standard sights. This was endorsed in Botswana by one shot over water preventing a closer approach with a 100 yards off the shoulder shot at a good warthog when I had the heavy rifle because we were really after buffalo, and the pig was drilled straight through the heart. For this weapon I had standard factory soft nosed and solid nosed ammunition. No way was I going to risk my beautiful Boss game guns in the knockabout of an African safari, so I took a Remington 1100 semi-auto twelve bore which I had been testing for fun, and this did all that was required in Africa.

Tony and 'Skips' with the basic transport — a four wheel drive pick-up.

The camp was much as I had imagined, adequate, businesslike, with everything required but no attempt at super luxury, and to start with Tony and I were together with the team of 'Black Brothers'. Water had to be brought once a week from 80 miles away in a truck, four wheel drive with a Perkins diesel engine. In such a set up how vitally important were relations with the White Hunter. The whole success of the trip can depend on this, you share all experiences, you depend on each other, even in the most dire emergency. For the client there is everything to learn. Tony was ideal, young, fit, born with a rifle in his hands, a superb shot, and with infinite knowledge, not only of the game, but on a very broad front, the country, the weather, plants, birds, beasts and even insects. A sense of humour and a delightful way of imparting information. I could not have been more fortunate. One outstanding thing I remember was his phenomenal eyesight. He used open sights, so fine that they were almost invisible to my eyes. He could pick out game in scrub invisible to me, and if, for example, one came out of scrub to look across a broad flood plain, I might say: "Tony, I see some beasts beyond the plain, out against the trees on our left". With one casual glance, he would reply: "Yes, there are 7 beasts, 3 of them are sessaby, the rest are hartebeest, one with quite a good head, but not good enough". I doubt if I could have matched that with the best field glasses. Incidentally, 7x is the highest magnification you should use in Africa, more than that seems to magnify the heat shimmer in the atmosphere, and it is also quite good for picking up game quickly and not needing too steady a hand or rest. I was familiar with this because 7x also happens to be the best choice for use in a yacht at sea.

Tony with the result of my first shot in Botswana — an old kudu.

A key man in the team was a half Hotentot tracker, a dimunitive little man with skills in tracking quite incredible. Put a bullet into a beast and if it went away he could follow the trail of that one beast through almost any country and amidst the abundant trails of others, until you eventually came up with it and could finish the job. This is one of the first things you have to learn in Africa in complete contrast with Scotland, there you seldom if ever shoot a moving beast, and if you did so and wounded it, it would probably be lost. In Africa when you get your chance, even if the beast is moving, you take it, relying on the tracker, and in course of time you become more expert. To give some impression of the figures, I suppose I reached the point where I would bring off about 3 out of 5 moving shots. Tony would probably bring off 6 out of 7. We also had a Botswana Game Scout, a nice old boy; he worked in happily with the team, had a good fund of knowledge and was good on spoor. His job, of course, was to check that nothing we did was outside the rules or beyond our licences.

Gradually, beasts began to come in as opportunities offered: wildebeest.

So on that first night I settled into camp with a sense of the wonderful, vast space of Africa; the stars appearing twice the size and the wonderful silence until a lion roared; the majestic signature tune of the African night. Tony inevitably had a vast fund of knowledge on clients and their personalities with some of the characteristics of different races. Some of these tales will appear as we proceed, but a trivial and nice one illustrating the importance of small things in these conditions. One day in the Kalahari one of the boys came to Tony and told him that he had found a little cut in the tent occupied by a client, and he had reported it fearing possibly that Tony might spot it and blame him.

Thinking no evil, Tony asked the occupant of the tent if he had noticed it. This was met with a firm 'No'. A thought rising in his head caused Tony to take the client with him to the tent in question, there on the ground outside there was a little carpet about a foot in diameter of beautiful little yellow butterflies. They had come seeking moisture from a damp patch in the sand. All was now revealed, the client reluctant to go out into the cold loneliness of the African night had relieved himself through the little slit in the tent. Surely there was a combination of yellow butterflies and a very red neck.

Little Hotentots rejoicing over much meat — a hartebeest.

When are we going to get to the hunting? But if this seems out of proportion, remember that the bulk of the time is not spent with the rifle at the ready on a beast, but in the sheer joy of living in the wild, and that anything to do with this is added importance, and one of the happy things I remember is the relationship with the Black Brothers. This was free and easy, the racial element at a minimum, all played their part, all had their skills and all were part of a team. Our first day out, travelling in the four wheel drive pick-up revealed quite a lot of game, but of no particular desirability for the rifle, though of intense interest to me, and then suddenly a gun bearer banged on the roof. The truck stopped and the word was passed that he had sighted a good kudu bull, unusual out in the Kalahari as they prefer areas with more water. Out and look, there it was, Tony could pick it out easily in the scrub, but I could not, my eyes not yet attuned to the light and the beasts, I simply could not see it; 3 weeks later I should have had no difficulty in doing so. So now it looked as if an almost unique opportunity might slip away, as the kudu took off at a swinging run. Into the truck and Tony drove flat out in a half circle, designed to intercept the kudu's path. In due course, stop again and out, and there at the same swinging run the kudu was crossing a sandy dip, 150 yards away and angling slightly away from us. ''Take him now'', was the word and my rifle came up to my first shot in the Kalahari, the kudu bull, very visible but travelling at 8 to 10 miles an hour. I hoped the computor in my brain would solve the co-ordinates and give me the right answer as I fired. Unbelievably the kudu went end over end, exactly like a hare shot in the head, but the more impressive with the size, an incredible sight, drilled into the mind never to be forgotten. Was I lucky? What a good omen, and so we had a trophy in the bag that might have eluded us for weeks or altogether. I think that shot was also important to the Black Brothers. I felt that from then on I had their confidence, and enthusiastic backing in all I did. It was a good bull, an old beast, past his best, so I think that no harm was done by taking him out at this time; skinning was completed and good meat for the camp.

That evening in the magic hour at dusk, after a limited shower and a frugal drink of whisky, Tony said, ''Do you mind if I ask you how you took that shot''? I could answer readily as I had the picture in my mind. ''I tried to swing through at the level 2/3 up the body at the shoulder and touch off about 10″ in front of the chest''. ''Fair enough'', said Tony, you were only a trifle high and well forward, the bullet broke his neck just where the spine joins the body at the shoulder''. I knew that, of course, he wanted to know if it was a pure fluke, if I had some clue, or if I was in fact an experienced shot at running beasts. The days ranged on, experiences came and went, my sight improved, my rifle handling improved. The weather was marvellous and

Making biltong.

gradually beasts began to come in as opportunities offered. Nearly always there was something every day. I had occasion once or twice to use Tony's general rifle. This was a continental make taking the Holland and Holland ·375 magnum cartridge, possibly the best all round rifle cartridge for Africa. Tony had a heavy rifle but rarely used it. I met one hunter who used a ·275 Rigby but he was the exception; few hunters in Africa use less than ·375. Of course Tony's rifle had sights so fine that, as I have said, they were no use to me, and his rifle had another peculiarity that will appear later.

I have no intention of giving a day by day report, nor a shot by shot account, nor a beast by beast survey. Sometimes we cruised in the four wheel drive pick-up, sometimes we walked, we even took little Dick Dick and the like with the gun loaded with heavy shot. I began to get the hang of the spoor, but above all, the marvel of shooting on the move, confident as I have said that if you put a bullet into the beast, the Hotentot tracker would go into action. It might take up to 4 hours but you always got your game. If the time fitted when we had a beast, we would make a little fire and while the skinning was done and with the fire down to charcoal, we would lightly grill the fresh buck liver for a timely meal. Amusing, Tony said, some Americans would not eat liver like this, apparently only if it was wrapped in cellophane and came out of a deep freeze, could it be pure. I lost an Eland because in very rough going the Weatherby took a wallop, and after missing three shots I realized that the telescope was hopelessly out of kilter, and we had quite a job resetting and resighting it, from scratch when we had returned to camp.

One day a little Hotentot trotted out of the scrub into the camp, he could communicate with our tracker. Where had he come from? From his tribe three days away; how did he know of our camp, or where we would be? And his reply. "I knew there would be meat", and so he settled down with us quite happily, helped to prepare skins and heads and eating enormously. One morning he came to say goodbye, thanked Tony for meat in his own way, and said: "I go to my tribe". "Where are they? They have surely moved away from where you left them", and his reply, "I will know where they are". Leaving us to guess whether he would find them through tracks and follow, or whether he would just know and go direct, and so that marvellous, little, diminutive man trotted off again as he had come, a tiny figure with a leather skin around his loins, a sort of bag holding one or two ostrich eggs for water, a little bow and tiny arrows, and in his primitive mind, senses and knowledge unapproachable to more civilized people.

Hotentot women and house. These people are about 12 inches shorter than the average white man.

KALAHARI

Day followed day, all fascinating, all enjoyable, some featureless, some with a special memory, we might instance the day of the ostrich, the day of the oryx, the day of the eland, this was the case of a long running shot, the bullet a little high, a little back, the skilled tracker and the ultimate triumph. A miracle here, how can such an enormous beast akin to the domestic bull in size be fed and in good condition in that waterless country? Tony said that they had small bladders and a very efficient kidney system, which meant that they lost little liquid in urinating. The necessary liquid intake must come from somewhere, and most of it can only be from grazing on the drought resisting shrubs with roots that go so deep that they can bring water to the surface and provide moist fodder for the beasts that live on their shoots. After the day of the eland there was the day of the biltong. All hands turned too, we butchered that massive beast, and with sharp knives reduced all the flesh to strips, carefully and cleanly cut to the breadth and thickness found best by experience. This was then soaked in a chemistry which Tony produced, again born of experience, and I never did find out what it contained. After an hour or two in this, the strips were carefully spread out on the shrubs surrounding the camp until they were thoroughly sun dried, and we had a magnificent supply of biltong, delicious and nourishing. A strip or two in your pocket, chewed as required would see you through the longest day.

Another day our water truck was due but did not arrive. This was serious, so we set off in the Land Rover and found it about 35 miles away on its return journey with the water, but immobilised. First they had got stuck in the sand, then they had somehow got air into the fuel system, and then they had run their battery flat and failed to start again. We set to, bled and primed the whole fuel system until we were satisfied, but then how to start the big engine? The Land Rover could not tow the truck in about 3″ of sand, our Land Rover battery with jump leads was quite inadequate, we did not even try this. The drill was to thoroughly chock one back wheel, jack up the other, then one man in the cab at the controls, a long, strong rope wound round the rear tyre of the jacked up wheel, top gear engaged and at a given signal, all hands pulled like hell. The engine fired up, a shout of triumph and charging merrily the truck completed its journey with the vital water supply. You have got to be both ingenious and self-sufficient in the Kalahari.

FORESIGHT
1/12″ DIA.

RIVERDALE MODIFICATION OF EXPRESS SIGHT FOR OLDER EYES

BEAD AS
SMALL AS 1/32″

STANDARD EXPRESS SIGHT

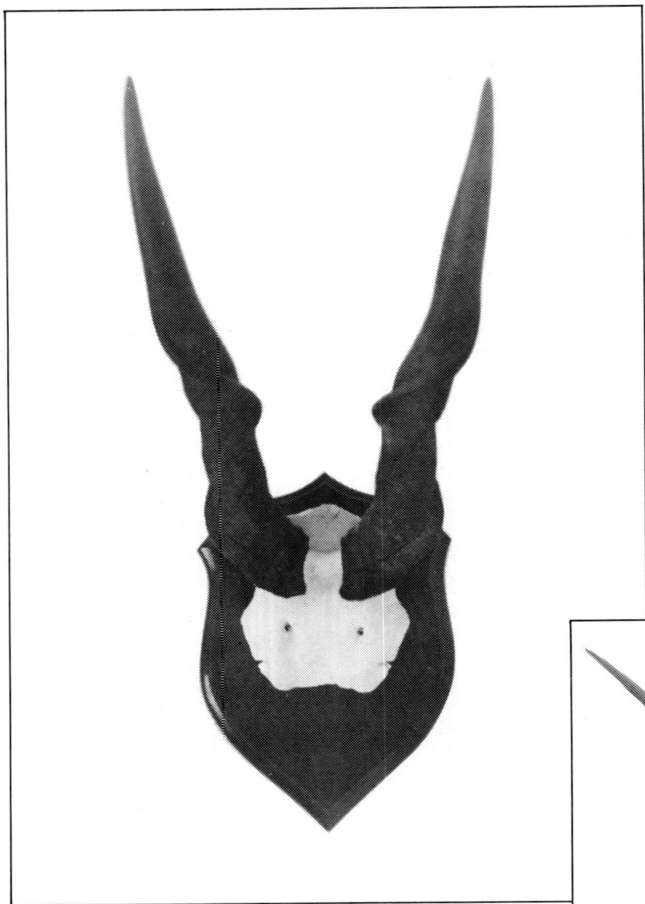

Eland.

An old cow oryx.

OKAVANGO

Always ahead in our plans had been the prospect of the Okavango. I had become quite intrigued and worked up about this and we now moved into our first camp, driving in with a reduced number of vehicles, no need now, for example, for a water waggon. The reality surpassed any expectation, it was unbelievably beautiful; behind us was quite an expanse of water, not far away, a beautiful river with pure, cool water coming down from the hills of Mozambique and containing excellent fish. Our tent in a glade surrounded by high trees, and looking out over a flat plain to more distant vegetation. The whole habitat seemed ideal for game, there was everything, forest, scrub, flat plains, wonderful feed, water, papyrus reed, swamp, and as might be expected, abundant game and a tremendous range of species. It had remained undisturbed and perfect, it was uninhabited, no 'black brothers' with their hunting and their ever devouring cattle; a perfect paradise. How and why had this been preserved? One simple answer, it was the kingdom of the Tsetse fly. This peril similar in form and habit to the English horse fly or the Scottish clegg, was the ever present menace. From sun up they started a relentless attack which only ended with sundown, (and then, of course, the mosquitos took over in their myriads until dawn). One hoped that with numerous bites one would not contract sleepy sickness, owing to the absence of man with his vector in the life cycle of the causative parasite. We found that the best defence was always to walk in pairs, both armed with a powerful fly switch to defend yourself and each other. Anyone in the slightest degree allergic to their bites would be swollen up, a hospital case, fleeing the area in days. If relatively unaffected by the bites, it still added up to a considerable stress factor, so much so that Tony had had clients simply unable to stand it, and who had been forced to leave the area. In my case balancing this against the game paradise was no hard task, and made it all worthwhile.

Giraffe: I dearly love giraffe; at rest they are statuesque and beautiful. Their make-up is interesting and ingeniously adapted to the requirements of their abnormal form and height. Their gait which appears, superficially, to be awkward is, when observed closely a wonderful, co-ordinated, almost slow motion poetry of movement which always fascinated me.

Zebra: Whenever and wherever I have encountered them, they always seemed to be in wonderful condition. I simply cannot remember seeing a zebra looking thin and poor or miserable.

In this area we could go out on foot or with the vehicles. If going out in the Land Rover with the heavy rifle for big game at first light in the morning, one would see the little partridge type birds out feeding. Disturbed by the Land Rover, they would scurry back on foot to their protecting patch of scrub, pause for a brief moment to look round before diving into cover, in that brief moment, a swift, accurate shot with the ·22 rifle would do the trick, and provide a popular and delicious evening meal; and with the water pans there were occasionally duck and a knob-nose goose, often far out on water pans. Tony and I both bagged one or two of these at about 120 yards, the bullet would kill them all right, but you were aiming about 12″ over their backs. The great virtue, of course, with the ·22 rifle was that there was no risk of the noise disturbing larger game that was your main objective. I simply revelled in the sight and study of the animals, lovely tsessaby, their beautiful coats forming a camoflage with the differential reflection caused by the different direction of the coat. We were being very selective in our shooting. I got by chance, a really good wart hog with magnificent tusks. We were out after buffalo, I had the BSA ·458 in my hands and the pig was over 100 yards away across water. No option but a lucky off the shoulder shot got him in the heart and bowled him over.

Perhaps our main objectives were buffalo and elephant. There was frequent elephant sign, but most of it was not fresh, and the buffalo, we would pursue an old bull from land into swamp, arduous treks, and without result. How often must I have seen a buffalo head peering at me from the edge of cover only to disappear before I could use the rifle, how often must I have seen the back end of a buffalo disappear into reeds or swamp, and it was quite a time before finding for once a really good old buffalo with his massive head on our side of a little herd in the open in the early morning, that I at last got a shot. This was a heart and lung shot; he went away with the herd out of sight, but then there was a long, mournful bellow, and Tony said: ''You have got him, he is dead, they nearly always make that one bellow'', and so it was. Of all the many trophies I had collected by this time, I still think that the buffalo gave me the greatest thrill.

Tony had taught me that it was wise when after buffalo, to take the first shot with a soft nosed bullet, as it would almost certainly be a heart lung shot, but to have in the magazine and to follow the solid steel cap bullets, the reasoning being that after the first shot, your buffalo would either be coming at you, head low with a large area protected by the massive boss of horn so that penetration might be vital, or the buffalo would be going away, and only deep penetration or the smashing of a large bone would have any effect.

One night we went out after crocodile, a very new and strange experience, sitting in the bottom of a dug-out canoe, rifle in hand, very wobbly, with two natives, a paddle on each side and one of them holding a flashlamp. The procedure was to find a crocodile by the eye reflection, stalk him to reasonable range, and then the shot, a very small target indeed from the wobbly seat in the canoe. If you got him, a mad flurry of paddles, rush in and grab him before he sinks, if you fail he goes to the bottom and stays there until putrefaction has generated enough gas to float him to the surface, by then in a truly disgusting condition. When I got one good crocodile, honour was satisfied and we thankfully retreated to get behind the mosquito net and away from the mosquitoes.

We came across a little tribe of Hottentot bushmen, a rare chance to see and study the all too small remnants of a wonderful people. We gave them a hartebeest we had shot. They were delighted, we had earned their gratitude and they became even more open and friendly; they have, of course been studied and excellent books have been written about them, much of which we were able to confirm in our observations. Yes, it is true that with the males, the penis is normally erect. How and why evolution developed this is a mystery, one would have thought that it was detrimental in their hunting and stalking lives.

Another delightful story which we did not witness is a courtship custom; a young man from one tribe attracted by a young girl from another, would stalk her, and eventually contriving to get her alone, on her own, away from the others, he would plant a little love dart from a little bow in her behind. If she turned on him tearing it out, it could be taken as rejection, obviously she didn't fancy his advances. If, on the other hand, she left the dart in place, and walked on away from the camp, that could be taken as a sign of approval and that the course of true love might run smooth.

At last came the opportunity so long awaited, and 'The Day of the Elephant'. In the Land Rover we came across the track of an elephant. The experts quickly confirmed that it was a large, old, solitary bull, and the track was fairly fresh, travelling steadily. Even I could appreciate that the size of the beast was determined by the size of the track made by the forefeet, but the experts could tell from that track his age and weight. The age because the foot was not smooth, but broken up and creviced by cracks, the larger and deeper these became, the older the beast would be. Tony's verdict: ''I think he will almost certainly be travelling to join other elephants''. We left the Land Rover and followed on foot, making a fair speed and hoping to overtake. It was an arduous trek, much of it over good going on dry land, but also into swamp, across a river, swamp again before welcome dry land. The procedure for crossing a river was to send a tall black brother across, to gauge the depth, then one of us would cover the river with a ready rifle against crocodile or hippopotamus while the other crossed, to cover the crossing in his turn from the other side. You waded across, holding your rifle above your head, and I remember crossing such rivers when for some yards the water was over your head and you had to hold your breath until your nose surfaced again, and the game trails through the swamp would usually have you travelling on an average up to your knees in water, but where elephant had passed through their great weight would have punched holes at least a foot deeper, and so every few strides, your foot would go down into one of these nearly to your waist in water and having to haul yourself up before you could proceed. I think the main risk in those trails was that some blundering hippopotamus disturbed might make a rush for the water, it would be difficult to get out of his way and one casual chomp with the massive jaws of a bull hippo would be a fearsome menace. After some hours of this I for one was feeling the pace, and we paused on a patch of higher ground while one of our black brothers climbed up a tree to spy as far as he could see ahead from that vantage point. How welcome was a cry of ''elephant''. Fatigue forgotten we were galvanized into activity and on our way. Soon we could see them and assess the scene. Tony had been right, the old bull had joined others. There were several elephants, mainly cows and calves in a patch of scrub and forest, but our bull was standing in the open beyond the end of this cover. The obvious approach through the cover was denied to us by the other elephants. We should have to creep along the side of the cover trying to avoid disturbing cows or calves, and hoping to get within range of the bull, but this plan was threatened by the wind. If we went too far the elephant in the scrub would get our wind, and so it was that we arrived eventually at a point on the edge of the scrub where we dared go no further, there were elephant close to us, but not seen, in cover on our right. The wind was dodgy and our bull about 60 yards away. That is a long shot for an elephant, enormous as they are, it increased the difficulty of placing a bullet in one very small area. Although it was an off the shoulder shot at this range, I decided to take the head shot with the ·458 BSA. The elephant very slowly turned round 180° and stood, I think my shot had just, but only just missed penetrating to the brain, but it was close enough to stun. Reloading quickly I put another shot into the heart lung area, and almost at the same time Tony fired, a head shot from the other side and it was this that was decisive. That enormous beast sank slowly to its knees and rolled on its side dead. Tony had fired to make sure, because if the elephant had been able to travel, it had only a short distance to go to a major river, it was also the boundary of our territory and we should have been in dead trouble and almost certainly lost it. We could not see where my first bullet had gone because it was on the ground side of the head, my second shot would have killed it, but not instantly. There was now a disappointment, as we had first viewed the bull it had a good tusk appropriate to its age and size, a really worthy trophy, but we now found that the tusk on the other side was broken at half distance. Imagine the force in accident or in battle that would be required to smash a 6″ thick elephant tusk in half. It is almost unbelievable, but it had happened. My main impression apart from the usual regret, was the unbelievable size and weight of that beast. We now had to retrace our steps on the long trek back to the Land Rover only reaching camp in the dusk, exhausted but triumphant. In the morning the boys went out to chop out the tusks, the usual miracle, they would go straight across country to the beast and when they arrived there were four lions feeding on the elephant, but they had had their fill, and belly full of meat they retreated quietly when the boys shooed them off, so that they could get on with their job and bring back the tusks. Also there were the wonderful forefeet, I have one of them now, the great toe nails and pared down to a translucent amber with the cracks and crevices to form a fascinating tray, and so at last I had achieved my elephant.

After a day or two the time had come to leave this delightful camp and embark on another new experience.

THE RIVER CAMP IN THE OKAVANGO

We drove out and spent a night camped by the river on the outskirts of the nice little town strategically situated to give access to the Okavango. We had been joined by another rifle, and a young white hunter who had been trained by Tony. The rifle was a member of the Diplomatic Corps of one of the smaller European countries; there was plus and minus in this addition to our numbers. It was pleasant to have another and new member in our discussions of an evening, erudite, travelled, experienced and good company, but there was something, I didn't ask and Tony didn't say. I think he had horned in on hunting for free as a quid pro quo for introducing some new clients to Tony. He had been out before, he was experienced, quite a good shot, and lucky, for example, he got a good buffalo bull within half a mile of camp, when I had been hunting for a week!

It made no difference to my hunting because I went with Tony and he went with the young man who was a delightful character in Tony's mould. Occasionally we would all go out together, but that was seldom.

Off again into the Okavango, but this time we left all the vehicles at the bank of a river and embarked in a launch and two dug-out canoes. Strict orders went out from Tony and our gear was checked and sorted down to the bare minimum for subsistence for 10 days. It was almost a case of cutting the handle off your toothbrush to save weight, and even so the launch was almost dangerously overloaded. Off we went up the river towing the dug-out canoes and but slowly overcoming the current. I managed to get out a rod and spinner and one could easily catch voracious fish about 1½ lbs. in weight which were excellent eating.

At last we reached our destination, this was an island where a steep landing was possible to unload our gear, and here we set up camp, very nominal and vestigal this time. The island was not large and unless one left by water you had to wade through a swamp to get to solid land. One might describe the terrain as like the last camp, absolutely delightful but with a higher proportion of water, river channels and papyrus swamp. The hunting went on as before without any very special day. I saw roan and sable antelope for the first time, but not in our shooting objective. There was one rare occurrence, I admit that I saw little but a red tawny flash, but Tony was highly excited. ''Do you realize'', he said, ''that you may have seen one of the wonders of the world? I have only seen it once before, and then I had a good look at it. As far as I know there is no example of skin, skull, or skeleton in a museum or elsewhere, and its existence is doubted or voted impossible by some''. ''What on earth are you talking about''? I said at last. ''What you have just seen'', he replied, ''is a cross between a leopard and a cheetah'', I collected a python about 8 ft. long, a beautiful skin. The natives ate the meat with a relish as a rare treat. Not to be left behind I tried it and found it good if not specially delicious.

Subtle tentacles of feeling had made me aware that the boys did not have a high opinion of the new rifle, though there was nothing open or derogatory, but at last something was revealed. I have already said how important small matters can be in relationships in the wild, and compared them with what could happen on a long ocean voyage in a yacht. Our friend had secreted a bottle of whisky. This was against orders and cutting down the weight we had left all alcohol behind. If now he had pretended that this was done inadvertently, that bottle of whisky would have been so welcome that he might have got away with it. But no, not daring to produce it, he was reduced to having a good swig of an evening when by himself in the tent. Tents were now cut down so that we now all shared. Alas, he didn't realize that even the fairly feeble oil lamp in the tent silhouetted him against the tent wall, and the rest of us could see exactly what he was doing. Not a word was said, but I can report that that is one of the ways in which to avoid becoming one of the world's most popular men.

I suppose the main objective was now Sitatunga, that strange web footed antelope of the swamps, and one of the few in Africa with a twist in the horn. Several times we would see one, but always slipping away through the reeds, and I never had my rifle on one even for a brief moment. Splendid days, splendid memories! Of course the tsetse fly and the mosquitos were as bad as ever, but it was with real regret with the approaching end of my time that we prepared to come out from that camp, returning down the river as we had come, more lightly loaded this time and within the limits of safety. So back and out, picking up our vehicles, making our way first to the town, and then along the track to Gabarone, the capital of Botswana, and not far from the border with Africa. Here the safari disbanded. Tony had a sort of base and headquarters, and he met up with another white hunter with whom he had some sort of partnership arrangement. I imagine sharing surplus clients when one of them was overbooked and the other had a vacancy. I happened to hear them. Tony asked how the other man had fared with an American client. The reply, ''Not good, not bad, better than some but a bit trigger happy. How did you get on''? ''Wasn't your chap a bit long in the tooth''? ''Oh no'', said Tony, ''we were quite all right, and the boys called him 'The Tough Old Buffalo', and as you know they never make a mistake in their judgement of people. Do you remember the one they called 'The Mean Old Woman'?'', and they drifted off into other reminiscences and out of earshot. I think that was the moment when the thought formed in my mind. 'If I can ever do another hunting safari in Africa, I would not want to shoot elephant, or lion, or many species, perhaps one or two antelope for the pot to keep one's hand in and possibly a couple of lovely tsessaly skins, but the objective would be a really tough old buffalo. There would be no question of conservation, no question of endangered species, I should be looking for an old boy that had been driven out of the herd and was living alone, bad tempered, lonely and wicked. Its wide sweep of horn worn thin at the ends, and the bosses solid over his head, and over all I should be offering him a dignified death, far better than lingering until with his teeth failing and his strength ebbing he would be taken by the lions or even worse still, done to death by hyenas, and remember, if I made a mess of it, such an old boy would hunt me till he died, unless I died first.

My weapons had performed predictably, no complaint if not ideal. I have it in mind to discuss this subject in another chapter. My only real complaint was the recoil. I had fired well over 100 rounds with the heavy rifles, many of them checking or sighting in. I had a bruise on the bone on the second finger of my right hand that took weeks and weeks to disperse. I don't know how I had continued to fire without flinching abominably. On return to London I went to the tropical medicine boys for a check against malaria, bilharzia or sleepy sickness in particular, and I didn't want this to crop up and make a mess of my activities later on. All clear, but a wise precaution. Discussing things with Christian, there was a certain reluctance about the bigger trophies, on a 'where shall we put it? basis', but an absolute rejection of one solitary, large elephant tusk. "That would simply look ridiculous in our house", so I sold the ivory, and got a good price for it to pay for setting up of the modest number of other trophies I had sent home. Prominent in my study, and prized still, even above my lion, the massive head of a 'wicked old daddy buffalo'.

LION

I anchored that lion. He was thrashing about with the lioness behind him and it took two more shots with the same rifle before he was still.

Reports came in from a camp 100 miles away of lions strolling about and practically coming into camp every morning for breakfast, whereas we had seen none. A difficult decision. We had few days left before we were to move on in the opposite direction. Was it worthwhile moving down to the other camp and back again just for the better chance of a lion? But the matter was decided next morning. We found lion spoor crossing our track, a lion and a lioness. The lion full grown, but probably young. How, I wonder, could they know that from paw marks in the dust? Obviously we must follow this up, and so we did, partly in the pick-up and partly on foot, sometimes easy, sometimes very difficult, sometimes they were together, sometimes they parted and appeared to be hunting in a desultory sort of way, coming together again without pattern. For perhaps 2 hours we followed the spoor until at last we saw them, and they saw us in the pick-up. Like other beasts, it always astonished me that a strange, smelly machine was practically ignored, while a man on foot sent a widening ripple of alarm. These lions did not like us, they ran and disappeared into a patch of scrub. Tony, reasoning aloud: "I should like to have a good look at that lion, he is young, they don't have a big black mane down to their knees in these parts". They had moved quite far and fast as they ran from us. It was not getting to the hot part of the day. "If we back off they will think we have gone and will probably stay and rest in the shade of the scrub. We can make a wide circle and come up behind a further patch of scrub beyond them. Then we can stalk through the scrub and see what they are like, and we should be able to stalk them on foot, have a good look at them and decide whether we try to take that lion". We struck off as planned and eventually came to rest some 40 yards from the far side of the second patch of scrub as we had intended. Quite leisurely we were preparing to come down from the pick-up when the leading gun bearer said: "Look Bwana, lion coming". The two lions had appeared at the edge of the scrub and doubtless annoyed to find us there at all and once again in front of them, the male was preparing to charge. "Rifle, quick!" from me. The gun bearer thrust it into my hands, and as I grasped it I realized it was not my rifle. In the emergency the gun bearer had seized the first rifle and it was Tony's rifle. Perfectly adequate medicine for a lion, with a ·375 Magnum expanding bullet, equal to or perhaps preferable to my Weatherby ·300 Magnum, but it had the sights that I could hardly see. No time to change, no time to hesitate, but as the rifle came up to my shoulder, another thought. We had in the camp between us six weapons, I knew them all and with all of them except this one, you pushed the safe forward to fire, but with this one rifle, God knows why and how dangerously different, you pulled the safe back to fire. The lion was now really charging home and closing fast, about 30 yards away. I pulled the safe back, and fired using the rifle like a gun, rather a downhill shot from the pick-up. I anchored that lion. He was thrashing about with the lioness behind him and it took 2 more shots with the same rifle before all was still. The lioness had not really joined the charge, but was waiting ready to join in, and she now circled at about 50 yards range. A freak situation that had suddenly turned dangerous, Tony and the tracker who were in the front of the pick-up in the cab, without weapons and helpless, I and the gun bearer were in the open pick-up behind. If the lion had closed in we could not have used a rifle, and the chances were that he would have mauled us both, while Tony would have been completely powerless to help, and would have been mauled by the lion or the lioness had he got out of the cab. Tony was now out of the cab with his rifle in his hands, and I had my own rifle in my hands. I asked him if the lioness would charge. ''No'', he said without hesitation. ''Will she not follow, or even ambush us''? ''Or return''? ''No'', he said with complete conviction. ''Once she has decided to go, that is the end of it'', but we had to fire shots over her head to make her take that decision. I had my lion, he was young, but good, and I have always been thankful that it was not a case of walking up to a well fed lion, resting in the shade and shooting him, but in this case it was for real. Equally, I have always been thankful that I kept my cool and that I remembered the safe that worked the wrong way. ''Lucky you remembered the safe'', was Tony's remark that evening. To me, that restrained remark was an accolade.

More and more I was reminded of the similarity of this life with a sea voyage in a yacht, with particular reference to the tests of personality and human relationships. Perhaps less definite here, perhaps less confined, but in the context of a possible element of danger and in the reliance of the team, there was no doubt here that all was well, and we were welded into an efficient unit.

Some of you may remember the tale told to the grandchildren, ''How Skips didn't get a tiger''. This lion story similarly became a legend belonging to the great grandchildren's generation under the title, ''How the lion nearly got Skips''!

I had my lion, he was young, but good, and I have always been thankful that it was not a case of walking up to a well fed lion, resting in the shade and shooting him, but in this case it was for real.

FEAR AND DANGER

Behind the whole subject of big game stalking there lies a maybe slight but deep sub-stratum of risk and danger. Fatalities are so few and infrequent that they are barely a statistic, and this is surely due to the skill, dedication and courage of the white hunters with whom nearly all clients take the field. The risk and danger tends to polarize on very few species; lion heads the list with their tendancy to charge and the speed and killing power. Elephant certainly; though here the risk is more likely being trampled on by a cow elephant defending her calf and appearing suddenly behind you in thick cover when you did not know of her existence, while in pursuit of a bull. The bull itself may charge. Buffalo certainly, quite arguably the most dangerous, they are large, powerful, very fast, and a wounded buffalo may not only hunt you until it dies, but has the intelligence to lay an expert ambush. There are also well documented occasions when a wounded buffalo seems to absorb astonishing punishment and many more bullets without apparent effect. Rhino surely a lesser risk, a blundering charge and you would be unlucky indeed to be caught by this. Hippo? You could be chomped or trampled by a hippo blundering back to water along a trail in the marsh, or your canoe could be upset by an attack in open water. Leopard? Hardly in the major danger category, but included because of the principle of the white hunter to finish a wounded beast, and following a wounded lion or leopard into cover is surely in a special category. What then does a white hunter think about this? I had many discussions with Tony and, from his knowledge and information from others, I formed a belief that the white hunter's ultimate nightmare is losing a client, but a far more frequent nightmare is the occasion that might lead to a loss, when for some freak reason he has a client in danger, (more often than not of course, through the client's failure or fault), and if for some freak reason the white hunter is unable to back him up with his almost unfailing rifle. I tested Tony on this in one of our discussions by asking him this question: ''No matter how it might arise, but if, Tony, you were in the ultimate peril with but a fraction in time and distance before a client was mauled, what weapon would you prefer to have in your hands''? The fact that Tony had thought about this, and deeply, was revealed by his instant answer. ''In such a case Skips, I should like a double ·470''. Indeed as our discussions proceeded he said to me: ''If you ever find a good double ·470, which is not more than a King's ransom, buy it for me and I will take it at any time''. It was many years later that I did find one and acquire it, but by this time Tony was no longer going out on hunting safaris and so I kept it myself, and I have it in my own collection. We may come across this again later.

Let us now turn back to my lion, and analize this from a different angle. You could I suppose have a very easy, straight forward and low risk lion; imagine the old gentleman, well fed and content, lying in the shade under a tree taking his ease in the heat of the day with his pride around him. What more simple than to approach without arousing resentment and with one well placed bullet from a suitable rifle, you have your lion. If such an opportunity had happened to me, I feel that I should not have wanted to take a lion, and I have always been glad that my lion was for real, but how quickly the simplest occasion can become a mess. Tony, talking freely to me now about near disasters, produced a case where a client, in very short order, had produced not one but two wounded lions. Apparently he had made a mess of one, then made a mistake and shot at the wrong beast and made a mess of that as well. When Tony had sorted out the resulting mess and stopped an ultimate charge, in his words: ''Quite close enough, thank you'', he turned to his client to find him, rifle on the ground, chalk white, paralized with fear, and yes, apparently it really can happen, he had evacuated his bowels in his trousers. One wonders what story he would tell when he returned to the Fatherland with his lion trophy.

There are no prizes in guessing the nationalities that appear in Tony's tales, after all he had experience, and what experience, of at least six nationalities. There are racial characteristics, but surely the reaction to danger and fear is personal not racial or national. Timing and short space of time and distance are so critical. In the case of our lion, if we had arrived a few minutes sooner, Tony and I would both have been out of the truck, on our feet with our rifles in our hands, and if the lion had then appeared and had charged, it would then have been to Tony a normal occasion. Had we arrived a few moments later, Tony would have seen the lion at 40 yards and would have driven on to a safe distance so that we could reassess the situation and have another think, but we had arrived at exactly the wrong moment. Tony was in the driver's seat without a weapon, three of us were up on top in the back, just preparing to get out. Let us now apply a figure or two, from the gun bearer saying ''B'wana, lion come'', to my anchoring the charging lion, you are talking about 30 yards and less than 10 seconds. Forget such distractions as wrong rifle, invisible sight, safe working in the opposite way and all that! Suppose I had missed that shot? There would, I think, have been just time to reload and put in another shot. Do I hear somebody saying: ''Of course you were really all right because you were in the truck''. But no! That in fact was a potentially fatal element. The lion could have been on top of us in the truck in one bound at the end of his charge, and then we could neither scatter nor use a rifle; nasty, very, very nasty, and the lioness was not charging but following up ready to join in when her lord and master had made his kill. Does somebody else say: ''Why didn't Tony drive on''? The simple answer to this is that from his lesser height, he did not see the charging lion until it was too late.

I liked another tale of Tony's, this time with buffalo. A herd may stampede, and this may be triggered by a variety of reasons. It could happen that a herd, ignorant of your presence, may stampede towards you rather than away. On one such an occasion, Tony shoved his client behind a none too thick trunk of a thorn tree with the words, ''Stay there, keep still''. He then sprinted to find another tree for himself. This was some 30 yards back, also none too thick, and he reached it just in time. When the herd had thundered past, he went up to his client, to receive a furious attack. ''You lily livered so and so, you coward, you are supposed to be looking after me, and all you did was run away to save your arse, leaving me to shoot for my life''. Tony repressing anger as a white hunter must do on such occasions, found a wonderful riposte, ''And is that how you defend yourself?'', he asked, pointing down at the foot of the tree where lay four unfired cartridges. This character completely panicked, thinking that he was shooting fast to save his life, had emptied his rifle without firing a shot. I could continue, there are many tales, but that may be enough to promote some thought about the thrills without which, I suppose, big game stalking might lose one of its strongest charms. As to preference, somehow I think my own would be buffalo, but the native Massai with their proud traditions of courage and initiation of manhood considers the lion and only the lion, not the buffalo, nor the elephant, as the ultimate test.

Of all the trophies I had collected, the buffalo gave me the greatest thrill.

My right hand is where I placed the first shot. From this side there was no indication that the tusks were not symetrical.

ROE DEER AT LAST

Roe deer continued to elude me, had I been unconsciously influenced by the low regard in which they were held in my early youth? Was it lack of active opportunity or pure chance? Meanwhile roe deer had been growing in numbers and growing in importance and they were at last a part of the stalking scene in their own right and there was I thinking quite a lot of experience, and I had never killed a roe deer. My start on roe deer when it came was pure chance. Visiting a sister-in-law living in the Lake District, she took me to Grisedale to some party as she was friendly with Bill Grant. When I was introduced to him an instant attraction developed and we were soon in a corner in full discussion. I shall be ever grateful for this introduction. After some exchanges Bill Grant came up with: "You ought to take up roe deer stalking, you would find them fascinating in themselves. Besides", he continued, "the day is bound to come when you can no longer take the hills for the red deer, while the roe deer, lower down in easier country, shorter distances and in better weather would give you sport and continual stalking for many years to come". You were absolutely right Bill, though neither of us at that time could see that 25 years later when Bill Grant was retired that I should still be stalking red deer, but now to strike while the iron is hot. "How do I start", I asked? "That's quite easy", he replied. "I will put you in touch with Gordon. He is enthusiastic and has a knack of imparting his knowledge. You will get the hang of it with him, and I have no doubt about the outcome".

So started another friendship with Gordon and his family, and I started out for the roe deer not a thousand miles from Carlisle. I have a vivid memory of my first roe deer buck, shot from the shoulder down a woodland ride, and again Bill was right, I found the little 'Will O' the wisp' roe deer absolutely fascinating. An intriguing difference from the red deer apart from the terrain and the time of year. With red deer, in the main you spy them and you stalk them. Rarely do they depart on their own business while you are making your approach, but with roe deer, you may see them, you may plan a stalk and as like as not you may never see the beast again. How often do they just vanish without trace. As the season advances they can be almost quite hidden by grass, bracken or herbage. They are seldom still for long and once lying down it is difficult or impossible to spot them. I think their sight might be superior to the red deer and equally sensitive to wind and scent. They are also intensely influenced by the weather conditions, particularly a cold wind. You can go through an extensive area on one day and see perhaps 40 beasts and have some chance with say 5. On another day in the same area you might see 4 beasts only, all just crossing a ride and have no chance at all. I have stalked for a week in unfavourable weather and killed just one beast almost by chance, almost at the last hour of the last morning. I developed a preference as I progressed with roe deer for stalking in the morning, and more waiting in the evenings that introduced us to 'high seats', the almost universal way of pursuing roe deer in Germany is from the high seat, but curiously it was a long time and many years and many high seats before I was successful. Often I would spy beasts from the high seat, and on occasions descend with difficulty to stalk them on the ground with success, but the many stories of roe deer literally gambolling under the high seat never seemed to happen to me.

Once in a lifetime, a three-horned roe deer.

I started my roe deer with the ·30/06 I used for red deer, and had no difficulties, but feeling that this was rather a cannon, I eventually converted to the ·243 calibre, and found this quite successful. I began to appreciate the tapered post as my favoured reticule. The continental telescopes with the thick bands, an advantage for dusk conditions, but for all round use I preferred the Leupold Duplex.

Roe deer are so beautiful, so dainty, so attractive especially in their summer coat that I never tire of watching them. I may have more to say about the weapons when I am discussing rifles. Additional experience was to go up in January to help with the doe cull. This less rugged than the Highlands, but still rugged enough. I learned that you at once forget roe deer if you see a fox which becomes a preferred target, usually at long range, but a great satisfaction if you succeed, and there are always new experiences. I once shot a fox way down a valley in a small open space. Shortly afterwards a roe deer doe came out with a fawn. Cautiously she approached the fox, satisfied herself that it was dead and harmless, and then quite deliberately and obviously educated her fawn demonstrating that this was a bad thing, striking it with her forelegs. Fascinating to watch.

Bill Grant had been more than justified, I became more and more entranced and as I gained experience on roe deer, I realized the infinite variety and possibilities of their behaviour, and so, as the years went on and I had more time I proportionally spent more time with the roe deer, until the great day came when I had my own roe deer and my own forest, but that is another chapter.

A MEDAL HEAD

Late in April one year I was at Eskdale Muir for a week. The weather throughout was discouraging, mainly wet with cold winds. Is there anything more discouraging to roe deer than a cold wet wind? Beasts just did not show themselves, and after being out alone or with a ranger for 4 days, I had not brought in a beast. Touring an area, with the ranger in a van, in good weather which could show you over 30 beasts, and provide a chance to stalk 5 or 6, in these conditions you may but see 5 or 6 all crossing rides and none offering a chance of a stalk. I did not mind as it was a pleasure to be out and about as long as I was not letting the side down with the urgent cull. On the Friday morning my last day and unchanged conditions I was out with one of the young rangers. We found ourselves at the far end of the area near the forest boundary to open country, and in an attractive little valley. Peter said: ''There are three buck in this valley, I saw them all a week ago, and we could take any one of them''. But we now saw nothing although spying across the valley was good with the trees only about 6 years growth. Slowly we drove round the head of the valley to the end of the road at a turning point. Back as we had come still slowly, still spying tentatively when we reached the otherside, again. Still nothing. Round a bend and along, I raised my hand. Peter knew well enough to slow the car gently and stop, I had seen something. Yes, a beast on the other side about 60 yards below the road was on its feet, a buck. It was about 400 yards away and no way could we stalk from our present position; we should have been open to view the whole of the way down to the bottom of the valley. We could have had a go from further on the road, then down to the bottom of the valley out of sight, back up the valley bottom and a stalk from below to the position of the beast, but this would have been a very long haul, taken a long time and more than likely the beast would not be there any longer when we reached its present location.

It seems that the beast must have been alerted when we passed above it in the car, heard the car turn and go back. I reasoned that as that had not moved it or alarmed it, we might do exactly the same thing, but this time stop the car at the turn, stalk down the road, wriggle across and make our approach from above. I suggested this to Peter and he agreed. Slowly and carefully we took the car back to the end of the road to carry out our plan, finally stalking diagonally down through the young trees. Everything went to plan. There was the beast on its feet, alert but it had not moved. Peter stayed back and I went forward the last 25 yards to take the shot. There was little sound from the strike, and I lost sight. Peter came up and we found the beast 20 yards down the hill, the shot had been correct. I came up behind Peter and he was worried. ''I don't know what Ronnie will say about this. Look at it, it must be a medal head''. Concentrating on my shot with Peter's words, ''3 beasts take any one of them'', in my mind, I had not noticed it. ''He must have come right over the hill from the forest to the east and he would have driven out the lesser buck and taken over the head of the valley as his own territory''. ''Don't worry Peter, the other beasts will be back again within 48 hours, and you will have the situation as before''.

When we got back to base, Ronnie, understanding and tolerant as ever was not worried. ''No harm done, an extra beast from outside and you deserve a good head against all the cull beasts you have brought in''. David my second son who loved coming with me but did not himself handle a rifle, used to say: ''They ought to give you a medal Father for the worst head not the best one''. Ronnie put this one up and it got a medal for the best head in Southern Scotland that year, and so at long last I had a really fine roe deer trophy and again it was an accident. You never know your luck, an odd chance on the last hour of the last day of a week's stalking.

GOLDEN ORIOLES

It came to pass that I was in Ischia with Christian. Why? After a strenuous week in Naples with meeting all the days and junkettings by night, at an International Chamber of Commerce Congress, we badly needed a quiet week before returning to the usual stress of life in England. Why Ischia? We knew it as a delightful island because we had visited it in my yacht on former occasions, the perfectly circular and well protected harbour formed by the crater of an ancient volcano. It was in those days, virtually unknown, and in complete contrast to Capri with its notoriety, deriving much from Gracie Fields. It is true, if my memory serves, that Anthony Eden's sister had married an engineer on the Ischia – Naples ferry, but I have the impression that this unlikely romance did not endure.

A pleasant five hour ferry journey from Naples, a delightful small hotel, simple but sufficient, lovely walking in the hills and woods, good beaches and the sea just becoming warm enough, and so the stage is set.

One morning about noon, a blue-rinsed American tourist, a typical example of the species, arrived back at the hotel at a dead run, dishevelled, distressed and breathless. She gasped out: ''I was in the mountains, I saw a bandit, he had a gun, he came after me''. A pause for more gasps: ''I am checking out'', and so she did, departing with some thankfullness by the next ferry to what to her would be the safe civilisation of Naples.

Christian and I looked at each other: ''Sounds interesting, let's go''. We took to the hills, and sure enough, we found a bandit. It may well have been the very same who had put the American lady to flight. So we made friends with him without difficulty. He had with him a dog, a mongrel dog of indistinguishable type, possibly the breed might have been known as the ''bandit'' dog. He also had a gun; this was likely to be 100 years old, about 16 bore, a muzzle loading flintlock, well worn, and I judged, a potentially dangerous possession, and his occupation? He was walking through the chestnut groves locating golden orioles by their calls in the nesting season, and shooting them sitting to feed his dog! This, perfectly logical, even laudable from his point of view, but if you are an English reader, you must attune yourself to the custom of a country where anything may be shot, songbird or not, at any season, and for any reason at all.

This character took us back to his house, a small hut out in a tiny valley high up in the hills, with a small, struggling vineyard which was his livelihood. From a cave he brought out a bottle of delicious wine, some bread, cheese from goats' milk, and made us welcome to a satisfying meal. From him we learned that the wines of Ischia, both red and white, could be exceptionally choice as we had already discovered at the hotel, but apparently they do not travel and were almost unknown even on the Italian mainland. He also explained the distinctive long, thin, double tapered casks which we had noticed. These were designed to hang, one on each side of a mule, so that it could negotiate the rocky and precipitous mountain tracks to take the wine down from the hills. When we eventually departed, international relations firmly established in great amity, we had enjoyed ourselves and had had a delightful day.

I feel a slight pressure building up that might be explained as: ''What on earth has this to do with stalking''? The answer of course is, 'nothing at all' unless you become filled with a burning desire to enter a contest and endeavour to establish a record bag of golden orioles, taken in the nesting season with a ·22 rifle. What a lot of information we had obtained from a bandit, at the instance of a blue-rinsed American widow. The best islands are not the best known, the best wines are not the most expensive, the best bandits can be delightful characters, and I suspect that any dogs would relish golden orioles.

HILL STICKS

It might be said that there are stacks and stacks of sticks and sticks of every kind and form for every need. The smart gold-plated topped malacca cane that our grandfathers walked to church with, the bishop's crozier, the shepherd's crook, the gnarled and twisted stick that Harry Lauder walked the stage with while singing: "There's somebody waiting for me in an old cabin down by the sea". This surely was supposed to be sad and sentimental, but the whole house would be rocking with laughter. There is the Irish Shillelagh, the swagger stick, the Indian policeman's lathi, the stick with the ram's horn head beautifully carved (I have one such which displays a leaping salmon), and finally the thumb stick for the hill, the traditionally formed and surely essential equipment for the stalking man.

Our thumb stick should be the height that comes easily to hand when the fore-arm is just above horizontal with the elbow at the waist. Nature always wonderful, grows the material for sticks thicker at the bottom and tapering to the top, for the very good reason that this form is correct to withstand the stresses to which a young tree is subjected as it grows, but if an engineer considers what is required for our hill stick if it is to be as light as possible while as strong as possible and making the best use of the material, it comes out thicker in the middle tapering gently at the top and tapered again, but slightly less to the bottom, to withstand the stresses man imposes upon it in its new role.

Now to achieve this form, no sooner said than done. Thanks to modern glues with which a joint between two well prepared surfaces of wood can be joined to produce a union stronger than the wood itself, we can construct a stick from three sections in the ideal form required; I have done this and it works. The more usual materials are ash and hazel, but many others are possible; holly, yew, briar and cotoneaster for example, but what would an engineer do if he were not tied to natural grown wood? Probably a double tapered, thin wall light alloy tube. They do not come like that unless specially and rather expensively contrived. Nature's nearest equivalent to the light alloy tube would be three sections of bamboo; splendid material but more difficult to make the joints without liners. All this seems to be leading to something, and I move from the 3 pieces, ash or hazel, to a double tapered balsa cane with six slim, tapered bamboo sections glued to it, very tasty, very sweet, very strong, very neat, but hours and hours of skilled work, analogous to craftsmen making the split cane fishing rod. When I had used this with success for some time, it was accidentally broken by abnormal stress (my dog bolted). Shrinking from the hours of work necessary to repeat it, I gave thought to a simpler form for a Mark II version. Starting with the same double tapered light weight balsa core I prepared sections of suitably sized bamboo canes nearly half their diameter and joined as shown in the attached sketch. Four sections will do, five is perhaps gilding the lily but attractive. Complete this with a suitable ferrule at the bottom, hard wood will do, rubber is possibly better for silence and grip. Can we make a further improvement? Our thumb stick is required to be about 6″ longer if it is to be used to steady the rifle for a standing shot. We could deal with this by using an appropriate length of

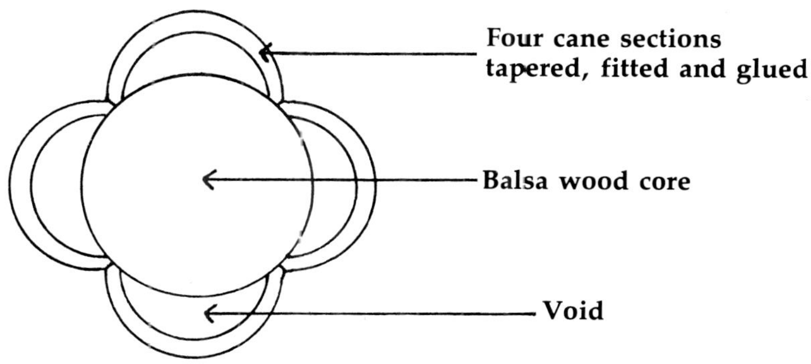

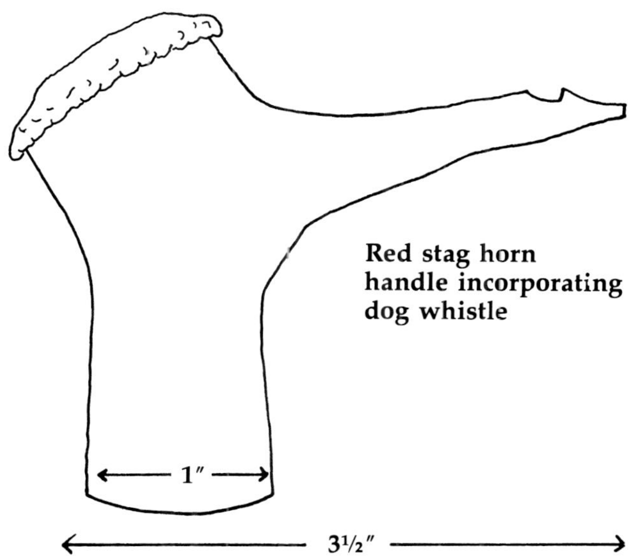

Mark II split cane hill stick

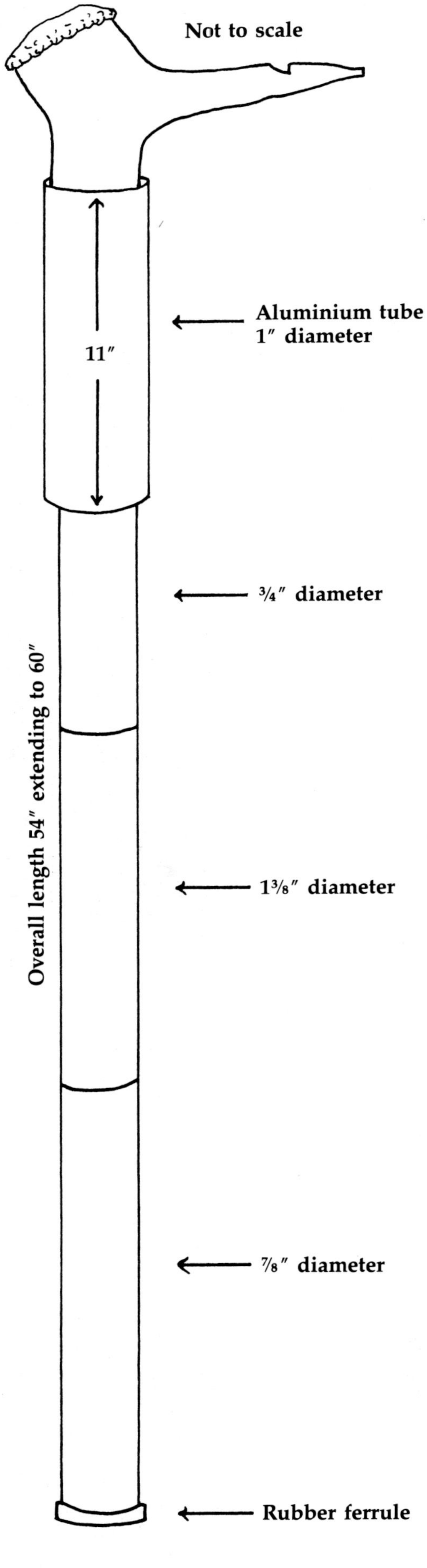

alloy tube sliding up and down on the stick. A neat way of doing the slider is to glue on to the stick a layer of old tweed, this, lightly greased, serves excellently with the alloy tube. A bayonet lock can be used at the different heights, but in practice a few turns of plastic tape does the trick just as well.

Now for the top of our thumb stick. There is probably nothing better than a section of red deer horn as sketched, and you can finish the branch as a whistle. This, of course, should match your dog whistle. Don't ask me how to do this, I don't know, but I have done it by trial and error. You seldom shoot off a stick for red deer, far more frequently for roe deer. This Mark II version weighed 12 ozs. total, it is as strong as 'be damned'. I added three bands of red tape, unnecessary for strength, but making it visible and easy to find when left behind on the final approach to a stag which may, of course, lead you a considerable distance away.

I have now had and used a stick in this Mark II version for many years. Stalkers, apt to be a little suspicious of anything new and not traditional, do accept and approve it. Nothing made by man is likely to be absolutely perfect in all conditions. One old stalker trying it and hefting it, came up with the verdict. "It'll blaw", and he was right, in a very strong wind its own light weight may cause it to be deflected and not go down to test the ground exactly where you wish. This inspired my retort to the old stalker, "Useless to blether, in heavy weather, if like a feather, your stick won't go doon". But I have found two more uses for a hill stick, even this special hill stick. Not only the third leg, and an aid to balance, a tester of doubtful ground and a help on a steep hill, it also enables you to stand still, absolutely still. If you can do this, a beast may stare at you without the fear caused by even the slightest swaying movement. My final use is on the occasions when you pause while the stalker goes on for a 'spy'. A welcome chance to catch your breath and ease your muscles when not worthwhile at the time to sit or lie down. Stand facing uphill, feet well apart, hill stick forward, bend down and put your chin on your hand on the top of the stick. Something like a third of your weight comes off your legs, all muscles can be relaxed, you are slightly lower and less visible, and perhaps less like a man standing if in sight of a beast. I have found this of great help. Is the effort necessary to produce this type of hill stick worthwhile? Yes and no. It may not be cost effective in time and effort, but in satisfaction, original thought, pleasure in your skill of hand, and the continuing joy in using something that you have made yourself that works well and is perhaps original — the answer must be yes!

AUSTRALIA AND NEW ZEALAND

I first made a visit to Australia in the middle of the 1920's, and it made such an impression on me that it is worth a mention although I admit that I did little work with a rifle. It really was a primitive country with a small population, and vast areas though much of it was virtually uninhabitable. In many respects life was rough, sometimes very rough. I had occasion to do a tour, motoring in the outback of Western Australia. The car was an Austin 20, and you took with you survival equipment, a timber winch puller with a long length of wire rope, planks on your running board, a roll of mesh for getting out of sand patches, and just about every spare for the car, except a crankshaft. One experience you had to learn was that if you were travelling on a dirt road, parallel to a fence and you startled a kangaroo between you and the fence, it would endeavour to race ahead and cut across your bows. If you maintained speed and the kangaroo misjudged it, a horrendous accident with some hundreds of pounds of kangaroo coming at you through the windscreen. You would wait in a little township for two or three days on the chance of another car going your way. This more than doubled your chance as if one car broke down, you could go forward or back in the other, and there was little risk to life. If you broke down 100 miles out, a strong man carrying water bags might walk in, but unless picked up by a car he might die, the alternative, to lie in the shade under the car, conserving energy and drinking minimum water from the radiator, hoping that somebody would come by before it was too late. Gates to open in fences, a real chance of taking the wrong road in roadless country and ending up nowhere. Getting stuck in sand, or even immobilised by a flash flood from infrequent rain. One unique sight in the back country was six tons of petrol in cans on a flat car with lorry wheels drawn by a team of camels. This might well rank as the most improbable method

Aboriginal family at home.

Petrol delivered by camel power.

of petrol delivery. You carried a gun and rifle but rarely used them. Lovely memories of sleeping out by a water hole after a supper of steak and mushrooms on a wood fire and billy tea. During the night the thump, thump of the kangaroos as they came down to the water hole. This is not really a tale of motoring in the outback, we are more concerned with hunting, and of this there was very little. Elsewhere in Australia I shot rabbit, duck, with the gun, but used nothing larger than a ·22 rifle. One kangaroo hunt on horseback with dogs, and a hard pressed joey throwing out the young kangaroo from her pouch. Luckily there was no drama here as the daughter of the house wanted to raise a young kangaroo, and the kangaroo mother would have a dormant small kangaroo in the pouch ready to take over.

New Zealand, a land of tremendous charm, again the small population, self sufficient, but here much more for the rifle. In various locations I was out after wild boar or deer. In those days deer, whilst abundant had not become a pest, and with a good guide stalking was possible and great heads might result, but the country was rugged, access to a stalking area might be up a stream bed, and if rain came down you might be immobilised in the 'High Country'. Getting trophies out was arduous and difficult and vast areas of forest stacked up the odds against you. Alas the day was to come when the deer multiplied until they were threatening their own survival, causing erosion and environmental change and damage. They were then declared a pest to be destroyed by any means. A horrible system developed of shooting them from helicopters above the forest line and bringing them out suspended from the helicopter. This was all season and without regard to any cull system, no limitation on age or sex. I have seen with my own eyes a helicopter coming in with five or six carcasses suspended beneath it. Happily the situation shows sign of improvement, and with luck deer will no longer be a pest and can be a worthwhile tourist attraction with controlled hunting, but there is another development, deer farming in some areas has threatened to become more profitable than sheep, so much so that there is difficulty in obtaining good breeding stock. Why is it so profitable? It is not just the meat or the hide, it is largely because Chinese gentlemen believe that the velvet from the horns is an aphrodisiac to increase their sexual powers and rivalling the powdered rhino horn the demand for which, in Africa, is threatening the extermination of the rhino. A substitute chemically and physically similar would be provided if they used hair clippings and finger nails, but that won't do for the old Chinese gentlemen. In England the removal of antlers in velvet is prohibited. I think this is right and I am glad that it is so.

Now 60 years on, New Zealand has changed, not so dramatically as Australia, but the population has increased, the Maori population even more so, and a fine people they are. There is the problem of the Cooke Islanders. More industrialization and changing markets, but to me the charm of New Zealand remains enshrined in many lovely memories.

Clinton Canyon, Milford Track, South Island, New Zealand.

WHICH RIFLE?

The Forestry Commission choice for their rangers' rifles was the calibre and cartridge known as the Winchester ·270. The E.F.G. by no means so definite but this was, perhaps, their predominant choice. This amounted to a pretty formidable mass recommend. If you are starting up with your own rifle and consult a dealer, he is likely to give the same advice and the same answer. I have no quarrel with this and indeed, I have a very fine example in this calibre, but it is surely interesting to look back at my experiences and review the possibilities to see what we can discover. If we say that the possibilities range from ·222 to ·300 Magnum a choice, though still not complete, would reveal: ·22/250, ·25/06, 6·5 mm, the Winchester ·270, Rigby ·275 high velocity (7 × 57 mm), 7 × 64 mm, ·280 Magnum, ·303, ·30/06 (·308) and ·300 Magnum, several makes.

Perhaps the next step is to eliminate some of these, giving reasons. Out go ·222 and ·22/250, simply because they are not legal in England though they are in Scotland. Surely with your first rifle you should choose one that is legal throughout the British Isles? I have another reason, popular as these smaller calibres have become, I find the experts quite dedicated to them, but consider the stalkers using rifles constantly and throughout the year, they tend to be better shots on average than the amateurs and their clients. For this reason and finally, if they ever have a shot they don't like, perhaps because it is rather far, or a strong cross wind, they can leave it, knowing that they are likely to get that beast on another occasion, next week or the week after, but the amateur up only for a day or two feels impelled to take the shot.

I should next strike out the ·300 Magnum as way over power for roe deer and unnecessary for red deer. I have tuned a Weatherby ·300 Magnum which I had used successfully in Africa, and tamed it sufficiently to shoot red deer stags in Scotland successfully, but I regard it as an African rifle, and quite unnecessary in Scotland. With the same feeling I eliminate the other Magnums, for our purposes they don't give any sufficient advantage to compensate for the disadvantages of more recoil, more flash, more flip, providing only a small velocity increase at long range. I think I have said already that my feeling is: "If a rifle doesn't do the job to your satisfaction at less than 3,000 feet per second, get a bigger one".

There may be a connection between skill and power, the less the skill the more the reserve provided by more power. In the U.S.A. with their tendancy to pursue the limit, they load up towards 4,000 feet a second, but I have a belief that bullet performance then becomes unpredictable. A head of grass seed might well deflect the bullet and depending on the position of the strike, and whether bone is encountered, the bullet may go through like a knitting needle or literally splash and shatter on a shoulder blade. The expansion may be irregular or unsatisfactory.

We have now considerably reduced the field, and can consider what remains. Suppose we take the energy at 200 yards as about 2,000 foot pounds. It is probably the longest shot you are likely to take unless you are up against a wounded beast at longer range. We are now down to four weapons. Does this agree with actual experience in general use? I have said that I don't like ·243 for red deer; I have had splendid results with 7 × 57 in Rigby form ·275 high velocity, splendid results with ·30/06, preferring it to the Winchester ·270 because of the versatility and range of bullet weights with which it can be loaded. I have of course used ·270 with equal satisfaction. Does it perhaps spoil a little more meat than the ·30/06 with almost complementary power? If we then say the extremes are ·243 and ·30/06, we find we are now concerned with one. I now use the ·25/06, a single shot at that, but with the Nosler partition bullet of 117 grains as my standard. I kitted up a friend with one of these in bolt action form for a specification:—

(1) To take to Scotland when invitation and opportunity offered.
(2) For use on a large estate in Hampshire for a cull of about 10 roe deer, 2 or 3 fallow deer and foxes ad lib, in the hands of a keeper, keen and an excellent shot. He told me that he felt a little disappointed when I first produced this weapon, but rapidly became fully convinced and full of praise as he has done consistently well with it, finding it particularly valuable on foxes at long range. I am thankfull that this had worked out well, and slightly humbled by the thought that I could have well suggested another.

Are we now back to two rifles, the 7 × 57 and the ·270? Should I then go for the slightly more modern ·270? Remember that in realistic terms it is the rifle plus telescope. Rifles are now so good that it is not necessary to pay the top prices. You shoot what you see through your telescope, and at the price you can afford for the outfit don't economize on the telescope, favouring this rather than the other way round. You will never use iron sights in practice, so you need not pay for them. For a beginner, again no hesitation about the reticule, 4 × and good light gathering power for a beginner the reticule is not too important, with experience he will find what he prefers, and very probably end up as I have done with the Duplex.

Where do you get your rifle? If your money indicates a secondhand rifle go to an experienced dealer, preferably in your own area, so that you can have continued contact. Discuss with him your plans, consult him, and get him involved, you may need his services, and it is in his interest to see that you are satisfied. Buying at Auction? Possible, bargains are possible, disasters are possible, but this is unwise for a beginner as you depend entirely on your own judgment, though the auctioneers' descriptions are astonishingly good, so it still remains "Caveat emptor". There can be pitfalls, and who can judge the accuracy of a rifle barrel by inspection of the bore which may well be dirty or full of oil and grease. So this method is definitely out unless you are prepared to gamble and back your experience and know how.

Well we have gone a long way to arrive almost at the same point from which we started, hoping that it may increase your confidence.

TRIUMPH OR DISASTER

If you can meet with triumph or disaster and treat those two imposters just the same
(KIPLING)

Time passes, and here are are in October 1987. My 86th birthday is behind me and I am still determined to go out on the hill. We are in England, not far from Penrith, and on ground adjoining Martindale, which I believe was one of the oldest deer forests in England. John, a stalker from the Western Isles, characteristic and at times difficult to understand. The night had been dreadful, heavy storms, thunder, lightning, heavy rain and strong squally winds, but today and after the storm atmosphere, bright intervals, some heavy cloud, showers threatening but holding off, and above all good visibility. Out on to the road, up the hill leading to the grouse lunch hut. The Argocat on a trailer behind a hard pressed car. Spying as we went in, it would appear that the rough night had brought beasts into sheltered corners low down and we saw beasts up the glen to our left with some stags, but John, knowing well, and with 5 stags already taken off the hill, dismissed them; a good 10 pointer, a 9 pointer, a young 8 pointer and a stagie or two. To our right, and not far away a beautiful young 8 pointer, we could have taken him but definitely a beast to leave, though he had not at this stage with the rut just breaking out, more than 2 or 3 hinds with him.

The Argocat comes off the trailer, a reluctant start and we are away, John driving, I alongside him in the cab, and a young helper, Bert, behind. Mechanised in these days and for me a life saver. On the same ground 15 years before you would walk the whole distance. You might have long drags getting a beast down to a point where it could be picked up, but now I must admit that I stopped dragging stags when I was 70. I can no longer stalk on ground which is too steep or broken, and I could only manage to do near-in stalking without the invaluable aid of the Argocat; a wonderful piece of modern technology with its 8 pudgy little wheels, all driving and exerting a pressure less than the human foot; capable of almost anything unless you get a belly-straddle on a rock or a steep bank it could not climb, but then it is light enough to be manhandled by three men. Still subject to the mechanical and electrical ills afflicting man-made mechanism, it is even amphibious.

We went back to the Argocat for a cup of coffee and a piece to let things settle down.

So, away up the hill to the ridge and along, leaving the Argocat occasionally to make a foray, to spy into the valley on one side, or the broken ground stretching away below on the other. Eventually at about 12 o'clock we spied hinds, about 12 of them spread up the hillside beyond, below on our right and with them, a stag. John's long, high-powered telescope resolved this as a poor type of 6 pointer head, definitely a cull beast that we could attempt, but now the approach and the stalk. The approach difficult but not impossible, peat hags, and by gulleys, though shallow, but then we should have hinds above to our left, the stag the other side of the hinds, low down the hill. John, knowing the ground better than I, was pessimistic. It did not look as if there would be any way in from 300 yards, with the hinds spread up the hill and commanding fairly open ground. "Oh well", we will have a go and see how it develops, but no, 10 minutes later a hind and calf, unseen, unknown, had walked up the hill, walked round the peat hag straight before us, and not 40 yards away. Away they went, instantly alarming the whole bunch. End of that stalk, nothing we could do or could have done. Had we proceeded down the hill we should have run into that same hind and calf, in a position that we could not pass. Best go back to the Argocat and have a coffee and a piece, let things settle down and try again. So 30 minutes later we set off in the Argocat on the original plan, and two stops later we found the same beasts, they had settled down perhaps 1½ miles from their original position and somewhat similarly disposed, if anything more difficult to approach. This time a different tactic evolved, we would walk away from the Argocat, over the hill to our left, away from the beasts, and well sheltered from any intervening beasts, to the boundary wall, along that, along a fence to emerge more or less above and not quite as far as the bunch, now involving about 28 pairs of eyes against us. This involved a walk of perhaps 1½ miles, and then we had an entirely new situation, there were hinds high up the hill to our left in a commanding position. As we faced them the wind was from our left at 45°, but we did not know how far along the hill the beasts extended below, we should have to watch that herd, it might indeed become critical, but of immediate concern another hazard, sheep, wild, scary, unpredictable. We had to do a definite sheep manoeuvre stalk to get past a bunch that might run and upset the whole performance. Similarly sheep to our right again by passed without disaster, but there were two sheep still on our right watching us, not alarmed as yet, but preventing what might have been our best approach, a little to our right for the wind and down. We had to virtually crawl past the sheep and go slightly left, still commanded by those hinds high up. Let us admit that things were not looking good at that stage, we didn't known where the beasts were below in relation to the wind, we didn't know where the stag might be in relation to the other beasts, there was no way forward not commanded by the hinds up on our left. The only chance was to crawl, and this was not hands and knees but a flat crawl like a snake, some of it over open white ground. In such locations I would be on John's right, close to him to reduce the size of our area as seen from the deer. We would make three or four wriggles, gain a few feet and stop, and repeat this until we had gained a critical 30 yards or so, to where a little hillock offered slight shelter, but that hillock might be only 18 inches to 2 feet high. We dared not crawl up it and look over. We had to crawl round its right hand edge and still almost in view of the beasts. Choosing our ground with care we went on, still flat crawling, 25 or 30 yards at a time, now heading across the slope, now heading down, now 45° to right or left using every inch or clump of rushes. How far this total was, how long, I did not know but it was taxing, and had it not been downhill I could not have done it. At last a small peat hag with heather atop; hidden at last from the menacing hinds, we could peek round and suddenly the picture changed; there were the hinds, the main bunch, spread out some 200 yards from us, safe from the wind, our only menace being one hind and calf level with us on the hill and only 70 yards away, but the stag fairly high up the hill, away beyond where there were one or two more hinds — about 350 yards. No way could we move any further or at all. There was nothing to do but wait on. The stag started chasing hinds, he rounded them up and drove them in towards the main bunch and as he did so he was coming our way, 300 yards, 250 yards, 200 yards, time to ready my rifle and try to get into a firing position with my elbows down, the rifle steady and the telescope on the stag. I then admit that for a moment I lost myself through the fairly narrow view provided by the telescope, hinds and the stag were running, at one bound the stag disappeared and my rifle was on the hinds. John, ever watchful, kicked me in the ribs to warn me. Everything went calm, the stag was lying down beyond most of the hinds, about 250 yards away, hidden in a little hollow in some rushes. Again nothing to do but wait on, and with experience I kept moving my hands so that my muscles would not lock, put my head down to rest my neck muscles, shut my eyes or changed the focus, relying on John to report any change of scene. He was on my left a few feet away, slightly above. At last the stag got up, came towards us and started moving hinds again. Things were looking better, indeed quite good, and then came the 'moment critique' the stag standing perfectly and broadside on 150 yards away, 20° downhill in a splendid light. And as I sighted the fine hairs of the reticle in my telescope on the vital position, just above and just behind the top of the heart, ready to touch off the trigger, when with a kick in the ribs from John, stopped me. What the hell? There were two sheep straight in line between me and the stag. From my view point the whole body of the stag was clear, I would have bet you 98 to one on a dead stag and a clean kill. I would have given you a thousand pounds on the life of those sheep, but from John's point of view a few feet away and a foot or two different in altitude, it appeared that a sheep had only to put its head up to stop a bullet, and so with no reason to suppose that we should not get other chances he had restrained me; but no, in the next 15 minutes we had the stag end on facing us, katie-cornered, partly hidden. In line with hinds, in line with sheep, and worse, tail on and moving away from us, while the light was declining, a threatening heavy rainstorm coming up, but still, at any moment he might turn and give me a shot. During all this the hind and calf, 70 yards away, had moved down the hill, but then invisible to me but just seen as the top of a back by John, another beast, a switch stag, little

John's long, high-powered telescope resolved this as a poor type of six-pointer head, definitely a cull beast that we could attempt.

bigger than a staggie, appeared from nowhere, and working down the hill, no doubt keeping well away from the big boy who would have attacked him, and this stag was now only 30 yards from us. Remember I didn't know that he was there, and fiddling restlessly to try to get my rifle correctly aligned on the ever moving stag, I moved my rifle slightly and I must have been moving my head slightly. The stag put his head up, looked straight at us, saw me and in a moment the whole hill was in motion. Desperately I followed the stag with the rifle and at about 200 yards he checked and turned sideways. I had an instant chance. I touched off the trigger, but impelled by the need for speed, and perhaps a cold finger from the long wait, I touched off a tiny fraction of a second before I had intended, and the bullet went harmlessly over his back. No further chance, all gone and out of range. Ah well! If I had pulled off that shot, I should have been tempted to feel that it was a wizard shot at the end of a wizard stalk, and a recovery from disaster, but should I have taken that shot at all? Was there not too much chance of a wounded beast and another sort of disaster? Wearily to my feet, muscles working badly after the long crawl, and the long lie, plod up the hill and so back to the Argocat, and a welcome cup of coffee, Bert had a hind and calf pass him close but down wind and had returned unseen. The whole performance from first to last had taken 4½ hours. There was no time to go out further from home. We worked back spying as we went and saw nothing of interest to us, and so to the end of the day.

Do you call it a disaster with nothing achieved, 'No', to me that was the essence of deer stalking, the thing that still turns me on, the fact that we hadn't got the beast of little significance, I am no longer bloodthirsty, and I have the memories fixed in my mind. A pity that I cannot draw a little diagram, but I hope that you can follow the proceedings. That night after a good hot bath, a dram of malt whisky, tired, likely to be stiff tomorrow, the dominant picture in my mind, the fine hairs of the reticle over the stag's heart, the sheep in front and the kick in the ribs from John.

MY FORESTS IN SCOTLAND

It was in 1968 and for various complicated reasons, unnecessary to detail here, that I bought an outback sheep walk in Eskdale Muir and embarked on the creation of a forest. Partly I suppose because the initial motivation was in search of a financial safeguard, I little realized how important this venture was to become in my life and when I was starting an entirely new chapter. As my career had been mainly industrial there had always been an underlying feeling that I should like a closer contact with the land and country life. Now at last I was a land owner, and it was a family possession. I often thought how much better than an inherited estate that might have been entailed, and thank heaven I had escaped a perilous and unmanageable mansion which had become the nightmare to so many properties. In our case a prime objective was to plant trees. I did not try to develope a fishing and sporting estate at the same time, though very willing to exploit any possible advantage in this direction. I liked the conception that the area had once been part of the great Ettrick Forest, destroyed by man for timber, for sheep and to discourage outlaws. Down in the peat there are still the remains of trees and indications of what had once been a very different outlook.

Fingland Hill. My forest in Scotland.

Two years later I bought another area, this time at Carsphairn. The forest was called "Fingland Hill", and I still do not know a satisfactory derivation of the word 'Fingland'. The other forest was called "Deugh Water", after an attractive river rising in the area and flowing past the forest. As to the trees, I remember one winter day in 1969 at Fingland Hill when with Christian I was doing an inspection at the top of the area with the forester. It was cold, very cold, there was a piercing wind with the promise of sleet. Our labrador, taking a poor view of this and following an inherited urge for protection, began digging a hole in which she could curl up for protection from the wind. The trees, pathetic little morsels, about 12 inches high on bare turned over furrows, blown by the wind, so that it was a wonder that they were not torn from the upturned sod. Very conscious of this discouraging scene and the impression it was likely to produce on an owner, the forester was saying. "We often feel an owner should not see his trees for at least 5 years". How right he was! Faith was required, but the will to live and grow triumphed over wind, frost, snow, voles, aphids, possible forays by sheep, hares, rabbits, and birds such as black cock. The aphid when much magnified, an ugly little monster with red eyes, adapted to the discouraging occupation of sawing away at the vital pine needles. Now 20 years later those pathetic little wisps are 40 foot high with quite different problems of thinning and future marketing.

It was fun to be able to talk about "My forests in Scotland". It could conjure up the vision of thousands of acres. In reality of course, it was hundreds, and I could equally talk about "2 areas in Lowland Scotland in which we are growing trees as a family venture". I like to tell the truth, but both statements are true and there are different ways of so doing. My son built a caravan in the Fingland Hill Forst, and this became a valuable resource for all the family, a place of retreat where one could find peace, relax the spirit and recharge the batteries.

It so happened that Ronnie Rose was appointed by E.F.G. (Economic Forestry Group) to manage wild life on the property just as I bought the land, and we were at once in contact. As I came to appreciate his conception of the management of wild life, I was a backer and a member of the team. I must here pay tribute and say how the enduring friendship that has developed enriched my life and enlarged my knowledge and resources, with an entirely new understanding of wild life, conservation, control and management, and I had recource to his vast knowledge; did I seek the correct form in Highland dress, Ronnie could tell me at once, did I want to know the origin of the Farquharson rifle, Ronnie knew the whole story. But above all I came to know his objectives and theories on deer control for the benefit of the deer themselves and having regard to the forestry interest involving the sporting side, the economics and the public interest. I hope I was a help to him in the early days, as I was then I believe, the only owner attending frequently and taking a personal interest in these problems, prepared to go and do it myself as I learned more about the game. One can only add examples from the memory, there are so many. At the beginning, in the area under his control there were but some 50 roe deer, and some of these were afflicted with liver fluke or lung worm so that he did not wish to breed from them. I think I shot the first such buck, it seemed terrible to be taking them out when there were so few.

It went like this: out together one day he spotted 2 roe deer up a little valley and sent me up on my own while he waited and observed from the bottom of the valley keeping my labrador with him. I stalked carefully to the top of the valley, where it came out below a forest ride. I had seen nothing and now waited while Ronnie came up to join me. He had seen a third beast a doe come out of the valley and coming to the edge it had seen me, alerted the others and taken them away. We walked along the road for perhaps half a mile and then the three roe leapt up below us where they had been lying down and fled before us along the flank of the hill. As they ran Ronnie said, ''I want that buck, you can get him''. I was not even sure which beast when they checked some 200 yards away, but Ronnie said: ''The left hand beast now''. I touched off a shot I should never have attempted on my own, as apart from the distance the beast was almost tail on to me. ''Got him, well done'', said Ronnie. We walked in, no sign. Dusk was closing in, my labrador 'Jet' was not entered to roe deer, but again Ronnie said, ''Why not try Jet?'' and when released she soon found the trail and disappeared. In a moment or two she was back again. We followed, she had found the beast, dead in a ditch about 60 yards away and ran repeatedly to and fro between the beast and ourselves leading us to it. Very useful as otherwise we should have had to come back and do a fresh search next day. What a contrast 20 years later, the area is vastly increased, now a complex of many thousands of acres, 75 miles of forest roads, a deer population of perhaps 5,000, an annual cull depending on many factors, and much influenced by winter weather, of perhaps a thousand. More rangers, more stalking clients from England and from overseas, and in those 20 years, 4 generations of Ronnie's family: his father, retired and now gone, who had been the head stalker at Balmoral, Ronnie and his family, Ronald his son, now a trained forester and ranger, in turn married and his children starting to grow up. How I value from the daughters now grown up, the same affectionate greeting that used to await ''Uncle Skips'' when they were small girls, and Ronnie at his best, relaxing in the caravan and talking freely of reminiscences with myself and Christian, Mark and Susan. Marvellous stores of knowledge now enlarged to the deer of almost every European country. I must not be led further into Ronnie's story. I know but just enough to appreciate that his tale should be told and written by himself, and I urge him to do this.

THE MASTER BUCK OF FINGLAND HILL

In 1969, I commenced planting up an area at Eskdale Muir, known as Fingland Hill. It so happened that Ronnie Rose joined E.F.G. at the same time, and I was able to collaborate with him, from the start, in an initial cull of poor diseased roe deer, and with his plans for working up a balanced population of good quality beasts in harmony with the forest operations.

Because there was a small established woodland by the burn at the bottom of my property, roe deer were present and a pair found the enclosed area free from sheep, much to their advantage. As trees began to grow, the population increased. In 1970, a splendid photograph by G. Taylor showed a roe deer fawn. I like to think that this was the buck on my property. It is also possible that he was sired by a gold medal head shot, (rather by accident) only about a mile away.

In 1971 there was no cull, and so as a yearling, this buck escaped. In 1972 I killed a young cull buck in the early morning by the little wood, and while Ronnie took it back to the road, I stalked up the burn and watched a party of five beasts, probably the total population at that time. One of them was a very good two year old buck. That was probably the first occasion when I began to know him as an individual. Ronnie also saw him in the valley the same year.

In 1973 this buck was so good at three years of age that he was left deliberately, and in 1974 at four years old events took a different turn. Powerful and aggressive, now established with a territory, he killed two young beasts and the bodies were found, one of them skinned and photographed had 14 stab wounds, five of them penetrating to the lungs. This might have indicated a killer with a spike head, but no, the head was normal but with tynes long and sharp. Better, we thought, if we could have taken the slain as useful culls instead of painful deaths and wasted carcasses. And so in that year we had the Master Buck of Fingland Hill. With the trees now four years old it was still possible to go to a point on the approach road and spy the whole valley basin through glasses. If beasts were spotted, one could plan a stalk and go in to watch the beasts and get to know them, even if no cull was intended. In 1975 the buck was seen frequently and extended his area. If more rivals were killed, they were not found. The population was now 8 or 9.

In 1976, the trees were growing, but stalking was still good, and this year we took a different view. The master buck was now so dominant and so aggressive that he was holding too large a territory, and preventing the establishment of three or four families which the area could now hold, and so the decision was made. ''If chance offers, we take him''. With this decision a new relationship started.

One evening I spotted him and stalked him, lost him, but guessed that he would cross the hill and go down below the road on the side of the main valley. I was right, and from that road I saw him again. I think he also got me so I retreated, moved quietly up and waited in the road ditch. Half an hour later he came out, crossed the road without a pause, mounted the high bank and checked for a moment the edge of cover. It was late, the light was bad, he had given me no time, and I took an off the shoulder shot, as I thought at 80/100 yards. I did not see what happened. The recoil and the blast of the rifle had blinded me. Reload and walk in. To my horror I found that in that light and in haste I had completely misjudged the range. It was 170 yards. There was no sign, it was too dark to search effectively. I went back to the caravan and had an almost sleepless night fearing a wounded beast. In the morning Ronnie came up, and we went over the area, noses to the ground like bloodhounds. A tuft of hair, ''brisket hair'', said Ronnie, and a spot of blood. It became plain clear that he had jumped into a drain and crawled up it, but after two more spots of blood all signs ended. The shot that at 80 yards should have pierced the heart, had just grazed the brisket three inches lower. My relief can be imagined, and when the well known deep hoarse bark was heard above the caravan that night, I knew that no damage had been done.

The next noticeable stalk was in the evening when I had a keen young man with me. We sighted our buck with a doe from the peak of the top road. He was moving steadily to the left, so we stalked swiftly through the trees, well clear, to the road he would cross if going to graze in the valley that side. I lay up on the top side of the road watching the edge of the trees, young David was in the ditch across the road, where he could watch the slope below. After the interval which seemed so long, but which was probably 20 minutes, David gave me a frantic restrained signal with his hands, only inches above the road. I started to crawl across, I was too late. The buck had managed to cross the road, unseen by me in a little hollow, and had paused for a moment at the lower road edge 100 yards from David in a perfect position. He then vanished and we saw no more of him that night.

So to a morning stalk with Ronnie. After an abhortive general prowl round, we were returning to the caravan but stopped in the valley above. Ronnie saw a doe and guessed that it might be his. We decided to stalk to her and see if the buck appeared. We had not gone more than 100 yards, Ronnie leading, poked his head around a tree, and looked down a track. There was the buck staring at him from 20 yards away. He had seen or heard us and had come down to investigate. Away he went, but we had a splendid look at his head and judged it to be 12". We moved on to a view point and watched the doe. ''He will go back to her'', said Ronnie, and so he did. It was a long shot, but I had no chance to get set, or to take it before he was out of sight again. We followed the same plan as in my evening stalk when I had touched him, but this time more to the left and not moving down the hill to the road. ''There he is''! Ronnie had spotted him moving between large trees by the boundary fence, far below. We stalked carefully, half way down the hill to a rocky outcrop above the road, and looking down a clear ride to the boundary. Time to consider. "It is too far", I said, "May be the only chance" from Ronnie. "He will come out on to the ride from the larches and may stand". My thoughts ran thus, "With this rifle, a Ruger Single Shot ·25/06, sighted 1½" high at 100 yards with a Nosler bullet and my own load, shooting 30 degrees down, I shall drop 5" to 6" at that range, the light is perfect, there is no wind". I could settle myself almost like a target shot. "If he stands well, and I feel happy, I will take it". Ronnie agreed. The buck stepped out exactly as expected and stood perfectly. I fixed my sight just on his withers and touched off. The buck bolted 40 yards towards us and dropped dead. A heart shot. "Fantastic" said Ronnie. We went down a long way. There was a moment of doubt and a moment of dismay. I had been so concentrating on the shot, and Ronnie, certain it was our buck from the interrupted view in the larches, but it was not. It was a good four year old stranger which had come in and challenged him and had been driven down. We went back, triumphant in one way, with no harm done, but a little downcast. At the same time the hoarse bark rang out again. Was it challenge, triumph or derision? He had stalked round behind us holding close to the top of the hill.

I put up a mark with a roe deer heart size target by the boundary, and a little notice from where the shot was taken. "It can be done, but don't do it"! This is shown by Ronnie to visitors as a warning, not as an example.

Many more times, I or both of us went out after him, stalking or waiting, more often than not we did not see him at all. There was ample food in the trees, no need for him to show himself, and he was now cautious and cunning. At the end of that year, we decided that his condition was so good (as we had seen from close up inspection) that we would leave him deliberately to the next year.

Another phase appeared to start here. Ronnie was taking a party in a small bus on a guided tour of E.F.G. operations. Driving round Fingland Hill, he told them about the master buck. No sooner had he done so, than he trotted out into the road in front of them, gave them a splendid view, and strolled quite slowly back into cover. This and other sightings produced the theory that he could sense when he was being stalked or when he was being admired, or that he could tell (as crows and magpies surely do) when a man has a gun or rifle in his hand.

1977: Would he appear in the spring, or had ill befallen him during the winter? He did appear, but had either extended or shifted his territory, and now seemed to be lying up by day in a different thicket. Remember that those little trees had now reached the point where they made stalking impossible or very difficult. Early in this spring, when grass was scarce, he developed a habit. When it was almost dark, he went down into a valley to drink and have a bite of the sweet grass by the burn. But this was only when it was almost dark and for a brief time. Just as settled routines and habits aid the bank robber, we said this made him vulnerable. He was then seen with blood pouring down his face after a fight, and we realised that he was reaching the age when he might be successfully challenged or even driven out.

Stalking started one morning when we sighted him chasing a young buck, but he broke off and went away back towards his thicket. We could have shot the young buck, but left him and made all speed round a wide circuit to a ride he might cross. Ronnie as ever, thinking like a deer, and right as usual. But the luck always ran with the buck and not with us. Had we been earlier, maybe a chance, but he had also made speed and so we met on the corner and that was that.

One evening we stalked him up the valley, but he got us and ran up the hill. I hastened up the road, he crossed 100 yards away, but as usual he did not stop, barely checking one stride from cover. An instantaneous and instinctive shot off the shoulder, but as the shot crashed out, he had taken off. The vital spring forward and he was gone. That was the second time I had actually fired at him. We gave him a day or two to settle down, and tried again. One night we were waiting and he stalked us. Barking at us from only 30 yards behind in the trees. Another night, Ronnie saw him below the road from the car, but we did not check, rolling down out of sight, until I could roll out of the car without given any sign. Back and crawl across the road. We hoped, of course that he would think the car had gone, but oh no, he was not fooled, he had moved 50 yards back and 50 yards up so that he could cover the road edge. He saw me at the same moment as I saw him. Rifle up, but as I did so, I realised that he was peering round a tree, his vital parts hidden, but even then, before the rifle could bear, he was gone.

So, we come to the final and fantastic episode of that spring. We saw his doe unusually far out over the valley, and we saw him. We stalked down through young trees, without being seen, and reached a point from which further progress might have left us unsighted, but to stay placed us far off. This time he had not a care, but he went further, crossed the burn to a grass bank and stood. Is this it? The first time he has been standing in sight, side on and I have been lying down with a steady rifle. Sure, it is a long, long way, sure it is very dark, but I can see. I squeeze the trigger. A brisk click! A misfire. Though I reloaded like lightning, he had heard and he was gone. Ronnie and I looked at each other speechless. What were the odds against this? One in 500? Why did it have to be this vital shot? On this special beast? Is one superstitious? Was it meant? We went back to the caravan. I took the cartridge that had failed from my pocket, loaded it, pointed the rifle at the bank, boom, it fired normally.

My wife, Christian, an interested supporter, but a bit bored with all the talk of the master buck, now adopted the positive attitude, "You will never get him, no rifle and cartridge you have will kill him". Furthermore, with devastating but contradictory logic, she announced, "I do not think you want to get him, he has got you into a state of mind".

With Ronnie, it was different. This buck had become special to him also, but he was dedicated to my getting him. He admitted now that the buck defied him and did things differently. He admitted he had hardly known a case where a beast was saved so often by extraneous circumstances as well as his own cunning. We both agreed that we must not lose. To let him be driven out, wander away and die, would not only be cruel, it would not be fitting. I said rather than that, "You must take him when you get the chance, as you are here all the time". But I knew that Ronnie would not do so, and in fact no chance occurred. Ronnie's son Ronald stalked him several times for practice, found him, went in close, observed him and out again without disturbance. He could see a sort of mark or growth below his left pedicle, and scars from former fighting. We said of course, that he knew that Ronald had no rifle with him, so that he could come in and out without difficulty.

So ended 1977, and he faced the increasing hazard of another winter which was hard.

1978: Great was the relief when he was back again on his rightful territory. Had he been driven in and relinquished some of his area. In May his hoarse bark was heard regularly at about 8.20 p.m. above the caravan. Ronnie was showing a young Dane around and the buck appeared 30 yards away and stood, so that the Dane, fantastically impressed, was actually able to take a photograph. Ronnie, of course, knew that this time he was chasing a young buck and when he suddenly saw two men on the road, he had been momentarily caught out, undecided whether to continue the chase or turn back. And so he had stood for the photograph. This also had shown Ronnie that his points were much shorter. He had definitely gone back this year if only slightly the year before.

The trees were now closing. I sat out for him four times in the evenings, and each time had him within 100 or 150 yards, but he never showed himself. Then one evening, after a prowl round in the car, we were rolling slowly with engine stopped, down the top back road, watching the forest edge. Suddenly a buck ran across the road 150 yards ahead of us. Was it the master buck? was it a young buck? or was it a chase? Our attention thus drawn, the car rolled another 15 yards, and that was too far. We saw the doe and the master buck had been grazing close in and near a shoulder at the forest edge, on a patch of good grass near an old roadstone quarry. If not disturbed by the other buck, we should have seen the doe in time, and an easy stalk might have settled the business. This was the 14th stalk and he had been saved again fortuitously. On a morning spy, from the top road, Ronnie saw a beast chase another across a ride, and into a patch of Norway Spruce below us. Too fast to see for sure, but he thought that it must be the master buck as his face looked white. We were badly sighted and had to stalk down 150 yards to a ride. 30 minutes wait, no sign. Ronnie moved round and saw the chased cull buck. We followed him with two sightings, but had no chance. He was scared witless, and so we returned to the car defeated. Then a discussion. He must have abandoned the chase of the young buck whilst we were going down and turned back before we could see. At that point, we said, "we must think like an old deer", and Ronnie suggested I go back and post myself at a good place on that site that very evening. It was dreadful weather, I thought it almost hopeless. There was a strong cold north westerly wind, with showers of rain. I was in almost winter stalking gear, although it was May, but at 1,000 ft, it was bitterly cold, and I remember thinking that it felt like sleet, but when I settled in a ditch sheltered by the trees, it felt much better. There was no sound but the wind, no movement, not even the call of a cock pheasant, and time seemed long.

I had a large area to cover, and so moved my head gently from side to side, scanning without pause, using glasses only for an occasional look at openings in the middle distance. Suddenly, awareness of movement, more sensed than seen, away to my right. There was a buck, 50 yards away, emerging from the spruce at the corner of two rides. It must be the master buck. Big head held out straight, grey face. With no pause he trotted purposefully and diagonally away from me across the ride. I was facing the wrong way, and dare not move. "He is going to go straight into cover", but no, he turned away in the ditch at the forest edge, the same ditch that concealed me. Now slowly, I turned, slowly I raised the rifle, his attitude quite hopeless and moving away. With one turn and one step to the right, he would be in cover, but he paused to sniff and think, turned left, mounted the bank and looked down the other ride, but still he did not show his shoulder, and did not pause long enough, but this did make him turn back more deliberately. He was still heading 50 degrees away, he was now at 75 yards. In a second he would make the final leap across the ditch and into cover. I was so keyed up that I was hardly conscious of thought, there was only one spot where the bullet could be effective at that angle. I was not conscious of firing. With this rifle and a muzzle brake, I was not blinded. I saw him go down, one horn showed and sank slowly. Reload, rise, stiff and cold, and walk in.

There apparently unmarked, lay the master buck. How many thoughts surge into the mind at such a time? The sudden strange feeling, not unfamiliar, of sorrow at seeing a lovely beast lying dead. I had almost expected a fantastic beast with a super head. I think he had once been 60 lbs, and we knew that he had been 12", now he was 55 lbs, and perhaps 9½" in good summer coat and splendid condition. Only then a feeling of triumph. Satisfaction at a good shot, more satisfaction at an instant kill. He could have had no sense of danger or shock, defending his territory not 500 yards from where first seen 6 years ago.I gralloched him and hefted the weight, tempted to complete the job, but reason prevailed. Not good if I struggled up 200 yards of steep hill with that weight. Not good however fitting, if Ronnie were to find me collapsed on the roadside with the master buck. So I walked up, drove in, and with Ronnie fetched him in the last light.

Anthropomorphism is dangerous, but surely the old buck must have thought something like this:

''They thought I hadn't seen them when but I had, so I doubled back unseen and did them in'', but then drowsing through the long day, they spotted me chasing that buck. He may have thought, ''They stopped me before I chased that young buck. Will he have the nerve to come back, come evening, I had better go and make sure''.

And so, at long last, on the 16th stalk, he had given me a fatal chance. 50 yards to the left, and he would have been on top of me. Had I been 100 yards right, he would have got my wind. Then only, the real moment of shared satisfaction as we had a dram and thought back over all the years. But life goes on, there were two culls still to take and probably that good four year old, six pointer, now in the valley at the entrance will take his place.

On my return home, Christian had the last word, ''I don't believe it''. So after 8 years, we come to the end of the story, that had become a legend, ''the Master Buck of Fingland Hill''.

The master buck. He had once been twelve inches and had weighed sixty pounds.

MECHANISATION

The theme that rises in my mind is to think about and examine the changes that have taken place since I first went stalking on the hill. You might then get a lift out with a car at the start of the day, but more likely you would be on your feet throughout, starting from the lodge where you spent the night, and returning to it by the same means. You would carry all the gear that you needed for the day, and accompanied by the pony and the ponyman, you would set forth with no mechanical aids of any sort. The 'walkie talkie' was a significant leap forward. This enabled you to keep contact between stalker and ponyman and with your base; an enormous saving in time. Terrible tales began to fly about of tycoons being delivered to the hill by helicopter, but this was generally dismissed as so far down the road, ''it's just not done'', even if technically possible. Although I have been thoroughly derogatory about the helicopter, I should be very grateful for such technology if I broke my leg, to be taken our safely to medical care.

Then the first mechanical contraptions capable of covering rough ground appeared. I remember the little three wheeled effort with tiller steering which would just accommodate one man and one beast. Even this began to open up areas on the hill previously impracticable because a long, uphill drag was required, to get a beast out of such locations. The Land Rover was I suppose the next step forward usable on rough approach roads and hill tracks hereto impassable, and thus speeding up the approach to the day and the distances to be covered to get a beast out. Improvement was inevitable and has developed. This is not the place to examine and compare in detail what is now available with either tracks or low pressure doughnut tyres, but it is surely fair to mention names, 'Argocat' and 'Snowcat'. The Snowcat may well be taken out on a trailer behind a Land Rover for a considerable distance up a glen to save wear and tear on the tracks, they may be expensive in first cost, they may be expensive in maintenance, and with fairly high fuel consumption, but they lead the modern technology with their ability to take, for example, 4 men and 8 beasts back from the hill.

Argocat — Green vehicle.

Snowcat. — Red vehicle.

I have reason to be grateful myself for this development as it has enabled me to continue my stalking into the years when it would have become impossible without some aid.

Telescopes have definitely improved, so have field glasses. Finally we have the Japanese inspired 3 and 4 wheel motorcycle based machines with low pressure tyres. I have not myself had the opportunity of assessing this development as stalking aids; are they perhaps more at home in the roe deer field than with red deer on the wilder hills?

A PEEP INTO THE FUTURE

Science fiction becomes ever more exotic, but in fact modern technology has advanced in a manner undreamed of 50 years ago and beyond what would then have been the extremes of science fiction. Another approach is the changes that have occurred in my lifetime. It is pretty staggering that I can say that I virtually started in the horse age with no aeroplanes, no radio, no television, no electronics and electricity really little beyond the electric lamp bulb and the electric motor. What of weapons? 100 years ago the Navy was still employing short range, muzzle loading guns. I find it quite extraordinary to think that even with the facilities then existing a super frigate could have been produced which would out sail and out range the three deckers, and if properly exploited, it could have established such a superiority that the Battle of Trafalgar would have been unthinkable and unnecessary. Pursuing the Naval theme, the big gun reached its apogee and achieved its dream when towards the end of the 1939/46 war, an enemy ship was sunk in the dark of the northern winter at a range of 15 miles without sight, but directed by radar, and at that moment it could be said that the big gun was obsolete, doomed to be replaced by the missile, even if able to operate only with efficient air cover.

The enormous leap forward of the percussion system had displaced the flintlock, but it was still black powder, low velocity, big bore. Today we have the supremely accurate small bore, high velocity rifle with superior muzzle energy and telescopic sights, but in our deer stalking world no need for the military takeover of automatic weapons with a high rate of firing; no need for night sights or heat seeking target technology, but where shall we be if we take a peep into the future?

When we go out on the hill I think we shall still be depending on human eyesight, still be immobilised by fog, with no new technology that could operate in bad visibility or over a mountainous terrain. Will our weapon have become some form of light, portable laser? Dealing death silently and at a flat trajectory up to perhaps 300 yards? Already we have mechanised means of covering rough terrain efficiently, and taking beasts out from the hill without the old tyranny of dragging and the pony, already we can communicate with the 'walkie talkie'; what then might the future hold? I don't think that we shall be a sort of super batman, but quite probably we shall be able to ring up for an air taxi, and be transported up to our base in Scotland economically in an hour. The helicopter will surely have gone the way of the sidecar, a Heath Robinson contraption, mechanically wrong in so many ways, but having a vogue for a time because of its ability to do something that was required and that nothing else could do. We only need more power from less weight and less fuel to unlock so many advances into the future, and of course, we shall have an electric battery of half the size, half the weight, twice the efficiency and twice the storage capacity to support the new technologies. What about energy direct from nuclear fusion?

I do see a possible advance in our future deer stalking to replace the 'Argocat' and 'Snowcat'; when you have traversed the hill in the then 'state of the art' vehicle, found your beast, stalked your beast, and killed your beast will you be able then to summon from base an automatic programmed transport vehicle that will home in on you, automatically traversing the contours. On this you lay your beast and send it back to base the way it came, leaving you free to carry on your stalking day. You yourself might have a back pack, giving a degree of levitation and a degree of propulsion, so that you will cover rough terrain with giant strides at 4 to 8 miles an hour, cross a stream or mountain obstacle; you might well be wearing a camouflage garment that maintains you with temperature and humidity under your control. The final stalk would be little changed, back pack left behind and the familiar thrill maintained. I don't see an automatic gralloch, there would still be blood on your hands, and so we come to the final assessment of the future. Will a day's stalking still be possible? Will it still be enjoyable? Will it still command qualities of human skill and judgment? Will you at the end of the day be able to enjoy your dram, and enjoy thinking back over an experience that is still demanding, still a challenge, and still worthwhile? I sincerely hope so.

ANOTHER ANGLE ON HIND STALKING

I read the article on hind stalking, its rigours and trials in winter, by Lea McNally in the January '88 No. of Stalking, with interest and admiration, would that I had his professionalism, life long experience, memories and expertise!

The article goes far to explain why so few owners stalk hinds through the season or at all. There is practically no participation by visitors from overseas, particularly Germans who are unlikely to be interested unless there is a trophy to take home. There are probably but few amateurs here dedicated to hind stalking. I have done enough to appreciate the dangers and the rigours without having had to encounter the full severity in the depths of winter, particularly when out alone, but as an amateur enthusiast I have another angle. I used to go in the fifties with 'B' an experienced companion. For three years we went to a great estate in the far north, 'not a thousand miles from Helmsdale'. We used to go in the second week in November, the stag season would be well over, the beasts settled down and the hills undisturbed for a few weeks and with luck we should get up and back again without being held up by snow, though I have known it touch and go over Drumochter even this early in the winter. I thought it essential to go with a friend to share the long hours driving, and for the pleasure of sharing experiences and company during the long evenings. There were favourable features such as uncluttered roads, the scenery often incredibly beautiful, the hotel where one might be treated as a welcome family guest, and quite likely the only visitors, and they might provide a sitting room to ourselves with a roaring fire where we could spread out our gear. Add a visit to the bar, and a quiet exchange of news and views with the regulars. We would have two separate beats in five days, perhaps exchanging beats on one or two days for experience. We would drive over of a morning, 'B' would drop me and go on to the other beat some 15 miles further. In the evening he would pick me up. At that time both beats had a Snowcat, which might be taken up the valley road on a trailer behind a Land Rover. On one beat the road went 12/15 miles up a glen and a strategy on some days might be to do one or two circuits with the Snowcat on one side of the road in the morning and on the other side in the afternoon, direction depending on wind and weather. Each half circuit might cover about three miles spying and stalking. The team might be the driver of the Snowcat, the stalker and the rifle, with an extra man whose function was to keep in touch between the Snowcat and the stalk to save time by signals and to help in dragging the beasts. I found that the tougher going and the harder weather were compensated by the shorter days, while the worse the weather the lower down the beasts would be, often just below the snow line. Add to this the break, and the rest in the warmth of the Snowcat at intervals was a help as I was no longer in my youth.

I consider that the stalking was often superb as compared with a dozy old stag in September, which might be dead easy compared with tackling the hillside with perhaps 50 or 60 beasts spread over it, and the need to deal with it with all those eyes against you. Another attraction for me was the rifle work. The professional with a rifle in his hands throughout the year might come to regard it more as a garage mechanic regards a faithful spanner, essential, useful, valued, but still just a spanner. We amateurs with much less use and familiarity tend to regard our rifle very differently, I know I do. Consider the situation, the team are trying to take a cull of perhaps 250 hinds, 125 from each beat in the six weeks before Christmas, with the odds that McNally describes against them, making it a formidable task. 'B' and I used to feel, and we agreed that if we did not take at least 20 beasts each in our five days, we were holding up the process, letting the side down and becoming a nuisance. It was up to us to show them that we could, and the rifle work was out of this world as compared with the amateurs usual shot or two at stags Often we would take two beasts or more out of a bunch. I am tempted to make what was for me a record never achieved before or since. Picture the stalker and I on a good day lying in the heather after a stalk. In a hollow before us and only some 80 yards away, a bunch of about 12 hinds, some lying down, some standing or grazing, completely at peace and without a care in the world. I discussed such a situation with the old stalker, and when I said, "This is my chance", he knew at once and we prepared with plenty of cartridges for him to hold. I was using a single shot falling block Ruger No. 1 rifle, the calibre ·25/06 with a Leupold 3 × 9 telescope set at 5X and with Duplex reticule. The single shot feature I regarded more as a special challenge than a handicap. All ready, here we go. I took a hind lying down, you must be sure of your anatomy for this, instant death, the beasts now on their feet, put another down swiftly, and they mill about confused before running perhaps 100 yards before checking to look back as if wondering "Where is Auntie"? The chance for a third beast before they are off again, and at another check; careful now they are getting further out, but OK, again and the fourth beast safe. A final run, they must be 300 yards now, can I risk it? Have no delay, the adrenalin is flowing strongly and with my forehand steadied, squeeze the trigger gently, and this time you will count 1, 2, 3 quickly before the welcome sound of the strike, and it was done. I had killed 5 beasts, all dead and clean shots, out of the bunch, inside perhaps two minutes with five shots from a single shot rifle. Wow! 'B' and I rated each other equally with a rifle and inexperience, and you can imagine how we compared notes and analized the events of each day. He was a left hander and shooting off his left shoulder with his left eye, made easy by using a Winchester under lever ·243 calibre with a good quality scope. I was keen to discover and to confirm or shatter my belief that I would rather not use my ·243 calibre for red deer, even hinds. After three years shooting with the ·30/06 and then with the ·25/06, we would be able to compare something like 75 beasts each, interesting, there was a difference. If over that number I had perhaps 10 beasts still on their feet, or making a second shot necessary, 'B' might have had perhaps 20. OK. He had killed as many, I don't think he had lost any beasts, but surely it is better to be over rather than under gunned, while the stalkers on examination in the larder made no complaints against us, and at that time of year any venison we took home was of superb quality. I remember when there used to be a tendency among the stalkers to find and take yeld hinds as they were not only culling but filling the requirements for the owner for gifts as well as for sale. I was doubtful then and now I feel sure that this is wrong. I should prefer to pick old hinds, barren, or old hinds with a late calf, that might well fail to make it through the winter, while such a hind would be likely to be barren or late again the following year. While every one such taken from the hill would leave food for a younger beast, I advance a plea that even for the amateur, there is so much to be enjoyed, so much experience and knowledge to be gained from hind stalking, though admittedly with some reservations against time of year and weather. I may well describe a special or difficult year at this game, but in various forests over perhaps 15 years, and with perhaps nine friends, some of them being introduced to the game for the first time, I have not only lived to tell the tale, but to value all the memories.

FREAK CONDITIONS

After a gap of a few years I again went up to Caithness for hind stalking in November. This time I had David, a young man of about 24. He had originally started coming out with me at the age of 10, and showing natural aptitude and enthusiasm, I had introduced him as he developed to fishing, shooting and finally rifle. I rate it one of the finest moments of my life when one year David came and said ''Skips, will you join my shoot''? Of course I would and I did so to our mutual satisfaction.

Now kitted up with a good rifle of his own, this was to be his first time stalking red deer. Now married, his wife Vanessa though due to produce the first child in another 5 months, came with us, made light of the conditions and was good company. We kept her going in the Argocat with hot water bottles and hot drinks. We drove up on a Sunday, a long arduous trek, and we should never have made it without the Range Rover as the roads steadily became more impassable for cars as we made our way north, and it was still snowing heavily when we arrived, late but thankful to arrive.

Next morning, Monday, it was bright with showers, but deep snow everywhere with drifts. We wondered if we should make our estate, but yes, it was just possible as there had been some clearance of the vital coast road, a lifeline for the whole area and its population. There were long faces on our arrival, with ''We shall no get far the day'', from the stalker. There were changes since I had been there before, the old stalker had passed into retirement (we went to see him later), and the present stalker whom I knew and was now in the cottage at headquarters, was no longer a young man. The Snowcat had gone replaced by an Argocat, cheaper to run and maintain and easier to transport. This time in deference to my age and David's inexperience, we were sharing one beat, my intention being for him to take some of the longer and more arduous stalks, while I relied more on the rifle and less on the legs. We set off up the glen but we didn't get far before there were impassable snow drifts and there was no way that the Argocat could cope with off the road conditions. What to do? Walk on and see what if anything we could make of it.

I must try to give a picture of the area that could be a reference as we proceed with our tale. The river, not large and with but few salmon owing to severe falls near the sea, ran down the glen. When low it could be waded but when high there were little wire footbridges at intervals to give access to either bank. The road up the glen, maybe 12 miles was on the right side of the river facing upstream. There were valley, flats at intervals alongside the river on either side ranging from not more than 30 or 40 yards to perhaps 100. On the right of the road particularly in the lower glen, there was generally a steep bank on the right hand with breaks in it where a burn came down. Above this bank the land ran almost unbroken up to much higher ground, the whole slope quite gentle and forming a grouse shooting area with pointers, but to the left the scene was very different. From the river flat there was a steep hillside, its crest as seen from the road, perhaps 200 to 250 yards, though there was much higher land beyond. The whole hillside was covered with the remains of old, stunted, scrubby birch, but in these blizzard conditions forming an attractive shelter for beasts. Spying to the right meant a struggle up the steep bank in the snow, any beasts then to be seen up the slope were in these conditions impossible to stalk, and it was a straight decision, leave them or shoot. We opened the score with one such at long range. Thus encouraged we proceeded with our best chance on the left hand. The beasts up the hillside could, of course, see us and usually moved up to the top, there they might stand and give a chance, but again at very long range. We had a little conference to work out our strategy, and this was our resultant plan. When and if a good but long chance offered, I would get set and take the shot, when either David or the stalker would also get into position and hold on the beast, not until they were ready would I take my final aim and fire. If I missed they would not fire. If I hit there was a second shot instantly available if the beast looked as if it might move. As this was to be the general if not the invariable strategy for three days, one must summarize. In the three days we took 17 beasts, of these 13 were to my rifle, I missed 2, and 3 needed the second shot, but all were safely recovered, an arduous task indeed for the young men. I stayed at the bottom of the glen, my excuse being that I had decided to cease dragging stags at the age of 70 and hinds at the age of 75. Fair enough!

What were the rifles and what were the ranges? My rifle was the single shot Ruger No. 1 ·25/06 with my own loaded cartridges and 117 grain Nosler Spitzer partition bullet, the scope a 3 × 9X Leupold with a Duplex reticule which I set from 5X to 7X according to the range. David had a BSA Monarch ·30/06 with normal 150 grain ammunition, the stalker had a ·270 rifle with a good 4X scope. Surely this was an effective battery? And both the others performed well. My rifle, of course, had my own made muzzle brake and other personal modifications. Now to the ranges; I should put the average at 200 yards, nothing less than 150, with one shot up to 300. Never in a lifetime have I consistently tried to cope with such difficulties, but this was a freak situation and it was give up and go home or take them thus. Each day the weather was slowly returning to normal, each day we got further up the glen with the Argocat and could penetrate further on foot. On the Thursday conditions were approaching normal, and David was able to have a stalk up a burn to the right and got one beast. I got a long one on the bank on the left, then by the bothy where the valley opened out and a stream came down, from the left hand side there were quite a lot of beasts in an area where some feed was appearing through the snow. We risked proceeding on the road until we were past the beasts and out of sight where we could stop and observe. David and the stalker then went down to the river, crossed it and stalked back down its bank towards the patch, and then made a more normal approach up the slope to the right to get on terms with the beasts. David then got three beasts, well done! He had graduated on hinds. I got a last one as we came back down the glen in the late afternoon. We were well satisfied and so were the stalkers, in freak conditions and against all the difficulties we had 17 beasts and none lost. It was 4 days instead of 5 because on the Friday we travelled back to Eskdale Muir to join an annual stalkers and owners pheasant shoot at the forest on the Saturday, home again on the Sunday. Vanessa had enjoyed it, we had coped with the unusual added experiences and memories, and David was at last fairly entered on red deer hind stalking.

IS IT A MIRACLE?

You can today set forth in at least 12 countries if you have enough pennies in the right currency and buy a rifle, you can have confidence that the weapon you have bought will do a 5 shot group inside 2″ at 100 yards, and this may be regarded as adequate for use on the hill. The ultimate, of course, would be to put 5 shots through one hole no greater than the diameter of the bullet. This may have been done for all I know and I am quite sure that ¼″ groups have been achieved, though this has little relevance to actual stalking in the field. Pondering on this the thought came into my mind that there is an entirely different way of looking at this achievement rather than simply taking it for granted. Take a little lump of lead and surround it with gilding metal, cunningly finished to an exact and special shape. Take a bar of steel and put an accurate hole in it. Taking the days of so called Damascus barrels it is hardly a fantasy to say: take a hole and wrap a band of metal round it, now go back to your bullet, for such it is, introduce this into a brass case with a primer at its back end, little different from the paper cap in a child's toy, but it took about 500 years before a Scottish clergyman successfully applied this to a firearm. This brass case which has become a cartridge must be filled with a chemical compound and this, when ignited, burns with extreme rapidity producing a large volume of gas, virtually without smoke, with very little smell and leaving very little residue. Again it took about 500 years to achieve this starting with a crude mixture of charcoal and salt petre (the I.R.A. produces explosive for their infernal machines from fertilizer). The cartridge goes into a recess in the barrel which started as our bar of steel; this must be built into a mechanism, the purpose of which is to allow you to hit the primer with a little pointed hammer when you release a trigger. For hundreds of years this was done by very crude means indeed, and it is only in the last 100 years that we have built up to the modern form.

If one must mention names and types, start with Lefoucheux — leading to the double rifle, Armstrong Whitworth — smaller bore, high velocity, longer bullet, Martini Henry — an effective military weapon for 30 years, Winchester — the repeating under lever, Farquharson — the falling block, action, Mauser — the bolt action, Fabrique Nationale of Belgium — a self-loading mechanism; all or their derivatives still in use.

All we have to do now is to put this into a shape that one can hold steadily against the shoulder, and squint along the barrel to align our rifle, for such it is, using a Express sight, a peep sight, a telescope or an optical system producing a red dot (ignoring for the moment the latest development in night sights). How many men, how many brains, how many original ideas and inventions. How much skill of hand, how much developed engineering has man produced to reach the present development? It is true that compared with some other inventions and developments, it has taken a long time, the jet engine, the hovercraft, television, the space rocket and many more have appeared so quickly. Never mind, I still think that it is permissible, particularly if you are fond of them, to regard our rifle as a sort of miracle.

The latest rifle from Parker-Hale with laminated stock, muzzle brake and a ten shot magazine. It has taken hundreds of years for man to achieve the modern stalking rifle's capabilities.

AN ADVENTURE IN NORFOLK

An estate in Norfolk was owned by a life-long friend. Every year we used to go and stay for shooting weekends with him and his family. Indeed for some years I had a share in the shoot and ran days on my own with my own guests. I had got to know the area well, quite often on shooting days we would see roe deer, more rarely but once in a while we sighted one or two red deer. My friend, as so often happens, was completely disinterested and I had to work carefully and diplomatically over a long time before I at last got permission to investigate with a rifle.

I would go out on my own, usually at first light, before a shooting day in September or October, coming in to breakfast and the start of the official day's shoot. I had only done this two or three times and had not brought in a beast, and when it happened I was out at dawn by myself and working along the edge of extensive woodland on my left, to my right before me a broad, extensive valley, on the right of which lay another large area of forest. There was a strip of useful cover in the valley, and on my side of the valley fingers of cover stretched some way down the slope, nowhere very large or very thick, but a good deal wider than overgrown hedges which perhaps they had once been. Coming out of one of these fingers I saw a red deer leave the far forest on the right about ¾ mile away and move slowly out as if intending to cross the valley. There were about 8 beasts, too far to examine closely, but certainly antlers showed. I made my way along my forest edge safely covered by another of the fingers ahead, I passed through this and as I did so, a pair of roe deer which no doubt had been walking up from the valley trotted out and ran in a semi-circle on the open ground around me to eventually enter the wood on my left. Jumping neatly and gracefully over the wire fence at its edge, they were visible to the red deer now somewhat closer, but the red deer took no notice of them at all. There was still another finger of cover from which I could spy my deer at about 300 yards range, as they were now working up my side of the valley slope, 2 stags, but what stags! They were almost level, but out of this world compared with anything usually seen in Scotland. One was definitely an older beast than the other, though there was little to choose between them, and the heads were massive, with so many points that I could not then count them. I considered carefully, yes surely with the few hinds and the second stag so good, I could take out the older beast if I could get him, and do no harm to the future, but how? I was now almost upon it, I could not emerge from my finger of cover in their direction, I didn't want to cross the fence into the forest and make my way through the trees as this would be slow, noisy and I should probably lose my sight of the beasts, so I waited on. Fate finally favoured me for they turned somewhat in my direction, worked up the side of the valley approaching what I knew to be a very broad ride in the forest on my left. They entered this, and as the last beast disappeared I came out and made my way swiftly along the forest fence, slowing down and moving very carefully indeed as I approached the gap of the broad ride. At last, crawling, I came into the gap until I was able, by a post with a little cover from weeds, to come to my knees and get a view of the ride. The beasts had not disappeared, they were about 100 yards up the ride milling about, no doubt making up their minds and on the point of entering and going into the cover where they would like down for the day. Pure chance now, one or two out of sight on my side, one or two on the other, and neither stag remained in view. It began to look as though I would have to wait on until they had disappeared into cover and then follow on and take my chance, very much more difficult and very chancy, stalking actually in the forest, but then, out from my left side the big old stag stepped out, as if looking across the ride to see if any of his hinds had slipped away into the cover on the right. It was now or never, the distance about 200 yards. I was kneeling behind a fence post and could get a fair sight line resting my forehand against the side of the post. I took my sight and squeezed the trigger. Then an extraordinary thing, the ranks of tall trees on each side had the effect of absorbing the noise of the shot, the passing of the bullet and there was no sound of a strike, the satisfying thunk which is unmistakable. At the shot the other beasts in sight

A 'dropped dead' shot at 200 yards with a ·30/06 using a hand loaded 150 grain Nosler pointed soft-point partition bullet. This solo stalk at dawn produced a medal head and the 'all clear' for the future.

disappeared into cover, silence and nothing in sight at all. I reloaded quietly, watched and waited, nothing. I gave it about 5 minutes, and they were agonising minutes. Then I rose, crossed the fence that my post was supporting and keeping close to the left hand edge of the forest, walked slowly and quietly up the side of the ride, still nothing. I had covered perhaps 100 yards and then my heart stopped. Surely that was the point of an antler showing above the grass and weeds some 3 ft. high? A few steps more and it was certain, there lay my stag, the bullet had struck perfectly and he had gone down dead on the spot without a movement that I could have seen, and there he lay, something unbelievable, I was quite stunned. I pulled myself together, performed the gralloch and walked back to the Hall, cleaned myself up, and walked in somewhat late for breakfast, to announce: ''I have got a beast this morning and I shall need help after breakfast to bring it in''. First a stunned silence, and then the questions, tentative congratulations stemmed from little understanding.

Afterwards with the volunteers we went out with the Land Rover and were able to take it to the stag down the broad ride from the other end where there was a forest road. It took 6 of us to load that stag into the Land Rover. There was no way of weighing it, my guess was 26 stone, and the massive head was 17 or 18 points, properly measured later I think it made a bronze medal European standard. There was a very strange look, but a thoughtful one on my friend's face, which I interpretted as: ''This is meat, this is masses of meat, this is valuable meat'', and from that moment a definite change of attitude to deer on that estate. From then on I had a free hand, a likely young man on the estate was recruited and went out with me to train, concentrating on roe deer, which were numerous but not of very good quality. High seats were arranged and a programme made for cull of bucks and does. Today my head stands proudly at the Hall, a suitable display as it was too large and massive for my smaller house. The son of my friend, alas departed, now regards the roe deer as a valuable asset to the economy of the estate. The young man has become a competent stalker and licencees, usually a party from Denmark come across and take a valuable cull. Some does are shot in the winter, one hopes the quality has improved. Measures have been taken to reduce poaching, red deer are seldom encountered; they are indeed outrunners from Thetford forest.

ROCK TO RIFLE

The apes are just beginning to use tools and implements to solve problems such as using a twig to help them with an ant's nest. So it would be very early man who developed the habitual use of a handy lump of rock to throw at the enemy, and from that very early beginning we can lay down a set of criteria for weapons. (1) Materials readily available. (2) Any development of the materials to be relatively easy. (3) Not too time consuming, developing later to be relatively cheap to manufacture. (4) The weapon must be easily carried about. (5) Ease of application. (6) As great a range as possible. (7) As accurate as possible. (8) As deadly as possible. (9) Speed developing to swift reloading. (10) Finally becoming more important as development proceeded, reliability and absence of failure.

Primitive man proceeded to develop flint and stone tools and as the stage of development of man is indeed determined by his weapons, so the Stone Age, the Bronze Age, the Iron Age and the Steel Age. With the development of the spear pointed with flint we enter another field. Is the weapon in regular use in life, for hunting and obtaining food, or is it used against a foe? or both. Sometimes, as we shall see, one weapon serves both purposes, in other cases it does not and so requires a different form. So to the bow and arrow. It would be a nice argument I think as to whether this was as important or more important than the invention of the wheel. Certainly it was a giant leap forward, almost worldwide with many variations and in use equally for hunting and for war. Develop the sling, the discus and like sharp edged throwing objects for propulsion. A phrase in the language: ''The slings and arrows of outrageous fortune'', and another: ''I cast my arrow in the air and it must fall I know not where''. In warlike operations the bow caused the development of body armour. Not precisely the first, but certainly a definite stage in the development of the projectile and its defence culminating with the armour and the shell and right into our own times, the anti-tank weapon and the latest form of tank protection.

From the bow and arrow the crossbow, perhaps inferior to the bow and arrow in some of our criteria, but developed because its 'quarrel' or 'bolt' could deal with the body armour which was able to resist the arrow, so that you could still give your armoured opponent a ''sair dunt''. A significant phrase: ''I shot my bolt''.

I suppose there have always been 'oddball' weapons, one might instance in very early times the blow pipe, and in fairly recent times the catapult. Neither applicable to war. I can hear somebody saying: ''After all this preamble when do we come to gunpowder, and weapons, using gunpowder and projectiles propelled by gunpowder''? This is the moment, but I am not going to compete with the many excellent works on the development, from the Chinese noise making bangs to the detailed examination and accurate charting of every form of weapon and development up to the present day. This has been done and well done, and there are many reference books covering the subject. I can confine myself more to the 'how and why', and so we come at last to gunpowder and a matchlock weapon. Where do we stand against the original criteria? It appears to me that the matchlock in its early form shows up so badly that it is almost surprising that it survived and developed; with the resources of those days, the gunpowder, the matchlock and the bullet were all relatively difficult to produce. They were clumsy and heavy to carry about, they were apt to leave the bearer ill defended against conventional weapons. They were slow and awkward to operate, and suffered badly in the wet, with the difficulty of keeping the match alight and the priming powder dry, while it was quite a performance to relight the match. Accuracy was very poor, range no better than the arrow and crossbow. I think they must only have survived as a psychology weapon, in conjunction with conventional arms, so that a commander on one side possessing a troupe armed with the matchlock would have the advantage against an enemy not so provided, of being able to spread despondency and alarm by the noise they made and the fear, largely based on rumour of their powers of penetration and force. They were very slow to reload, altogether a pretty poor score, but they continued to survive and be used for 600 years until the 1800's, and as a final word, I remember a friend of mine in China telling me that he had seen a Chinese market gunner shoot a flying pheasant with a matchlock of very primitive form, fired from the hip, surely the ultimate exposition of skill in the use of a weapon so difficult in so many ways.

Surely an invention waiting to happen for at least a hundred years

THE WHEEL-LOCK

I am continually amazed that the matchlock did not develop straight into the snap haunce and the flintlock. But no, the different era and time of the wheel-lock comparable perhaps in the later days to the pinfire, an unlikely development in many respects, but with a quite extensive field of use and filling needs for a relatively short period. If we look at the wheel-lock gun against our criteria, it could be criticised on many grounds. It was in its time expensive, difficult and time consuming to manufacture, demanding great skills and ingenuity. As a result of this it was confined in the main to hunting rather than to war. It was also owned only by the titled and wealthy. Its success attributable perhaps to the start of the use of rifling with a marked improvement in accuracy, again much in demand for hunting purposes, but with the gain in accuracy, the rifle barrels became more difficult to load, thus detrimental to its use for warlike purposes. The wheel-lock also tended to be elaborately decorated for its privileged owners. Fairly limited in area of manufacture, fairly limited in numbers, but often a rather lovely thing in its own right. Were any wheel-locks manufactured in England? I myself have never seen one, and the nearest approach has been a weapon in a catalogue at Auction, described as "probably English", which would tend to indicate that English wheel-locks were known; if not, I find it astonishing, as although England may have been backward in the skills of manufacture of weapons, they were manufactured here and I should find it almost unbelievable if some gunmaker had not constructed this type of weapon in imitation of these from the middle of Europe.

So we come at last to the flintlock in all its forms, but before I launch into this, I cannot help another thought; early weapons using gunpowder, particularly small cannon, were often breech loading, using a primitive wedge system for obturation and we shall find that gunmakers were often quite obsessed and ingenious in the pursuit of breach loading weapons. But the muzzle loader remained paramount until about 1860, making the muzzle loading flintlock a prominent example of the works of man that persisted over a great and almost unlikely period of time.

A Japanese Matchlock.

THE FLINTLOCK

I find it a revelation that the notable feature of the flintlock era is the fact that it endured for more than 300 years. So simple, and allied to a well known method of lighting fires with a flint and steel contraption it had to be invented. I find it astonishing that nobody really got past it until the Reverend Forsyth, an amateur in Scotland came up with a practical percussion powder and percussion lock in 1805, and so the flintlock joins the select ranks of industrial development that cover an unusual life, a notable example being the crucible steel melting industry in Sheffield which was in action from Benjamin Huntsman's invention in 1750 which only finally died out in about 1950.

I shall make no attempt to describe in detail all the variations of flint and steel gunlocks from the original snaphaunce to its final development with a roller, a water proofed pan and the like, through variations with inside springs, outside springs, the Miquelet lock and many others. All this has been so well written up and for anyone wishing to study it there are excellent books dealing with every detail. During the period of its existence there were attempts at breech loading, I have a Griffin rifle, notable in that Griffin was one of the first English barrel forgers to challenge the Spanish for good quality guns around 1750, and the same maker with a breach loading by a screw under lever trigger guard, the precursor of the slightly better developed weapons of this type, the Sutherland, at the time of the American War of Independence. Incidentally one can quote this as one of the many, many instances where the military authorities apparently failed to see any virtue in a new idea and even if they tried it, failed to adopt it or develop it. There were also the attempts at repeating rifles. Just imagine the difficulties you are up against with the flintlock era? A repeater has to be some form of breach loader, it has to provide a means of separately loading ball or bullet and powder. It also has to prime a pan and cock the hammer, but it was done, and successfully by the German Kalthoff, further improved by Lorezoni, chief armourer to the Medici family in Florence, Italy, produced in England by Cookson in London (nobody seems to know anything about Cookson), and I myself have an excellent weapon made by Ellis of Doncaster who must have received a commission to make one from a local noble after Cookson had no doubt produced with pride and demonstrated shooting fallow deer in a park before astonished guests at the great house.

Of course, the invention and development of rifling was epoch making in accuracy, starting in middle Europe and spreading outwards, but in this era rifling cut against ease of loading so much that it practically precluded rifle weapons from military use. The long reign of the flintlock put phrases into the English language, a ''flash in the pan'' from the all too prone tendency to miss fire, ''keep your powder dry'', with reference to another obvious difficulty, and so the the 'Brown Bess' musket and the phrase, ''don't fire until you see the whites of their eyes''. What a picture this conjures up in the warfare of the period; serried ranks, muzzle loading in turn and stepping forward to fire their volleys; the inaccuracy of the weapon partly offset by the convenient habit of the enemy of marching up in a solid phalanx, and as feared, the military leaders were horrified at the thought of abandoning the use of this weapon, hanging on desperately until our 'brave boys' were too frequently being picked off by the marksmen of other countries with rifle weapons at longer ranges, but I have strayed into the percussion lock period, which should, I think be a separate chapter.

THE PERCUSSION LOCK

How astonishing as we have said that Forsyth should have developed this system. The whole story has been written up and needs no detailed description by me, but it does show up another tendency which was applied to almost every significant development of weapons, the old boys' tendency to stick to what they know and to resent and resist new inventions or development, usually younger and more adventurous souls were prepared to adopt new ideas; still each new development was apt to have an overlap of anything up to 30 years before it became paramount. In the case of the percussion system, this was delayed by Forsyth's master patent, but accelerated by the fact that the old flintlock could quite readily be converted to the percussion lock, which could be regarded as virtually universal by about 1830 in one form or another, with different forms of tube or cap hammer and access for the flame to the main charge. The added speed of ignition opened the era of game shooting at flying birds. Forsyth's patent had another effect in increasing the use and development of air rifles. This and various forms of pump up pattern could be quite lovely, could be repeaters in their modest way, and with no Geneva Convention in those days, were classed as weapons in the ''dirty tricks'' department and discouraged by the edict that anybody effecting them would not be treated as a 'prisoner of war', but bumped off at once. The air rifle might have developed further had it not required the separate pump, and had it not suffered from the difficulty of maintaining airtight seals. The development of the patent breech I think by Nock of London, further improved the firing of the charge, and unlike the flintlock era, the percussion lock span was compressed between 1805 and about 1860, by another development just waiting to happen. The breech loader with a cartridge, but here again we need another chapter.

BREECH LOADING AND CARTRIDGE

It just had to happen, and it happened relatively fast. It is impossible not to mention Lefoucheux, with his move forward, a drop down barrel system. The extraordinary thing about this period was the rapid development of a great number of patents, and the whole of it dominated by weapons asking for a cartridge which at first did not exist. In the middle came a very brief and extraordinary phenomenon, the pin-fire. I cannot help likening this to some other examples of our time, something so horrible that it ought not to have happened, but which filled the need when there was nothing else, and was, therefore, useful. My comparison here the sidecar on a motor cycle (until I suppose surpassed by the Austin Seven motor car), and in my mind the now universal helicopter. I feel that this simply has to be eliminated, it only awaits an increase in power, weight ratio, jet propulsion and fuel economy, and we should have a computer controlled jet system which would make the helicopter look like a mechanical abortion similar to the sidecar. Having disposed of the pinfire by the simple and obvious means of putting the percussion cap into the base of the cartridge, we take off into the rapid development from 1860. One must mention a few landmarks, the Jones under lever, for which he had little credit, though it was a useful type for 30 years or more, the Purdey bolt, the elegant Purdey snap thumb under lever, the Scott spindle, the Dougal lockfast action and many others, while on the rifle front and for military purposes developing from the Whitworth hexagonal rifling and the Lancaster oval bore, both developed in the last years of the percussion system, but persisting and well regarded and useful for 30 years into the cartridge era, though their original virtue of ease of muzzle loading was no longer required. We still have hammers, but the introduction of rebounding locks in the 1870's greatly improved these, though it was not long before we had top lever hammerless breech loader ejector associated with the mass game shooting and enormous bags towards the end of the 19th century.

Meanwhile two developments that never took hold in Great Britain, the Winchester Marlin type under levers of the United States, seen in every western film, and sold by the million around the world. Limited slightly by the power of cartridges they could absorb, and necessitating a blunt nosed bullet, the most famous of them the Winchester "thutty thutty" (·30/30), at its best shooting in woodland within 100 yards, but the result not always that intended: "I saw something move and thought it was a deer", and another hunter bites the dust. What better than the under lever for a left handed rifle man? Another American development little known in Great Britain, the rolling block, the best known manufacturer of this type perhaps Stephens. On the otherside of Great Britain on the continent, the Drilling, the most popular, and usually a double-barrelled side by side shotgun, and to keep weight within bounds more commonly a 16 bore shotgun with a rifle bullet adequate for wild boar in the Black Forest. Splendid weapons also sold in millions and in common use to this day, and if anyone doubts their efficiency they have only to join a German shoot and see redoubtable German ladies handling them with deadly efficiency.

I can see somebody saying "My godfathers, has he forgotten the Martini Henry". This was a rather delayed military development, the result of the competition in 1865 for a military weapon, the winner an amalgam of the Martini version of the falling block action allied to the esteemed rifling developed by Henry of Edinburgh. It may have been delayed but it was good, and it served the British forces well from 1868 until the 1890's. In between there was also a notable Great Britain and Scotland development, the falling block rifle, many forms, many makers, but perhaps the best known the Farquharson, reputed to have been a poacher near Balmoral. He is also supposed to have come up with this idea carved from a turnip having no other resources, and it is creditable and gratifying that weapons developed have continued to bear his name. I have a memory of this type of rifle in a cartoon. A blimpish sort of sportsman is running round a large rock in Africa pursued by a wounded lion; in his hands a falling block rifle, they were noted for poor extraction, but he is in such a predicament, the caption: "If I can only gain on him enough I can stop and hit the rifle on the rock to get the cartridge out, but if I gain too much I shall be getting near his tail end and he might turn round on me".

Some good things do not die, and I today use with satisfaction a single shot falling block rifle, modernised and made by Ruger of America. It has become my favourite rifle for roe deer and red deer with ·25/06 cartridge. Another reminiscence of the development years, in about 1875, Colonel Valentine Baker led an expedition, ostensibly hunting but really military, in disguise from Turkey through to India, but on the borders of Russia no doubt to find out what was going on and what the Russians intended. For this expedition they had great arguments, obviously the latest breech loading cartridge rifles must be the best answer, but this was contradicted by the fear if, for example, a mule bearing some of their ammunition went over the 'Khud' or the mountainside and was lost, they would be helpless. If, on the other hand, they took the outdated muzzle loading weapons, they could buy lead and black powder in almost any bazaar in almost any country and so would not be left defenceless. This argument won the day, and they actually departed armed with muzzle loading weapons, at least 25 years out of date.

So to the revolution only comparable with the Reverend Forsyth's invention, the Mauser bolt action of the early 1890's. This was the end of the road, happily combining virtues both for military use and the sportsman. It served our armies through both World Wars as the long barrelled Lee Enfield and the shorter barrelled Lee Enfield, only to be finally obliterated in turn by the quick firing weapons, of which perhaps the best known world name is the Russian Kalashnikov, in the hands of almost every guerilla force in the world from the I.R.A. in Ireland to Manilla in the Pacific Ocean. Alas the theory that pumping out a multitude of bullets quickly must be superior to the well-aimed but slower marksman. I find this sad, but change is inevitable "Tempera mutander et nos mutanter in illis" — "Times must change and we must change with them", who remembers their Latin nowadays. Have we reached the end of the road, Oh no! there are bound to be developments yet to come.

CHAMOIS

Early in the 1970's my friend John with whom I regularly pursued the wily roe deer, was talking about a past expedition to Austria, when, at the invitation of a German friend, he had a chance to stalk chamois. He had enjoyed it, he had been lucky, and had a pair of the delightful little curved horns on his wall at home. "I should like to go again", he said, "If I am able to fix an opportunity would you come with me"? "Of course", I replied, but two years elapsed before he came up again. "I have picked up my contacts and I think it can be done. I have to make a business call in Germany, I could do that on the way out or on the way back". We could cross from Hull to Rotterdam, the sturdy Subaru was good for a steady 85 on the autobahns and at the end of a long day's drive, we met up with his contact, in a small house with his wife and daughter. I slept with friends of theirs and next day we were off again. John's German friend in his Gelandewagen and so to Austria. Our destination, a little inn like an English village pub in the Austrian equivalent to the English village. Next day the process was interesting but not very efficient with much time spent in finding and meeting people, being introduced and passed on to others, but finally what seemed to be the vital contact, a very nice old man who had inherited a large estate. Yes, we could go up and try for chamois. What rifle? He produced a serviceable 8 mm bolt action repeater with a good telescope; detachable of course with the continental type 4 foot mounting which they use. Could we try this rifle? "Quite unnecessary", was the reply. It took quite a lot of tactful insistence before we were allowed to rig up a target across a meadow and have a go. Just as well, it was 2½" out, but we soon had it 'sorted'. Of course they immediately took the telescope off again, which I should not have done, and put the rifle to bed again in its case. I knew that they did this all the time and thought nothing of it, but I still prefer to fix my scope sight, sight it in and leave it on the rifle.

At last next day we go up the mountain, a road good enough for the Gelandewagen and leading ultimately to the Alp where the cattle would be taken to graze through the summer days. Up and up through well kept forest out above the treeline, glorious views and fine weather.

There was no pretence that I could go up and down all day in that steep country. My route would have to be more limited in range and contour selected by our guide. So along the top of a mountain ridge spying down on each side. We saw chamois as distant little black specks through the glasses, but that is all that we did see on that day, and those black specks were virtually on another mountain. Two days of this and then another contact, another session and another permission to go up another mountain by a similar road to a similar Alp, with a little building at the top. Again along the ridges until at last we saw a beast or two on our mountain but on the other side of a valley. They might feed across our way, they might feed the other way, they might go up over the ridge or down into the forest. I made my way to what I hoped was a well chosen spot on the nearside of the valley while the others walked on behind the ridge to get beyond the beasts. My beasts did not oblige and the others found nothing, returning three hours later. We turned towards home and trudged back along the ridge, the day was almost done and the light declining. Suddenly excitement, a chamois came out of the trees below us to our left. A scramble down the steep mountain for 75 yards, not my best going, and so to a tree, the rifle ready, it was a long way, a steep downhill shot, the light almost gone, and the beast was moving, and I had a strange rifle. I was unhappy, the sort of shot I would rather not have taken, but was this a typical chance? The guide was urging me on, he had all to gain and nothing to lose, but the beast decided the issue, he never checked and in a few yards it was behind a rock, out of sight, and the light had gone. That was how 'I did not get a chamois'. This was the only chance but I have the lovely memory of my rifle on that beast, the excitement, the wonderful terrain, and the experience of their magnificent habitat. The forests were beautifully managed. Every little chalet surrounded by at least two years' supply of logs, stacked up to dry for the cold winters. The sight of a big red deer stag in the forest low down, sawmills with magnificent timber, farms with attractive cattle. The evenings in the little pub were enjoyable, the local regulars came in to drink, sometimes there was singing. One evening there was a slight commotion which centred round a nice old boy. When we enquired it was revealed that his interest was in me, and eventually our landlord found out what it was all about. "Oh, that's old Johann, he used to be a good professional chamois hunter, somebody has told him that you are chamois hunting and that has started him off". He had always thought that the English were a little mad, but he is now quite convinced when somebody told him that you had been chamois stalking and he found out your age. It turned out that he was younger than me, and he had given up chamois stalking seven years ago. We went over, stood him a drink, and when he calmed down we listened to his wonderful tales of the chamois stalking experiences of a lifetime.

On an expedition to the nearby town we visited the gunsmith and saw some nice rifles of the local type, and I bought the correct hat, unadorned alas with no trophy, and a Lodencloth jacket, highly esteemed when I returned to England. It was time to return home, back across the long distance, John made his business call, and we stopped and had a look at Heckler and Koch with much of interest, and collecting their full catalogue to bring home.

Quite by accident another contact brought us an excellent day's experience with shotgun shooting in Northern Germany, our host very pro-English and with a wonderful collection of best quality English guns. His wife Hildegard, quite magnificent, a good shot with gun and rifle. She trained her own dogs and joined in every activity. They visited us in England, stalked roe deer and remained permanent friends. I suppose it could be said that this was a long and arduous expedition to Austria for very little, even perhaps futile, but No, it was very much worthwhile: "If you don't go you don't know". I had added significantly to my memories.

A VERY BEAUTIFUL RIFLE

I did not really need it, I should never have bought it, I might not even have chosen that calibre, but this is how it happened. I found myself owning this rifle by accident. It had been left in my hands as security against a loan, but as time passed and circumstances changed, repayment did not transpire, and the man to whom I had lent some money asked me whether I should be happy to keep the rifle. I had at that time no balance of values, but to avoid embarrassment and to help a friend, I said: "Yes of course, think no more of it".

I knew something of the circumstances which had led to the rifle in the first place; picture a man who had been left unexpectedly some money after a death in the family, and the idea came to him that he would like to take up stalking. Until then I think he had mainly been target shooting. Did he go and consult a dealer and purchase a secondhand rifle on advice, did he buy a new rifle? No, with the money in his hand the fancy took him and he went to Westley Richards. "I want the best English rifle that you can make today", and a considerable discussion ensued. This resulted in a continental action, the rifle made up in England in Winchester ·270 calibre, with a very beautiful stock, first class finish and engraving, complete in a beautiful case, and so I now had occasion to assess the rifle seriously. Consulting my friend and advisor in the trade, his reaction was: "Forget the rifle, do you realize what it would cost me to find and buy the piece of walnut to make a stock like that"? "And do you realize what it would cost to have that engraving done? What you have is unique, valuable, and if I were you I should insure it at once for a considerable sum", which he advised, but that was only half the story.

Examining the rifle as a piece of equipment that I should use and enjoy, the picture was not so good. Alas, my friend had stopped at the rifle, and the telescope had been added later. It was not a very good telescope, it did not fit my ideas, and it had not been well mounted. Going through the rifle there were other points, the stock was not the right length for me, the trigger pull did not fit my ideas, the forward sling attachment was in the wrong place, and I found that I had built up a list of about 12 points to attend to before the rifle was really the way I should like it to be. Of course I could then have made the decision, "the best thing to do is to sell it for what it will fetch", but I could not resist the challenge, and decided to complete the rifle. I set about this by obtaining from a friend in Germany a beautiful Zeiss telescope, the Duplex type of reticle and 4x and 6x magnification. When we had mounted this really properly, what a difference. Then, one by one, the other points were tackled, and so at last, I had a weapon, not only beautiful in itself, but completed and fitted to my ideas. We had managed to get the scope lower in height, and in so doing the bolt had been fitted with a 'butterknife' handle like that on the old Mannlichers. With my addiction to muzzle brakes, this rifle should of course have one. Although tempted, I resisted making it integral with the barrel, fearing that one day that might reduce its attraction to somebody with other ideas. I then went down into my workshop and made a muzzle brake; tempted in doing so to develop another idea, by incorporating reverse flow to the gasses I could surely increase the percentage reduction of recoil. Lacking machinery my muzzle brake had to be reworked to obtain the degree of concentricity required, but the result, at any rate to me, was both pleasant and effective. Certainly, it might increase the bang, but what does that matter when you are out on the hill, firing perhaps but one shot in the day? The rifle had a nice and attractive rubber butt recoil fitting (it was just too early for me to obtain and fit the latest energy absorbing rubber for this purpose). This I had leather covered.

When we had done everything we could, aiming at perfection, it could still be said that ⅜″ on the stock would fit better to the face. I shuddered at the thought of adding anything to that beautiful walnut stock. Was there another solution? Yes, but others may shudder at this, logical though it might be. If you are unable to add ⅜″ to the stock, what about adding ⅜″ to the face? The picture this raised of walking about with a pad on the right cheek attached by surgical tape was not very attractive, was there an alternative? Yes, I found one; make the little pad required, enclose it in plastic, and when required place the neat, little resultant object inside your mouth between your teeth and the right cheek. Try it, it works like a charm. No need to wear this except for a brief moment or two, it can be slipped in and out in a second. A beautiful example of how a search for perfection in one direction can lead to an unlikely but minor invention in another.

Have we now arrived at a rifle so beautiful that it should be left at home, polished as an exhibit? No, that is not my way. After careful sighting in with the correct ammunition, the rifle had to go out on the hill and be christened on red deer hinds. It is delightful to record that the practical result was as good as its looks, and so at last I had arrived. It was not only a very beautiful rifle, but it was also a functional success.

RIFLES FOR THE WORLD

When hunting men meet and talk, sooner or later there is bound to be a discussion on rifles. In my case this backed by actual usage, dedication, fascination, and a collection which I call: "The Rise and Fall of the English Hunting Rifle"; I am almost certain to refer to this again. I have given much thought to this subject, you have to lay down some requirements, and this is a difficult enough task. Suppose for example, you want to hunt anywhere in the world and can take only one rifle! You have then got to decide also, are you going to tackle dangerous game or not? I now divide the requirements sharply into two approaches: modern rifles as might be the case with an American, not short of dollars, who has not studied the past, and would in any case favour the latest. The second approach, accepting the past, might be the approach of a man like myself, not short of years, and guided by men who have hunted in the past, and the literature of the great days in Africa and India. Let us look then at the modern approach:— it is perhaps the easier. The type would be bolt action repeater, but do you exclude automatics or semi-automatics? I should exclude them, but am I just being out of date? Why should a modern automatic loading job be any more vulnerable to failure than a man who can jamb a cartridge at a critical moment by too short a stroke with the bolt?

Your American would almost certainly choose a Magnum, and probably end up with a Weatherby ·300 Magnum or similar; I only say Weatherby because I happen to have owned and used one. Winchester or continental or Holland and Holland, and may be even Japan, may now be just as good a choice. Remember also that as with motor cars, rifles tend to be more international. An American or a British rifle is not necessarily totally manufactured in its own country. This manufacturing of parts is governed by relative costs and exchange rates of the currencies involved such as a collapse in the U.S. dollars values in world markets, but I think we have arrived at our first answer, a modern ·300 Magnum.

Now for the next approach. I should not hesitate, my choice would be a Holland and Holland ·375 Magnum Bolt Action Repeater. Why? I can only say that having seen such a rifle, yes, handled and used it myself in emergency, I hold the opinion that this calibre and specification delivers a slightly more reliable wallop than a ·300 Magnum, although the ballistics on paper may be very similar in energy available, at the likely range. There are of course other prescriptions; I should be equally happy with a double rifle. With this I should have a 1 x 4X scope fitted, yes, they do exist, and I have one. With this you can use the double rifle at close range in an emergency with both eyes open and you see the same picture with both eyes, and your double rifle should be fitted to you like a best shotgun with its superior handling qualities in such conditions. With the scope at 4X you can imagine that you are lying over an ant heap to take a kudu bull at 150 yards. Are we quite finished? This will cover the world including elephant, buffalo and tiger, a grizzly bear in Alaska and a polar bear in the arctic (I should hate to take one of these even if they were not protected). You would have to make sure that there was not a local restriction against using anything less than ·400 calibre, for example against dangerous game. This makes it necessary to explore heavier calibres, and with this limitation one rifle should surely be a Rigby ·416; it had a great reputation in Africa, particularly as lion medicine, and would avoid the slight feeling of having a cannon with a ·458 or anything between ·450 and ·500. Of course there are the double ·577 and even the double ·600, but even if old fashioned, I feel that we can leave these enshrined in the past with our limit at ·500.

We now come to a different hypothesis, what if you are allowed two rifles? Does it not follow that a Winchester ·458 and a ·300 Magnum might then be your choice? But again, if old fashioned, what about the double ·470 for the heavier of the two rifles? This would have my own special type of open sight, but for others with different and younger eyes there would be no problem with the standard express sight. For those whose eyes positively demand the telescope, it would again be the 1 x 4X. The second rifle a ·300 Magnum has a wider option of sighting 2X x 7X telescope with the Duplex reticle might be a nice answer. I am repeating myself here, but Tony, the White Hunter in Botswana, was emphatic that in an emergency he would prefer to have the double ·470, and both his and my second rifle might be a double Holland and Holland ·375 Magnum.

Now into the unlimited category, what if you are allowed three weapons? Would you like a ·22 shooting game for the pot? You could have a gun or a lovely light rifle such as ·30/06 with its wide choice of ammunition. I should be tempted to go for the gun because you could have bird shot in one barrel and a Brennecke slug in the other. The American would probably plump for an automatic 12 bore such as the Remington 1100 (don't forget that FN were the originators of this type). With this type you can also have a compensator fitted or even a variable choke if you wish, and a plus factor in the type is that it also tends to reduce recoil. There is also the equivalent pump action. Back again to the past and the old boys such as myself would love a Paradox from Holland and Holland or the Explora from Westley Richards. I have a Westley Richards 12 bore Magnum Explora with detachable box locks, a really lovely weapon which could tackle a tremendous range from guinea fowl for the pot up to a wounded leopard.

We need hardly bother about more than three weapons, and so I come to my final counsel. I should do my best to reduce the recoil with any of the more powerful rifles, excepting only the automatic recoil operated type. Reduction in recoil would not only improve performance and increase enjoyment, indeed I regard it as essential in my own case.

Now for the howls of protest, the counter suggestions, the arguments and the different ideas. Let them all come. We shall see what we can learn.

IS THERE SOMETHING DIFFERENT?

A few years ago I think I should have produced the 'Darne Gun', a French production, well regarded, effective, quite elegant, with a considerable following over a considerable period of years. Essentially it was an action with a straight slide forward and back and no drop to the barrels. I don't think the Darne was ever produced as a rifle, but there is no reason why it should not have been equally applicable, though it was typically a side by side double barrelled gun. Production of this type ceased a few years ago, but I am pretty certain that some examples of the principle will be in production somewhere, probably as a single barrel gun.

Next we come to the ''Bull pup'' rifle. I do not know if the idea started in America, but this name did. I now turn to my long-term friend John Brown, the same John as in ''Chamois'' and many another foray. Forgive us if we are somewhat technical as I quote what he has written, but I feel this is necessary to show how difficult it is to develop something and describe the problems encountered and how they may be overcome by imaginative engineering.

***THE BULL PUP** — Definition:— Where the action of the rifle has been positioned as far back as possible to the butt plate, thus considerably reducing the overall length of the rifle.*

This necessitates a thumb-hole stock and moving the trigger forward of the action, this has been in the past a problem due to the long linkage to the trigger. However François Gex, a gunsmith of Sallanches in the French Alps has overcome these technical problems. He has developed an offset scope mount which is combined with the trigger assembly which includes a set and normal trigger unit.

This allows for any play in the linkage to be adjusted out. The scope mount and trigger platform is machined out of two pieces of high resistance duraluminium (AU4G), the barrel near the breech is carefully machined down and two grooves are cut, one at either end of the machined portion, into which fits a rubber 'O' ring as a moisture seal.

The two sections are thus positioned round the barrel, one piece dovetailed into the other very precisely and the whole unit then locked into position by two bolts on the underside. An adjustable rod transmits the movement of the trigger which is located in the base of the assembly; thus by removing the two screws from the action, the whole assembly can be removed from the stock, thus facilitating maintenance or adjustment.

This method of adapting a large calibre bolt action has been developed and honed over several years, you can even have a left handed bolt action, with detachable five shot magazine, fed from under the stock.

Pourquoi? The reduced length of the GEX carbine (approx. 10 inches) makes a considerable difference in use, getting in and out of a vehicle, climbing up a tree or high seat; stalking and operating in thick cover, or just being unobtrusive when travelling.

The point of balance is the thumb hole grip, which allows the rifle to be manipulated very quickly, most of the 3.3kg weight is in line with the rifleman's body, and when used with a stick, very effective shots can be taken quickly with practice.

With the centre line of the scope being just over 2 inches above the bore, a wide range of scopes can be used in the same mounts.

There is no noticeable difference either in recoil, muzzle blast or any other sensation when compared with a conventional rifle of the same calibre, nor is it more or less accurate.

However, if you change to a ''bull pup'' after many years of shooting a conventional rifle, it will seem rather strange; at first the ejection and reloading of a new round seems rather difficult but with a little practice this is soon perfected, as is the operation of the safety catch, it just means reaching behind instead of in front.

The British are renowned for their slow acceptance of ''new'' ideas, it is a known national trait, but if the ''bull pup'' had been developed first, and at a later date the ''long rifle'' came along 'who on earth would change to a long clumsy thing like that?' even if you can reload it 0.3 of a second faster!

C'est la vie.

John Brown '91.

You can see that John is not only a protagonist, he has become charmed and dedicated to this type of rifle. I have seen him in action with it at Deer Society Shooting Competition and in the field. Both equally impressive.

I have myself handled and fired the bull pup but I have not stalked with it. What do I think? Nothing made by man is perfect in all circumstances. If there were a serious malfunction or a blowback, it would be right up against your face. This however, is so unlikely that we can say ''Ça ne Fait Rien''. (Who remembers the ''San Fairy Ann'' of the 14/18 War?)

I should have liked to have one of these rifles in my collection. I think I should have chose the ·25/06 calibre and it should have had a ''Riverdale reverse-flow integral muzzle brake''.

I am sure I should have been seduced and become fascinated. Alas, it is now too late and so in the French idiom that has crept into this chapter, I must end with a non-committal ''Je ne sais quoi.''

Bull Pup — held in different positions.

Comparison with conventional rifle with the same barrel length which is 20 inches.

Photographs taken by T. P. R. Brown

INVENTIONS AND ORIGINAL IDEAS

When does an original idea become an invention? Why should one not leave things alone and accept that what was good enough for others must be all right? But no, there is an attitude of mind which seeks to improve, find out why, try to find a better way to achieve an objective, so devise something which is entirely original. The world of patents and registered designs is a jungle full of perils and demanding special knowledge. I have indeed a son who works in this world, enjoys it and is a mine of information, but mine has always been a strictly amateur approach.

Over the years I think I have learned that an invention should be utterly simple, easy to produce, without any specialized or expensive machinery, demanding little capital involvement, easily marketable, but above all, and this is the real catch, something that a great number of people badly need, or really want.

We move on to examples: My memory may not be quite accurate, but I have the impression that the zip fastener, now so universal, was in a sense a patent failure because a great amount of time, money and effort was necessary to devise the machinery to manufacture it. Until this was achieved the public had no chance to evaluate it and by the time it was accepted, the patent had virtually run out. A much more successful story is the 'cats eyes', so welcome on our roads at night. If my memory is correct, this invention was produced by the inventor and his family, manufactured by them, remained under their control and provides an example of an outstanding success.

Now to some of my own experiences; in 1922 for a variety of reasons I designed, and produced a yacht of a new type. I didn't patent it, I didn't know if it was patentable, but it would not have mattered had I done so because the idea met no success until the vast expansion in the numbers of yachts that took place in the 1950's. Yachts of the type I had pioneered in 1922 now worked up until they took some 40% of the market in small cruising yachts. I never made a penny from this, but it resulted in a lifetime of personal use and satisfaction. It might even be the one for which I am best remembered in the future.

In my industrial career I have invented if that is the right word, many improvements in manufacture and process; one tool, was patented, produced and sold as a successful commercial product for many years by my company.

There is a category which comes under the heading, 'just too late'. As a young man I thought up and made a sprung seat for motorcycles, submitted this to Terrys and received from them a very courteous acknowledgement to the effect that they had just gone into production with the identical idea, it would be on the market next month but, and for this as a needy young man I shall be ever grateful, they sent me a small cheque by way of acknowledgement and thanks for submitting the idea to them: 'just too late'.

There is another category, 'If only I could have thought of this at a much earlier date'? and this apposite to our present exercise as it deals with weapons. In the 1980's I devised and made a double muzzle brake which I applied to a Rigby double barrelled Express rifle, a ·470 calibre of about 1890. What were called 'Express' rifles of those days in larger calibres for big game hunting, often had a ferocious kick. My idea was successful and tamed the recoil. If only I had been around in 1890, and then produced this, my name might have been recorded in the 'Halls of Fame' alongside Colonel Forsyth with his wonderful gun rifle the 'Paradox' of 1885.

There is another category: 'how often do people in different parts of the world have the same idea at the same time unknown to each other'? This happened to me once in the early days when I produced a carburretor for motorcycles with a variable choke only to find that some character in Sweden had just patented the idea.

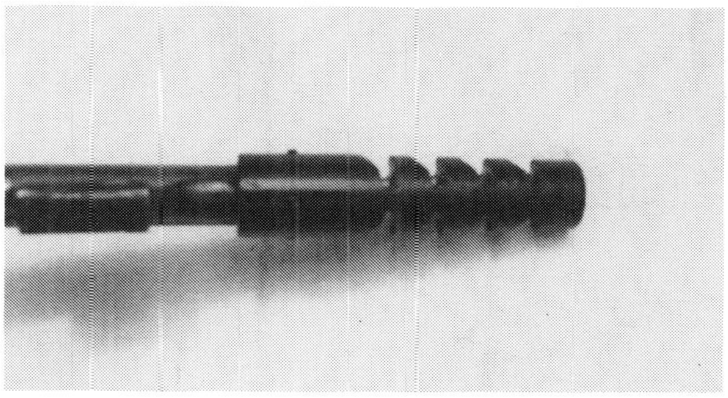

Riverdale reverse gas flow muzzle brake.

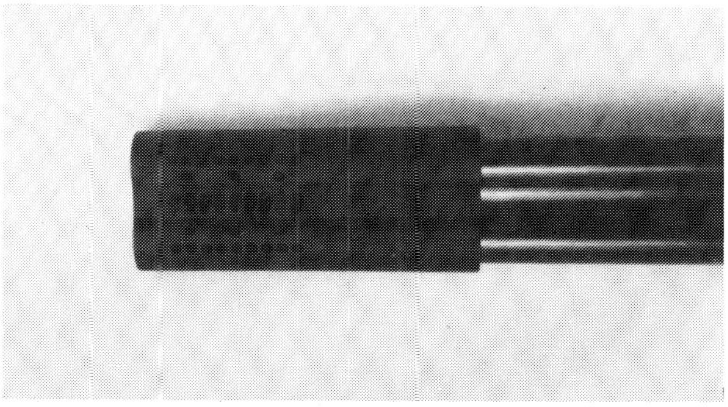

A double muzzle brake. (See Recoil Chapter).

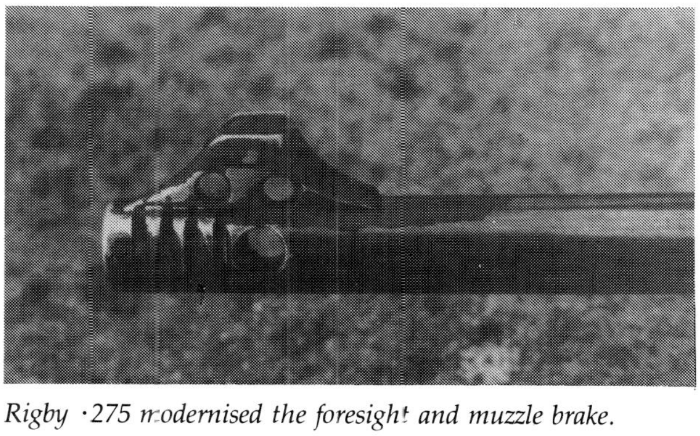

Rigby ·275 modernised the foresight and muzzle brake.

Tripod with padded rest.

So to another example in the weapons field, in the 1960's the idea came to me that a rifle with a taper bore might produce an acceptable way of achieving a high velocity without a corresponding or excessive pressure at the breech. It would, of course, require a special bullet, but this problem was easily solved by having a bullet with two rims which would fall back into recesses in the bullet as it progressed up the barrel and the diameter was reduced. Nice thinking, but quite by chance I heard that the Germans had tried this very scheme with an anti-tank weapon in the 1939/45 war. The ''Schweres Panzerbuchse 41'' as it was known, was a 28 mm weapon with a barrel that tapered to 20 at the muzzle. The 4·5 ounce projectile was essentially a hard tungsten carbide core enclosed in an alloy sleeving, and it was this sleeving that progressively ''compressed'' during its passage down the bore.

The muzzle velocity achieved was 4,593 feet per second, giving the small, hard projectile quite a penetration at close to medium ranges (apparently up to 55 mm of armour at 500 metres). This was, of course, quite effective against the older, less heavily armoured tanks of the day, but by 1942-43, newer and more heavily armoured tanks rendered the weapon quite ineffective. Also the increasing scarcity of tungsten and cost of production meant that the weapon quickly fell into disuse. By the beginning of 1943 it was only being used in the Middle East, and to a lesser extent on the Russian front.

The Americans apparently also experimented with a squeeze bore cartridge based on the ·50 calibre Browning cartridge, but its manufacture and application I have no information on.

Perhaps my final category might be: 'this would have been splendid if other factors had not changed', and here I quote what I called the 'clean hands dipstick' in the 1960's. In the 1930's the owner of almost all motor cars would be apt to check his oil level with the dipstick almost every day before he went forth with his car, and I well remember one nearly always got one's hands messy, and one was always short of a piece of rag or even newspaper with which to wipe one's hands or wipe the dipstick. But alas, by 1960, nobody dipped their oil anymore, it was only done by the garage at maintenance, or perhaps occasionally by the garage as a check when filling with petrol, so a gorgeous idea which I actually put on record as a registered design was no longer attractive.

I have already referred elsewhere to the 'Riverdale revolver' with the barrel at the bottom of the cylinder rather than the top, but, however original, I don't expect the world to abandon or throw away all the existing weapons to embrace my idea with a great shriek of joy.

I don't think anything has given me so much pleasure as some quite slight ideas which I have been able to produce in my own workshop, tested and evaluated, thrown out or approved, and enjoyed their use if successful. An example of this process came up when a young nephew of mine, aged about 10, was staying with me. On a day of hopeless weather when he was rather at a loose end, I said: ''Rupert, let us go down into the workshop and make something''. ''What shall we make Uncle Robin?''. Inspiration was badly needed and it did not Fail. ''We are going to make a 'mud spud'''. ''What's a mud spud?''. ''When you go shooting Rupert, you often have to walk across open ground, or a ploughed field for example, and if there is a thaw after frost, you find that you very quickly have two or three lbs. of sticky, muddy soil round each boot. Walking is exhausting and almost impossible, and it is difficult to deal with the problem. You see people looking for a stick or a gatepost and trying to wipe their boot sideways against it, not easy, and only partly effective. You see people finding a piece of stick with which to poke the mud off, and then 'like as not', the stick breaks and you have mud on your hands, and you have had to put your gun down to bend down and use the stick. Our 'mud spud' is going to provide the answer to all this''.

So to the workshop, we found a piece of hazel stick about ¾″ thick, it should be the length from the waist to the knee, if longer it would get in the way. Now we want a way of hitching it on to your belt, best done by making a belt hook of green insulated garden wire, attached to the top of the stick. Now for the spud, a piece of hard wood, about ¼″ thick, about 2″ wide, and 2½″ long, the bottom sides sharpened. This we dovetail and glue to secure it in the bottom of the hazel stick, and there is our 'mud spud'. In use you unhook it from the belt, and hardly bending, a few shrewd pokes round each boot, and you have got rid of the mud. So simple, so effective, and so easily made, I used Rupert's mud spud for many years, and it was much admired.

There are times when, in the early morning perhaps, the mind becomes active though the body is still asleep, and on such occasions you are apt to develop odd thoughts. I find myself thinking of ''Creatures great and small'', but I wasn't thinking of creatures, I was thinking of ideas, and I started reviewing and making a mental tally of the ideas of a lifetime. Believe it or not, by the time I had finished, not all on this one occasion, I had over 70, and perhaps 12 of these would be apposite to stalking and to weapons.

WAS IT A V.C. RIFLE?

Early in the 1850's a situation was building up that was embarrassing and causing concern in Government circles. Politicians were becoming alarmed as a ground swell of public opinion slowly gathered. Reports were coming in at more frequent intervals of occasions when our brave troops in the wide flung empire were losing men to snipers, armed with rifled weapons which had greater range and accuracy than the musket, and to which there was no effective defence and no reply.

There is an inbuilt resistance to change in all human beings; is it perhaps very strong in Great Britain, even to our detriment? Certainly if this is so, it was never stronger than in the armed forces. The Army Authorities were reluctant to make a move, the trusty "Brown Bess" musket had served well, and one could understand and feel sympathy for their predicament. Never perhaps since the days of the Roman Legions with the disciplined troops, the drill and the short sword had virtually conquered and held the known world. So now the trained and disciplined repetition volleys from troops armed with the 'Brown Bess' musket had dealt successfully with anything in a far flung and expanding empire ranging from the charge of fanatical Fuzzy Wuzzies to the French troops under Napoleon at Waterloo. The weapon in universal use was relatively cheap to produce and well known, it could be easily repaired, it was manufactured overseas, particularly in India, it did not jamb up in time of battle with repeated loading and the use of the dirty black powder. To change this would involve fantastic cost and dislocation when all the logistics were against it, and yet something had to be done. What was the reaction of the Government and the politicians? Then as ever, reaction to the public clamour was to find a way that looked as if something was being done when, in reality, the only desire was to do nothing hoping the problem would go away, or postpone action until it was somebody else's problem. One solution which became popular later was a Royal Commission, with a little bit of luck and steering in the terms of reference and the appointments, it might be 2 or even 3 years before a report came out, and it might then be possible to find reasons to pigeonhole it for future action, meaning never, but in this case somebody, I have not the faintest idea who it was, had a new idea. "Why not go to the brilliant engineer in Manchester named Whitworth? Give him a modest grant, and see if he can come up with something new based on the rising mechanical technology and engineering". Whoever it was deserves a resounding cheer echoing through the years to the present day. Whitworth accepted the challenge, the terms of reference must have been in effect: "Produce if possible a weapon acceptable to the Army Authorities, not too costly, and having the qualities necessary to meet any challenge by weapons now known to be possessed by potential enemies". In the records of another brilliant engineer, Brunel, there is mention that he had the idea of a rifle with polygonal rifling. One I believe was produced for him by Westley Richards, but immersed in more important matters, this was never developed and apparently no more was heard of it. Whether Whitworth knew of this or whether his adoption of the hexagon form of polyrifling was spontaneous, I don't know. He was, of course, also constrained by muzzle-loading, and the tendency of the dirty residue from the black powder to so foul up rifling that repeated loading in battle might become difficult or impossible. The Army would certainly condemn instantly any weapon that suffered from this difficulty, another formidable obstacle. Whitworth turned to the then modern machinery rather than the old gun trade practices. He established a range in a railway tunnel to obviate as far as possible the influence of variations in wind, weather and humidity on his testing, but the great breakthrough was the reduction in bore from the almost universal ·577 to ·450, and to increase the length of the bullet. We can forget the technical terms and the ballistic expressions, it is enough to simply look at a drawing comparing the previous bullets (if used instead of ball) with the Whitworth bullet. Could this longer bullet be stabilised in its flight? A necessity always present and stemming perhaps originally from the feathers on an arrow. Yes, the hexagon bore with a twist increasing from breech to muzzle would do the trick, and a round bullet with suitable wadding would adapt to the hexagon form. For accurate work and sniping, Whitworth produced accurate machined bullets in the hexagon form with the necessary twist.

So we can turn to the reaction of the Army Authorities Are you surprised to hear that in fact they turned it down? Who really expected anything else. A small number were ordered as a face saver; a company were armed with this and no more. There were, however, unexpected repercussions. It is said that if you produce a better mousetrap, the world will beat a path to your door. So in this case, as the knowledge of the accuracy became known the rising flood of volunteers built up a demand for this rifle, and they found it so superior that in their popular shooting competitions, there were virtually 2 classes, those armed with Whitworth rifles and those with other weapons.

We now come to another phase of our story. I have a friend, a talented gunsmith who is a grandson of a man who worked with Whitworth in the production of this rifle and he has many records of this product. So, when I acquired one I was able to check. This was a military type weapon, produced with superior quality wood chequered and beautifully finished, in a case with every accessory and cartridges. This had been sent to a friend in Denmark in the hope of influencing the Army Authorities in that country to adopt it. With this weapon was a letter in Whitworth's own hand, amplifying the instructions for use and including a target (reproduced here). This target measuring 18″ × 24″? Assumed no doubt to approximate the human torso area. On this, 25 shots, no doubt fired from a rest, no doubt with hexagon bullets, and probably in the tunnel, but wait for it, at 500 yards this shows 19 holes out of 25, and all the remaining 6 shots would have put the man out of action. This performance creditable today but simply fantastic and incredible in 1860 shows the potential of the achievement of the Whitworth rifle. Obviously the Danish authorities did not take up this rifle, and its subsequent history is unknown until it came into my possession at an auction.

As usually followed with most military weapons, a demand arose for sporting examples. These could be adapted from military weapons, but the records show that Whitworth also produced some. In those days sport with the rifle soon involved India and Africa, and in those areas dangerous game had caused the development of the double rifle. For many long years, the best protection against disaster when facing dangerous game. So one can understand a further pressure building up on Whitworth to produce double rifles. This was so far from the original intention that he was no doubt reluctant, but it was a mechanical challenge and I think this he was unable to resist. The record shows that he produced 5 of this type. One was not finished or sold, and was probably used to develop the machining methods for the remainder. Here again departing entirely from the gun trade, Whitworth produced a double barrelled by machining from a single block of steel.

What happened to these weapons? My friend has one passed down from his grandfather. Test firing it one day, he inadvertently pressed both triggers, firing both barrels simultaneously. The recoil was horrific, but no bones were broken, but the imprint of the 2 bullets at 100 yards was as if the target had been placed on the muzzle of the 2 barrels. Another, let us call it number 2, was sold recently in America, in good condition at a considerable figure. There is reported to be a number 3 somewhere in darkest England, lets hope that this story brings it to the surface, and number 4, well, it is mine. It has seen much service, it is a bit battered, and there is mild erosion or corrosion in the bores, but it is still serviceable, and a record of its performance is available.

What is known of the history of this weapon? Here we move admittedly into the realms of true or false, hearsay or imagination. I make no apology for letting myself go.

Imagine a valley in Afghanistan way back in the days of the Afridi wars. There a small number of forces surrounded by superior numbers of Afghans, have holed up in a primitive fort. Their situation is not desperate, they have food and water. They could hold the fort against any likely attack. They expect a relief force but who knows when that will reach them. Above all, they have plenty of ammunition. There is in my mind the legend of similar force at the last desperate assault, still with some powder but too late and bullets gone, firing sections of the wooden ramrod into the chests of the attackers, at short range and just as good as a bullet in such circumstances, but there is one bad feature in the situation of our particular scenario, a rocky outcrop on the adjacent mountain has provided the enemy with a point at which they could fire into the fort from above, this within range of their long barrelled jezails. Although not particularly accurate, they have already registered some hits, one or two men had been killed and more injured. What could be done? The post is beyond the range of the British weapons, the enemy well protected by rocks and an assault would lose too many men.

With our force is a Colonel Fortescue of Scottish descent, brought up to stalking in the Highlands and with many years of Shikar in India. He has a double Whitworth rifle and has been heard to say: ''In all my years of Shikar in India, the Whitworth ·451 double has always been my favourite rifle''. A daring plan has formed in this man's mind; before dawn he will creep out and relying on an area open to the fort as unlikely to contain the enemy he could reach the hill and stalk to a position which should place him above and to one side of the Afredi post. Here at first light he would be in a position to enfillade them and expose them to fire from above and behind just as they have been doing to the fort below. This plan succeeded and carefully concealed, Fortescue waited until the light was good enough and then with 2 successive shots from his accurate rifle, slew 2 Afredi snipers. Imagine their consternation and their reaction to the 2 shots which would mean more than one man. How many might there be? While this speculation gathered, Fortescue reloaded, another couple of shots and 2 more casualties. Demoralized and scared stiff, the Afredis fled. Fortescue made his way carefully, watching for possible enemies above, he closed in and with a final highland yell he took the post, and was able to signal to the fort below so that a sortie by a party could come up to relieve him as had been arranged.

How lovely it would be to read the citation on this act: ''With great gallantry and courage, Colonel Fortescue, single-handed, captured an enemy post, undefended''. Would that have gained the award of a V.C. and if so it might be the only award in which the word 'undefended' so appeared. In my imagination and in this case, I regard it as the ultimate vindication and a glorious tribute to the genius of a great engineer and the courage of a splendid man with the unique qualities of the Whitworth ·451 rifle.

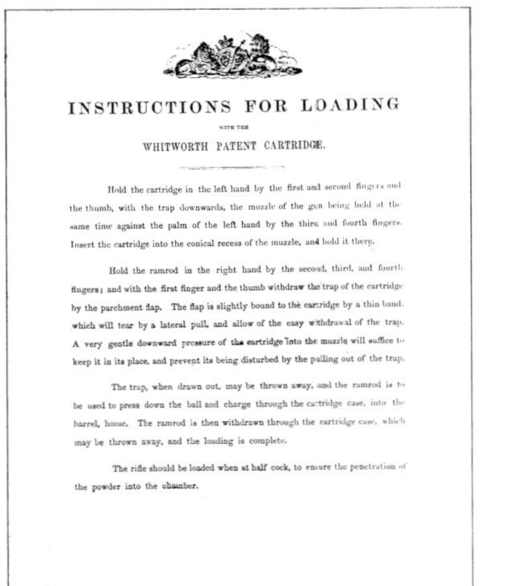
INSTRUCTIONS FOR LOADING

WITH THE

WHITWORTH PATENT CARTRIDGE.

Hold the cartridge in the left hand by the first and second fingers and the thumb, with the trap downwards, the muzzle of the gun being held at the same time against the palm of the left hand by the third and fourth fingers. Insert the cartridge into the conical recess of the muzzle, and hold it there.

Hold the ramrod in the right hand by the second, third, and fourth fingers; and with the first finger and the thumb withdraw the trap of the cartridge by the parchment flap. The flap is slightly bound to the cartridge by a thin band, which will tear by a lateral pull, and allow of the easy withdrawal of the trap. A very gentle downward pressure of the cartridge into the muzzle will suffice to keep it in its place, and prevent its being disturbed by the pulling out of the trap.

The trap, when drawn out, may be thrown away, and the ramrod is to be used to press down the ball and charge through the cartridge case, into the barrel, home. The ramrod is then withdrawn through the cartridge case, which may be thrown away, and the loading is complete.

The rifle should be loaded when at half cock, to ensure the penetration of the powder into the chamber.

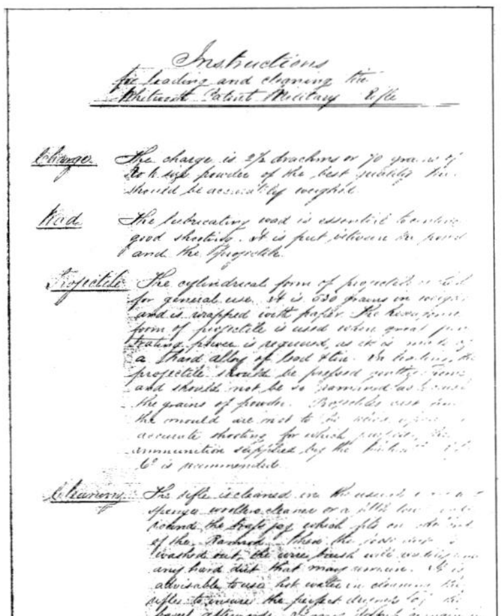
Instructions
for loading and cleaning the
Whitworth Patent Military Rifle

Charge. The charge is 2½ drachms or 70 grains of [illegible] powder of the best quality [illegible] should be [illegible] by weight.

Wad. The lubricating wad is essential to [illegible] good shooting. It is put between the powder and the projectile.

Projectile. The cylindrical form of projectile [illegible] for general use. It is 530 grains in weight and is wrapped with paper. The hexagonal form of projectile is used when great penetrating power is required, as it is made of a hard alloy of lead & tin. In loading, the projectile should be pressed gently home and should not be so rammed as to [illegible] the grains of powder. [illegible]

Cleaning. The rifle is cleaned in the usual [illegible] [illegible]

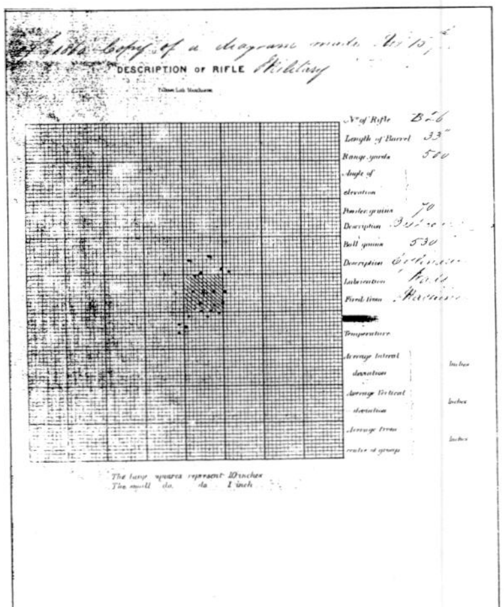

TINTS AND HIPS

This sounds like a foray in the colours of autumn, but it came to my mind as a spoonerism for 'hints and tips' and as I have written various chapters, the thought of an article on 'hints and tips' has hovered in the background. When I now bring it up and look at it, I find that a lot of them must already have appeared in what I have already written, with such examples as: ''Hill Sticks'' and ''Rifles''. There must, however, be some remaining, so let us have a go.

Blessed with feet that are very broad and with very high insteps, known by the family as 'bears' paws', wellingtons and their like have always been impossible for me. Any that I could get into or out of, left me slipping about inside, so in the old days it was genuine leather boots with tackety soles, none better but expensive then and very expensive now, and these have all suffered from the same difficulty, sooner or later they would develop a leak where the boot flexed just behind the big toe, and once they started to do this, I found no cure, and so was faced with wet feet for keeps or scrapping expensive boots which were otherwise no more than half worn. Now we have the answer, Norwegian boots with composite bottoms reinforced at the instep, and with fairly long leather tops. These with a thick wool felt insole are still lighter than the leather boot, and I feel that at last I have found the answer, but these (and many others) have no tab to take hold of and give a solid pull when putting them on. So to the first of my hints; take some tough webbing and one of the excellent modern glues and fasten on your own tab. This can be a loop glued inside and outside the boot, but I have it single glued inside the boot where it is tucked away, to be sightly in action.

I think I have tried all types of fabric in a garment from the old original ''Grenfell'' cloth, very good, waxed cottons, oilskins, and the latest technology ''Gore-tex'', but I prefer ''ventile'' even to Gore-tex. This was developed in the 1939/46 war to save the lives of pilots ditched in the Arctic convoys, dead in 10 minutes without protection from the cold seawater, it gave sufficient time for a destroyer to pick you up, good for morale. Ventile was developed for this purpose and did the trick. After the war I designed and was presented with a set of Ventile garments for seafaring in yachts, and very good they were, though too expensive to take off as a popular garment. The last of mine was consigned to the Pacific off New Zealand after about 20 years' service, so when they reappeared recently I just had to have these, and I find them good. Perhaps Gore-tex may have the edge for over-trousers, though with more rustle than Ventile. Underneath the lower man I don't mind the accusation of advertising ''Husky'' quilted underpants from knee to ankle, these are my answer. Climbing trousers are effective with double knees and double seats, an alternative to tweed, but here I have another hint. I find they tend to be short in the waist, and I have a 4″ extension sewn on, this makes them warmer, more comfortable, and avoids the feeling of the belt slipping off and their descending when you are crawling. Incidentally if your trousers have ever come down when you are crawling flat, it is one hell of a job to get them up again when you are absolutely snake flat. For the upper half of man I prefer a string vest as base, a thick shirt and thin sweaters in multiple layers rather than one thick one. It is easier to peel off and stow one or two of these, and if it is ''gey cauld'', 7 layers is about the most you can handle without being immobilised, and at the same time wear a balaclava underneath your deer stalker. If you have head gear that has not got built in 'tyer oners', bore a couple of discreet holes and make a lash on gear with spare bootlaces. So to the hands, and here I start with fingerless and thumbless mittens, not very thick, but for serious weather I have a pair of thicker mittens, knitted for me by a girl friend to my design. They come right up to the elbow, and the finger ends fold back to be secured on a pop fastener for the final act of shooting.

So we come to handling the binoculars, and here I have a different hint, I have a flap of thin leather on the binoculars (see photograph). When the binocular is hanging this flap is over the top and protects the lenses from dirt and wet. When you are using the binocular the flap covers your face from the eyes down and acts as an effective camouflage avoiding a white patch of face visible to the deer. If when crawling your binoculars tend to fall out into the peat, sew a length of strong elastic on the inside left front flap of your jacket, the binoculars tucked inside this will no longer fall out.

With flap.

You can now purchase an attachment for a rifle which provides 2 legs for a forward support. This has been well written up, I have seen it and talked to people who have used it, it works well. I have heard it criticised as being a little too short in the legs.

But ''Please Sir, Aie Sir, me Sir'', as the boy said in class, holding up his hand to catch the teacher's attention. Long, long before this gadget appeared I had made myself a tripod support for the rifle from a photographic tripod with the top removed and replaced by a padded rest (see earlier chapter). This was good, approved even by conservative stalkers in the Highlands, two of whom asked me to make one for them. It is useful to be able to clip this on to the person so that you don't lose it, or it doesn't fall out of a pocket, and for this purpose I find nothing better than the old strong paper clip. This came from fishing where you always have something that you want to attach and release singlehanded. Most of the expensive spring clips, bayonet locks and the like, really demand two hands for attachment and release. While we are at it, quite a nice cord attachment can be made by plaiting three pieces of string. Do you know that by cunning manipulation of eight strands of string you can plait a square shaped cord, neat and useful for some jobs?

Without flap.

So we come to a rifle cover; there is always an argument, when the weather is fine, do you bother with a cover for the rifle? If you have one is it padded or not with the argument about holding the damp and difficulty in drying, but in any case it must be easy to remove the rifle quickly and silently. Feeling slightly dissatisfied with these professional articles, I cast about and now use an air inflatable case which zips from both ends to the centre, and I find that this has many advantages; it is a splendid protection for the rifle in a motor car and when travelling. You can carry the rifle by its own sling projecting from the slot formed by not quite shutting the two zips on the case. On the hill you have it virtually without air in it, and its final bonus is that you can open it out and lie on it with or without air inflation when waiting on in a wet location, and even use it as a cushion in a high seat.

Turning to rifles, have I talked about the virtues of a broad trigger? I will not have a set trigger, either single or double, particularly for red deer stalking, I think it is dangerous with cold wet fingers, and it is one more thing to think about and it can be dangerous. I have actually encountered a stalker who all but lost his life, a client behind him after a successful shot, accidentally set the hair trigger as he reloaded, and as he lifted the rifle it went off, the bullet literally went through the hair of the stalker in front. I know how popular the hair trigger is on the continent, but there surely it is associated with shooting roe deer from high seats, a very different environment. On the contrary, a broad trigger gives a subjective feel of a lighter pull as it spreads the pressure over a greater area, while the actual trigger pull cannot be better than that you find on the first trigger of a best gun. In figures it might be just over three pounds.

Then we come at last to the telescope sight, tape to the rear end of the telescope a pad of foam rubber; when you mount the rifle, the end of this soft rubber just touches your forehead above the eye, and with this touch you know without any fumbling that the eye relief is correct and the eye concentric with the scope. The effect of this pad is also useful in excluding top light from the telescope and avoiding dirt and wet on the ocular lens.

I am quite sure that as soon as I lay this chapter down, I will have thought something up, but there is no harm in that, and what fun it is to try and develop ideas of your own. An untidy worker, I admit that the house tends to get littered with papers and bits and pieces. My wife, exasperated, has been known to say: ''Why can't you leave things alone like everybody else''? This is a perfectly reasonable point of view. Do not, and I repeat, do not try and explain why you do it, you will get nowhere, better to retire to your study and brood quietly by yourself on your ''Tints and Hips''.

A MacNAB AT 90

Around 1912, the well-known author John Buchan, wrote a cracking good yarn which always sticks in my mind as: ''Doing a MacNab''.

Against self-imposed Handicaps, two bored gentlemen with sporting proclivities, undertook to poach a grouse, a stag and a salmon, and the yarn describes the adventures that resulted. Ever since there has been sporadic interest in this, and getting a grouse, a stag and a salmon in the day in whatever circumstances, had been referred to as ''Doing a MacNab''. Keeping as I still do, a Project Book, which includes objectives far beyond time probability at my age, up came the idea of ''Doing a MacNab'' at 90. The idea came back again and again, and I began to formulate the project. Around my 90th birthday in September 1991, not necessarily in one day, the project would be to drive up to Scotland in a 90 year old motor car, shoot a grouse with a 90 year old gun, kill a stag with a 90 year old rifle, and take a salmon with a 90 year old rod. I think this might make the Guinness Book of Records, though that would not be an objective in itself. How then should I set about it? I should enlist the help of my son Mark to drive to Scotland in the Sheffield Simplex which would be 81 years old. I might indeed settle for Shap as a suitable objective, though it is in England. I should enlist the help of David with his German short-eared pointer Wilf. I can rely on Wilf to find, point and hold grouse while I come up and get in position. My weapon I think would be a Lancaster 14 bore, smooth oval bore of 1863. Although a rifle, this weapon throws a good, even, but rather wide pattern with shot, and with a little attention to head space it has been proved for smokeless powder and can take Italian made 14 bore gun cartridges.

Turning to the stag, the best weapon would be a Holland and Holland ·375 Magnum which I have and for which I have a 1X 4X telescope, heavy metal but dead certain and easy on my eyes. This weapon, however, is about 1920 and so only some 70 years old. One alternative would be a Webley and Scott Double ·500 of about 1895, again heavy metal, but all the more certain, this time with the handicap for my old eyes of open sights, which I should adjust to my own pattern as I did when stalking in Africa. Here I should rely on John Reeside, my old stalker friend to locate a stag in a suitable position, take me up to within my stalking capabilities in the Argocat, and so complete the job. I will not despise having one of my friends with me and covering me with a modern rifle in case anything went wrong, purely for the sake of the beast concerned.

So to the salmon, here we are far less predictable, but surely the river Eden might be a good prospect and it would be easier for me to take reaches of the river where a boat can be used. I shall rely on Mark's experience here, but I know the 90 year old rod is available, it is hanging up in the country hotel where I have often stayed in that area, it could be borrowed for the occasion, though I think I should use a modern reel and line.

Well, there we are, what fun to think about this even if it doesn't come off; it is a splendid thought and an encouragement. I shall do it if I can and here's hoping that it might after all be possible.

WENT THE DAY BADLY

For various reasons this stalking venture was a rather special occasion. It was my first time out on the hill with a rifle after a bad motor accident. Recognising the limitations quite apart from age, I realised that I should be confined to the rather lucky stalk which was short in the approach walk, not too much crawling and so forth. I had tested my rifle at hime and knew that I could handle it in spite of a wrist not yet fully up to strength. For this and other reasons I asked Nicholas to come with me. Forty years younger, I had introduced him to stalking and kitted him up with a rifle some years before and he had stalked with me more than once on different occasions.

This time it was to be an estate where I had stalked regularly for nearly 20 years, not a thousand miles from Penrith. So you see us going out on a day at the end of September, with a very high wind and the threat of driving rain showers. First check the rifles, and the first mistake of the day; Nicholas had managed to leave behind my special 'sighting in' target, and the stalker's target I didn't like, a 4 inch white circle surrounded by a three inch black band on an area not much more than 15 inches square. This placed at about 125 yards and firing lying down with the rifle over a rock I estimated might give us a wind error of from 1 to 3 inches in the prevailing conditions. Nicholas first with his rifle, a BSA Monarch ·30-06. He had fired two shots at 25 yards at my house, apparently OK centrally but about 2″ low, but now after 3 or 4 shots we were all over the place. I had a try and put 2 shots 3″ apart 8″ low at 5 o'clock. The stalker had a try and put 2 shots 3″ apart in a different location, but complained about the scope. I had also found it difficult and on examination we now found that there was moisture in the scope. It transpired that after moving house and under Police constraint, the rifle had been stored in a steel cabinet bolted to the wall in a cellar, obviously damp had done its foul work on the scope and probably on the woodwork and bedding of the rifle also. Nothing to be done, put the rifle on one side and forget it. So we have a go with my rifle, my very beautiful rifle (see other article) calibre Winchester ·270, with a beautiful Zeiss telescope and Duplex reticule. 2 shots 9″ low at 5 o'clock, 3″ apart. This in my experience allowing for the wind correlated with 2 shots at home which had been central 3″ low. Up 12 clicks on the telescope, yes, we have it right, again 2 shots 3″ apart, 3″ right, 4 clicks left. Yes the bullseye. So off we go, but this had taken us over an hour. On the way up the rough road to the lunch hut in the van, we saw deer up the valley to the left, and when we had got the Argocat going, we went out to investigate. Stalking in from the Argocat we found something like 20 stags spread out on an open hillside over 200 yards; 4 of the beasts that we could take, a difficult approach with much flat crawling, but, oh dear! There were 8 hinds on an open slope with a completely commanding view 150 yards above the stags. After studying the situation carefully, including the wind, the answer was: almost hopeless, better abandon it, look elsewhere and go back and have another go at this later if we failed.

So we got into the Argocat and went up to the 'great rock' a wellknown spot from which to make a survey and spy over a considerable area. 'Yes', beasts including a possible stag, far off, looked difficult, but the only answer would be to go in and see what we could make of it. This one a job for the younger man, so off they went, Nicholas with the stalker and a young keeper who had come out with us. I remained with the Argocat to contemplate nature, watch deer through my glasses, enjoy the peace and think, I hope, noble thoughts. With prudent forethought I had brought an extra top layer and an extra bottom layer, and I put these on; it wasn't cold in spite of the high wind and driving rain showers, but I had a hunch that it would be better to conserve heat and spend most of my time in the shelter of the Argocat. After three hours I began to think: 'if all has gone well they should appear at any minute'. It had probably taken half an hour's hard walking before stalking the stag. At four hours I thought they should be returning if they had to, for example wait on for a lying beast to get up or had got pinned down unable to go in or in trouble with sheep. At five hours none of this would do and at six hours I passed the point of no return. If they were not back in half an hour it would be dark and difficult to drive the Argocat out. I now began to think evil thoughts, could some accident have happened? Surely not, but in that case surely one man would attend to the injured man, the other man would come back to me to fetch the Argocat. Suppose they did not come back in another hour, should I try to walk out? No it might be beyond my capacity in my present state, and if I were exhausted and out on the hill, the wrong thing in every way. Should I try to drive the Argocat out? No, unfamiliar I might hit a rock, get it bogged or even turn it over in a deep peat hag. What was the rule? Never leave the spot on the hill where other people know you to be. If you do so you are only compounding bad possibilities, and suppose I had gone out and they came back, they would be faced, after a long trek, with a long walk out and they would not have any idea where I was or the Argocat, or whether I was still with the Argocat. So to the ultimate thought; if something really serious had happened and they had not returned, what then? One answer only, make myself as warm and comfortable as possible in the shelter of the Argocat, sit the night out and wait for a rescue party in the morning. Not pleasant, would not do me a lot of good, but not critical, the weather was not cold enough to present a serious hazard, and I was well clad. In the event of course, I heard voices quarter of an hour later and the party returned. What would be their tale? I give this only in outline as I was not present myself. First a long walk out for half an hour, then difficulty in making the initial approach because of sheep. This surmounted a further approach, but tantalizingly about 100 yards beyond decent rifle range, the desired beast lying down, but again four beasts higher up commanding the approach. Nothing to do but wait on for a time, and then the only bit of good luck in the whole day, the four beasts up on the hill moved and went over the crest. It was now possible to crawl in to rifle range. Eventually the stag stood up, too much of an angle, wait a moment, now he turns, take him now, and Nicholas made a clean miss. Unusually he had the opportunity of a second shot a few moments later. This time a solid hit but the beast was still on its feet and the stalker who had seen this with his telescope reckoned the beast was mortally hit and should go down. Not good Nicholas, let us give you what excuse we can, an unfamiliar rifle, unfamiliar scope and my trigger much lighter than his rifle. Another difference, favourable this time, this rifle was fitted with my own gas flow muzzle brake and both Nicholas and the stalker had been astonished at the absence of recoil. I think the real answer was that Nicholas had fired something like a dozen shots that morning with no result other than to shake his confidence, he had not been able to practise at home and it was a long time since he had been out stalking. What followed was incredible, the stag could and did move. It never allowed them to get into range, one long shot at 300 yards, but the stalker, again unfamiliar with the rifle, also missed and with various difficulties they followed it for something like 2½ miles. They had reached the point of no return for different reasons, on the one hand it would be almost dark by the time they came back to the Argocat, now some six miles away as the stag had gone off in the opposite direction. Also Nicholas, though pretty fit, would certainly have had enough by the time they got back, and they began to worry about getting back to me, and getting out before full dark. So the ultimate disaster, a wounded beast which would certainly drop dead in the night, but which might well be difficult to find. A thing that should not happen but it does. Searching my long memories I think I lost one red deer and one roe deer, the stalker admitted I think, to losing two beasts, Nicholas so far had not lost one.

It was 8 o'clock before we came back to our lodging, Nicholas had had quite enough, I was glad to be in, it had been a long day for me although I had done so little. The evening dram did much to soften the impact of disaster, a good meal and an early bed. Went the day badly? Yes, very badly, it could hardly have been worse.

TWO DAYS ON THE HILL WITHOUT A RIFLE

September 1990 and time to make the accustomed foray to Shap Fell on the Lowther Estate with one or two cull stags as the objective, and this time again I would take a young man with me, the idea being that he would take longer, more arduous, difficult stalks, while I would be confined to shorter and easier opportunities if they offered, but danger threatened. I had recently had a complete eye check up, and this had revealed disturbing news, there was some deterioration of the retina due to age that could not be corrected. How would this affect me with the rifle? Try it and see. A check at home at 25 yards on both the rifle and myself was encouraging, the rifle was in good order and with 6 power magnification of the telescope I could see well enough. So up to the day, and out to the hill with my trusty young David in support. Entering by the customary road which led up to the lunch hut we prepared to check the rifles, but not this time, not here, there were beasts in sight which would be disturbed. So we backed out and drove 2½ miles to the other end and a site by the quarry where we could check rifles. David had checked his BSA Monarch ·30/06, but it took him several shots and some telescope adjustment before he was satisfied at 125 yards. My turn, and this was the moment of truth, yes, the target was clear enough and sharp enough, the bullseye was good enough, but oh dear! at this range the fine lines of the reticule were all bent and almost indeterminable indications. I might well put my bullets into 3″ on the target, but there is no target on a stag, and fearing the risk of a bad shot and a wounded beast, I made an instant decision that I would not use the rifle on the hill. So back round by the road and in again at the original entry, and before long we had a very good stag with a few hinds away down to our right, but judged too good so we left him and went up the track. Quite a lot of beasts now visible up the valley to our left, and John the stalker and David went off to see what they could make of this while I stayed in the van.

There had been a bad forecast for the day, the sky was low, showers threatened and there was a brisk wind, but so far visibility was reasonable. About an hour later David and John returned defeated, several attempts to get in to a cull beast had been thwarted every time by being completely overlooked by other beasts above them. So we went on up the track to the grouse lunch hut from whence they went out again to the left to approach the same territory and the same beasts from a different angle, still acceptable from the wind point of view and this time being able to approach from higher ground. After a wee walk I settled down to wait, but this time I had my reward, over the hill across to my left beasts started to appear, on they came, in format, not in a hurry, just gently moving of their own volition, mainly hinds, a few stags, difficult to tally as they were covering each other and moving about, but I made it about 34 beasts, the nearest perhaps 300 yards, an enjoyable kaleidescope to watch them for perhaps half an hour until they disappeared over a crest away up the hill to my right. Not long after they had disappeared, David and John came back, this time success. After a long and difficult stalk, a fairly distant and difficult shot had been completely successful and David had bagged a very good switch, good for the larder and a good cull from the hill.

On the hill with the Argocat but without the rifle.

Thus encouraged we had lunch in the lunch hut, heavy showers, and rain now descending, we argued the next move. Should we go out to the west to our right in the Argocat and see what we could find, or should we go back out, round at the other end with the object of coming back into the territory into which the morning beasts had probably moved. In the now bad weather this seemed a better option and nearer home, so we went round and in again. David and John went away up the hill on foot, forward again through the quarry and down the rough lane track leading to an abandoned old farmhouse. The wait this time was about 1½ hours, and they came back, again defeated, not this time by the beasts, but trying to get in, the cloud had come down and they had been completely isolated in the mist. After waiting a while they had been forced to come out and return.

That was the end of the day, interesting, and it could be judged satisfactory. David had to return south that night, leaving me for a bath, a dram, a quiet evening and an early bed.

The next morning John picked me up, and I was completely in his hands as to what he might do with me that day. Better weather, a little breeze, good visibility, the cloud higher and one or two bright intervals. I gathered his plan was to do a survey of his territory with a view to getting an up to date picture of the beasts and their deposition, useful knowledge for stalking in the next fortnight. Into wet Sleddale, and after a mile or so instead of continuing along to the last farm and beyond, we broke off to the right and went up into the hills, leaving the van and starting away in the Argocat. Almost at once we saw beasts. Every now and then we would stop and walk out to a crest or round a shoulder to have a spy. We passed through some territory that I had never seen, and going through a gate in the fence at one point, John said, ''I haven't been through this gate for at least three years'', and so we continued. Some of the going was not so bad, some was very rough indeed, and at last we came to the main out valley; well known and from which I had in the past taken many beasts, and then a strange occurrence. I had often been amazed both in this country and in Africa by the way in which beasts would tolerate a large, noisy, smelly vehicle, whereas they would have been instantly alerted by a couple of men walking in with rifles. So now a large, bare, empty, grassy hillside, below us there were 7 hinds, the vehicle was in full view, they took no notice of it at all, and we drove round them on three sides at no great distance, and still they remained placid and unconcerned; did this display another factor I have often suspected? It is well known in Africa that buck know instantly if a predator is hunting or not, is there something of the same facility in cases like this? Did those hinds know that we were not stalking? One thing is for certain, one man out of the vehicle with a rifle with no intention of closing in on them and they would have been gone like a shot. I wondered, but we shall never know.

So we came to the deserted farmhouse in the valley, and there we had our piece and coffee from the flask. While doing so I turned over in my mind a fantasy. How would a firm of house agents describe these premises, let us have a go: ''Desirable residence, a strongly built, old farmhouse, four up, four down and offices. Ample farm outbuildings, no electricity, no gas, water from the burn, outside sanitation, no mod. cons. Last inhabited about 50 years ago, would repay total reconstruction, approach by track on foot, by pony, or cross country vehicle only. Pleasant view of valley and surrounding hills. Situation, 6 miles from nowhere, 9 miles from anywhere. A perfect opportunity for anyone wishing to 'get away from it all'''.

Well, there you are, does it appeal to you? One wonders what life must have been like for the farmer's wife at the turn of the century. Enough of that, we were away again, and made a long circuitous return to our starting point, where we loaded up the Argocat on the trailer and prepared to make our way home at the end of the day. Do I remember a phrase when I was young? ''The outside of a horse is the best thing for the inside of a man''. There was a companion piece about the inside of a woman, I will not repeat that as some might not think it proper. However that might be and with unbounded admiration for the way the Argocat could cope with the most appalling obstacles and variety of terrain. It could be a very rough ride, you set your teeth, you hung on, and you hoped for the best. If, as can happen, you come to an abrupt halt hitting a hidden rock in bracken, you are flung forward violently and bang your head on the framework. The Scottish phrase for this would be: ''many a sair dunt''. I felt battered, bruised and tired at the end of that day. We had seen in all about 100 beasts, only about 20 of them stags, the remainder hinds, but the stags had included one royal, 2 or 3, 11 pointers, half a dozen good 9 or 10 pointers, smaller 8 pointers and lesser beasts. The rut had not started, stags were with hinds, but we saw no sign of activity and never heard a roar. I made the reflection which John did not dispute, that a similar survey in that same territory 15 years before would not have revealed more than 30 beasts, and hardly a stag amongst them. With the companionship and friendship that we had built up over nearly 20 years, we could discuss long term changes and developments such as this, and share a day like this with enjoyable and mutual understanding. So ended the day, we came out for a welcome cup of tea with John's wife, similarly an old friend and I can reflect: two comments thus came up in my mind, the first: how much I had enjoyed two days, two such varied days 'on the hill without a rifle'. The other, alas, the realization that now 89 with less than a year to go, I must abandon the thought I had had of a MacNab 90; sad maybe, but why complain, for 80 years I have had a good run and enjoyed my hunting, and I can still go out and enjoy a day on the hill.

THE "NOO"

Career Naval officers of the old school were so influenced by their early and long training for their careers that I remember a remark: "Are Naval officers really human?" Whatever truth or exageration may lie behind this was of course completely torpedoed by the influx of temporary gentlemen from all walks of life in the 1939/46 war, and I was one of them. One met some fascinating characters; I remember one, son of a high ranking Church dignitary, who on a guest night could display an incredible ability to chew up wine glasses. Another when we were stationed in Scotland used to exaggerate the difference between English and Scottish dialects and the need for a dictionary. This he extended into an even greater need for a Scottish/French dictionary, and on occasion he would develop this giving examples: "Bonne femme – Braw lassie, Banks and Braes, Mickle and muckle" and so forth, but this he said was not enough, colloquial expressions were equally important, such as "presently – tout a l'heure", and so to his closing and punch headline: "Le maintenant – The noo". At well over 80, time as I find it has changed significance, it may be true that appreciation of a period of time is in inverse proportion to one's experience of time. What an age a year can be to a child of six, how rapidly it slips past a man of 70, but I find tremendous importance attaching to "The Noo". I may be lucky after a long life of battles and accidents, all parts are still working, if at less speed and power, the eyesight alas, has failed for driving and the rifle but can cope with all outdoor pursuits without glasses. I still have my own gnashers, which is perhaps unimportant, and a scientific test of my hearing reveals that it is good for my age, but with a nasty gap caused by the many long years of shooting without ear defenders. Perhaps most important, the hand is steady, and the co-ordination of mind, hand and eye can still cope well.

So again "The Noo", there is the question: fishing in the spring? Yes no bother, but watch difficult wading. Grouse shooting – marginal, but hope for the best. Pheasant shooting, roe deer stalking, red deer stalking – time perhaps to lay down my spear. With the memory good, one has to perhaps resist the tendency to dwell overmuch on all the lovely memories of the past. If the mind is healthy, there is the pleasant tendency to remember the good times in preference to the bad ones, and so we come to the future. This when one was young was infinite, now one is conscious of limitation. Ignore this I think, as far as possible; continue to put items in the Project Book. If fate decides that they are never done, it is still good therapy. I remember the dear old Admiral when he was getting old saying: "If God is good, I would like one more passage in the North East Trades". I now stand where he did, and I also would like to sail the Atlantic once again. Without being precise on the date, it is a nice thought that I might climb the hill, and if I then drop dead with one of my life long friendly stalkers at my hand, how appropriate, and how much better than the drear possibility of decline. Almost inevitably there is the thought of what lies beyond: I have no great faith in harps and halos, and none at all in Hells bells and hot spots, nor do I go for transmigration of souls, though in parenthesis I cannot think of a happier life than that enjoyed by "Lark", the 7th of my labradors. I like to think that it would be possible to see selected scenes from one's life. How grand it would be to see and feel the wind, the rush and tumble of ocean seas and the feel of a yacht of your own design responding to your guiding hand. Gorgeous to look out from the top of the forest, "where the hills unfold". Above all I think I should like to see generations still to come, to watch them develop, to see them take to the hill, and learn a way of life, caring for the beasts.

"To watch with joy as each must learn
in his or her successive turn
"To Squeeze the Trigger Gently".

PRESERVATION AND CONSERVATION OF WILD LIFE

I feel there would be something lacking in this book if I did not make clear my position in the ever growing need for attention to this subject. In 90 years some things are a long time ago. I remember a Latin quotation long ago, which reads thus: 'Times change and we must change with them'. So it is that if one put back the time age clock, there are things that one would not do, or things that one would do differently. So in relation to the preservation and conservation of wild life, to this I would now add management as, in almost every case, man has interfered with nature and the environment, man has the responsibility of dealing with situations in the conditions that he has created.

In Great Britain there is an increasing area of Forestry, and increasing numbers of deer, roe deer and fallow, for whom the forest is the natural habitat, and red deer, adapted to open country but ready to revert to forestry where they can create enormous damage. There are also sika and muntjac, minor problems except that sika can mate with red deer. A very considerable problem has developed and the complication of the relationship of deer, their numbers and condition in relation to forestry (the age of the forest is vital), food supply, the environment, the growing interest of the public in the countryside, wild life, sport and the economy; one can also fairly include artists and photography.

In this discussion I think we can ignore the hunting of deer with hounds as a separate subject, usually confined to Devon and I propose to ignore the growing industry of the farming of deer in Great Britain, New Zealand and elsewhere.

Nobody is at odds with the farmer who, in general, tries to balance the herd with the area and the food supply. Trying to breed from the best beasts, maintain them in the best condition and cull the surplus to sell for food and profit. Surely we should attempt the same objectives in the wild? For the last 25 years I have not taken a beast out unless it was in a managed cull programme. For the last 20 years or so I have been associated with Ronnie Rose at Eskdale Muir in the development of his ideas for the management and welfare of deer in relation to forestry and modern conditions; I became an honorary ranger with his team. Ronnie Rose has had the opportunity of studying the state of affairs in nearly all countries in Europe, and his ideas have proved so successful that they are now being adopted and applied in an ever widening circle. Lectures and papers by Ronnie Rose are available; I am a disciple of his.

The sex ratio has to be established and maintained, the age ratio similarly, the climate, for example the needs of severe and mild winters. It is surely not necessary to say that poaching must be rigorously suppressed, not only for the obvious legal and social reasons, but in my mind more importantly because of the cruelty involved, and finally the fact that beasts are taken out regardless of age, sex or season. Poaching can destroy the management systems which are being applied to an area.

Turning to the world at large we had the horrifying examples of the past, to mention only three examples by land, sea and air, remember what happened to the bison, the sperm whale and indeed the herring and the passenger pigeon. Think of what is threatened at the present time, for example the red kite in Wales and the raptors, the rhinoceros in Africa, and the dolphin, that delightful small mammal in the seas and oceans. Surely the future is bleak unless wide international agreement can be achieved and enforced to prevent poaching and exploitation, to research and endeavour to maintain balanced populations. I need hardly add that I am now personally dedicated to these ends.

THE RIVERDALE FAMILY COLLECTION OF WEAPONS

Predominantly English Rifles

1. A representative Matchlock 1450 type – Japanese.
2. A representative Wheel lock 1550 type – Middle Europe.
3. A Lantaka bronze cannon 1″ bore South China Seas, circa 1600.
4. A Lorenzoni type flintlock repeating rifle – Ellis, Doncaster, circa 1650.
5. A breech loading flintlock rifle by Griffin, London, circa 1750.
6. A pair of flintlock duelling pistols – Nock, London, 1790.
7. A Rev. Forsyth patent double barrel percussion sporting gun, scent bottle locks, 1808.
8. A high power pump operated air rifle by Shaw, Manchester, 1815.
9. A W. and C. Smith double barrel percussion sporting gun, 1825.
10. Lyell, Aberdeen, double barrel percussion 2 groove deer rifle 28 bore.
11. Nock, London, double barrel, 6 bore 2 groove elephant rifle with gold decoration – Ceylon, 1830.
12. A Manton, London, single barrel percussion rifle, 8 bore, 1840.
13. A Lang Thompson patent 16 bore percussion collector's walking stick gun rifle, circa 1845.
14. A Scottish type belt dress pistol, circa 1850.
15. Three Armstrong Whitworth Manchester ·451 hexagon bore rifles: (1) A military type for test by the Danish Army; (2) A single bore sporting rifle; (3) A double barrel big game rifle. All percussion hexagon bullets ·536.
16. Lancaster, London, a double barrel 14 bore smooth oval bore rifle, breech loading 1863 with patent flat face cartridge, reproofed modern powder.
17. A Westley Richards, double barrel, breech loading pinfire rifle, 1865.
18. McCricrick, Kilmarnock, double barrel, breech loading ·500 bore tiger rifle, 1873. A. Henry barrels and rifling.
19. A double barrel breech loading, 10 bore elephant rifle by Rigby, 1875.
20. An Enfield Martini Henry breech loading sporting rifle ·577/·450, 1875.
21. Alexander Henry, Edinburgh, single barrel, breech loading, falling block rifle ·360, 1875, with 1½″ cartridge for roe deer.
22. A Purdey, London, double barrel, breech loading ·572 rifle, circa 1875.
23. A Tolley double barrel, breech loading rifle ·577/·500, Ipswich, 1876.
24. A Lancaster patent 4 barrel Howdah pistol ·476, circa 1880.
25. A Holland and Holland, London, rook and rabbit rifle ·380, circa 1880.
26. A Rodda London and Calcutta, double barrel, breech loading rifle ·450/·400 Express, circa 1880. A Rajah's tiger rifle, gold decoration.
27. Westley Richards Colonel Forsyth patent 1885, double barrel, breech loading 12 bore super magnum gun rifle, detached box lock. Explora.
28. A similar 20 bore Faunetta.
29. A Cape type rifle by Gibb, Bristol, double barrel, breech loading, 12 bore ·303, circa 1890.
30. A continental drilling double barrel, 16 bore 9·3 × 75 mm with Hercule lock, circa 1895.

(Continued)

31. A Webley and Scott, Birmingham double barrel, breech loading, ·500 Express box lock, circa 1895.

32. A Purdey single barrel falling block ·303 rifle, circa 1900.

33. A Rigby double barrel ·470 Express rifle, circa 1900. Fitted Riverdale double muzzle brake.

34. A Winchester rifle, circa 1900, 1896 type underlever ·30-30 repeater.

35. A Rigby game rifle sleeved to ·22 Hornet, circa 1900.

36. A Rigby 1912 type ·275 high velocity repeater, 1920.

37. FN Belgian International modern automatic target pistol ·22 LR.

38. A Sako Finland ·243 Forester bolt action repeater – modern.

39. A Weatherby U.S.A. ·22 LR semi-automatic – modern.

40. A Ruger U.S.A. No. 1 falling block ·25/06 modern.

41. Westley Richard bolt action repeater ·270 modern. Fitted Riverdale super muzzle brake.

42. BSA Birmingham BA repeater ·30/06 "Majestic" and BSA muzzle brake – modern.

43. Weatherby BA ·300 Magnum – modern.

44. Holland and Holland double barrel ·375 Magnum, 1912 type with telescope – modern.

45. Weatherby BA repeater rifle ·460 Magnum with muzzle brake and scope – modern. The most powerful big game rifle.

46. Webley and Scott double barrel 20B gun, box lock, modern.

47. A pair of Lang double barrel sidelock ejector guns, 1906.

48. A pair of Boss, London, double barrel sidelock ejector single trigger guns, 1921.

49. Ugartechia Spanish double barrel 12 bore sidelock ejector 2¾c – modern.

50. A ·22 LR rifle BRNO bolt action repeater – modern.

TOTAL NUMBER OF WEAPONS: 55

WORDS AND PHRASES DERIVED FROM OR ASSOCIATED WITH WEAPONS

Weapons have been so important to man in his development, way back to the Stone Age right up to the present day and into the future. Inevitably they have had an influence on the language. Without any connection with a glossary which I always find pretty dull, even if useful, I have put down at random some weapons derived words and phrases.

PHRASES

I shot my bolt.
I loosed an arrow to the air and it must fall I know not where.
A flash in the pan.
A quiver full.
Two strings to my bow.
Keep your powder dry.
Don't fire until you see the whites of their eyes.
Not by a long shot.
Spike the enemies guns.
Blown from the muzzle.
Stick to your guns.
Within a stone's throw.
Shoot from the hip.
Squeeze the trigger gently.
Hoist with your own petard.
A bolt from the blue.
A shot in the dark.
Lock, stock and barrel.
Son of a gun.
Praise the Lord and pass the ammunition
Draw a bead. (American)

WORDS

longbow
cartridge
harpoon
bunker
ricochet
drawbridge
mitreiulleuse
BSA
arsenal
kalashnikov
exocet
minute man
tracer bullets
rocket
flintlock
shell
grenade
artillery
rampart
maxim
wheellock
pinfire
sniper
magazine
castle
skirmish
Thomson gun
field fun
dagger
missiles
recoiless weapons
dynamite
obturation
crossbow
centre-fire
mine
slow match
salvo
portcullis
machine-gun
colt
recoil
bayonet
scud
trident
smokeless powder
incendiary
matchlock
rim-fire
mortar
bandolier
moat
bailey
lewis gun
Lee Enfield
sword
nuclear weapons
anti-aircraft
dum dum
shrapnel
battery
touch hole
a blow back
present arms
ground arms
sling arm
jezail (India)
muzzle brake
resleeved barrels
self-propelled bullets
sub calibre
carbine
side by side gun
revolver
bolt action repeater
half cock
detent
rimless
bazooka
trigger guard
muzzle energy
expansion
smooth bore
phalanx
the falling block rifle
chariot
spear
balista
throwing stick
Hitler's supergun
napalm
gelignite
the Forsyth patent Paradox gun rifle
tank
blue finch missile
Mauser
sabre
atom bomb
anti-tank gun
black powder
flak
multi rocket launchers
percussion lock
torpedo
lantaka
howitzer
parapet
gatling
Smith and Wesson
explosive
blitzkrieg
patriot
skua
fuel air explosive
sabot bullet
butt
a bullseye
six shooter
order arms
shoulder aims
trall arm
nipple
free floating barrel
tubed barrels
blunderbuss
volley
over and under gun
drilling (continental)
pistol
Brown Bess musket
automatic
flange
carronade
trigger
muzzle velocity
penetration
scatter gun
oval bore
Martini Henry
trajectory
sling
turret
boomerang
rifling
Hassam Iraq supergun
napthalene
Semtex
the "Cape" type gun rifle
sea dart
submarine
pump action
centre fire
the Darne gun (French)
Winchester patent underlever
repeater
bullet
ramrod
breech
safety catch
side lever
box lock
back action
firing pin
quarrel
dirk
bull pup rifle
peepsight
express rifle
cohort
navy
paratroop
troop
posse (USA)
batallion
brigade
regiment
platoon
holster
firing range
infantry
marines
grenadiers
Luger
super-imposed loads
FN type automatic
shot gun
Thompson sub-machine gun
gun carriage
wads and patches
chamber
top lever
under lever
sidelock
bar in wood
needle fire
skean dhu
broad side
telescope
rebounding lock
magnum rifle
army
airforce
squadron
commando
corps
division
army corps
company
cavalry
target
high seat
gurkas
fusiliers

WEAPONS AND ASSOCIATED DEVELOPMENT FOR 1,000 YEARS

Some significant Types, Inventions, Names, Approximate Dates and Periods

YEAR	DESCRIPTION
1000	Spear – importance declined but never ended, vide Zulu, South Africa. Sword – Importance declined, now mainly ceremonial.
1050	Bow – Held its own against firearms to 1650, continued for sport.
1100	Sling – Dying and almost obsolete. Arbalist – succeeded by cannon, circa 1450. Chariot – Dying as war weapon – see horse age.
1150	Galley – Dying – see sail age.
1200	Gunpowder – ?1250.
1300	Crossbow – challenged and paralleled the bow – ?1150-1650.
1350	Small Breech Loading Cannon.
1400	Harquebus.
1450	Larger muzzle loading cannon. Matchlocks – very important for 100 years, never died out. Japanese for 300 years and still found in Africa and India.
1500	Wheel Lock – Middle Europe, not military, died after about 100 years.
1550	Rifling – Middle Europe.
1600	Flintlock – very important, dominant to say 1800.
1700	Experiments with breech loading and repeating rifles.
1750	Brown Bess musket – British Army to 1855.
1800	Duelling pistols – French – to about 1820. Nock patent Breech ?1800.
1805	Sensation – Rev. Forsyth patent percussion type, dominant by 1820 to say 1860 – died about 1875. Some air rifle development.
1830	Sporting guns increasing. Big game double barrel rifles.
1850	Revolvers – colt needle fire, first breech loading and cartridge – Le Foucheux. Whitworth patent ·451 Hex rifled percussion Army trials.
1860	Army trials Martini Henry adopted 1867-1890. Lancaster oval bore rifles.
1863	Pinfire – died in 10 years. Dougal lock fast.
1870	Purdey bolt and thumb lever. Rebounding lock. The period 1850 to 1875 saw the most rapid development and innumerable patents, it was the middle of the steam age, say 1820-1920, first metal, armoured and powered ships. First B.L. and turret HMS Warrior. Locomotives challenging the horse and coach. Winchester Marlin USA under lever repeaters. Universal B.L. and C.F. cartridge. Choke bored guns. Express rifles. Rook and rabbit rifles.

Continued

YEAR	DESCRIPTION
1875	Farquharson falling block rifle.
1880	Maxim and Gatling, the early prototypes that became the machine gun.
1885	Col. Forsyth, India, patent gun rifle, Holland & Holland Paradox. Westley Richards – Explora. Cape type gun rifle – limited popularity, South Africa, typical 12 bore gun barrel side-by-side with ·303 rifle barrel. Drilling continental, millions sold, still popular, typical side-by-side, double barrel 16 bore, with rifle barrel beneath such as 9·3 x 73 or 7 x 57 mm.
1896	Winchester ·30-30 underlever repeater. Millions sold, still popular.
1900-2000	1900 was a starting off point for innumerable developments. The century to 2000 sees an ever accelerating rate of change, so extensive that only examples are possible. First we move from coal age to oil age, to atomic age. We move from iron age to steel age to alloy age. Telegraphy to world news by satellite. Photography through cinema, T.V. to holography. Aeroplane to spacecraft. Gun to intercontinental ballistic missile. Travel by train and ship to supersonic flight.
1900-1910	Aircraft – airships, sporadic development to date – Zeppelin R100. Automobile, cinema, X-ray, wireless.
1910-1920	First World War 1914-1918. Surely a war of the trench and the machine gun. First primitive air warfare, first tank, submarines.
1920-1930	Stainless steel, tungsten carbide (later used in anti-tank ammunition). Light alloys increasingly used. T.V., General tendency to higher velocities, smaller bores and lighter bullets.
1930-1950	Magnetic mine. Second World War 1939-1945. Surely the war of the tank, but air supremacy now vital.
1945	Atomic bomb, jet engine, radar, submarine and anti-submarine warfare, rockets, penicillin, nylon, terylene, napalm.
1950-1970	IBM missiles, H bomb, whole families of glues, paints, plastics, CRP construction, supersonic flight, carbon fibre, kevlar, titanium (Blackbird American high speed aircraft).
1969	First landing on moon. Hovercraft. End of the rifle, superceeded by quick firing weapons. Terrorists used Kalashnikov and Semtex.
1970-1990	Computers, advanced chip technology, Hydrofoil, SWATH, wave piercing catamarans, all potential weapon carrying sea craft, stealth bomb, stand-off bomb, space shuttle and fuel-air explosive.
1990-1991	Gulf War, surely the first war to be decisively won by air technology. Pollution, land, sea and air, global warming? Greenhouse effect. Fertilisers, pesticides, water supplies, oil pollution in sea.
2000 and beyond	What about the future? to do a modern Jules Verne or do we dip into the realms of science fiction? No matter, here are a few ideas: Power direct from controllable atomic fusion. End of reciprocating engines. All prime movers rotary. Cermet construction? Electromagnetic ship propulsion? General application of superconductivity. England to Australia travel in 5 hours. Hotol? Phototelephony? Spacecraft, space travel, space technology. Colonisation in space. Ultimate space weapon?

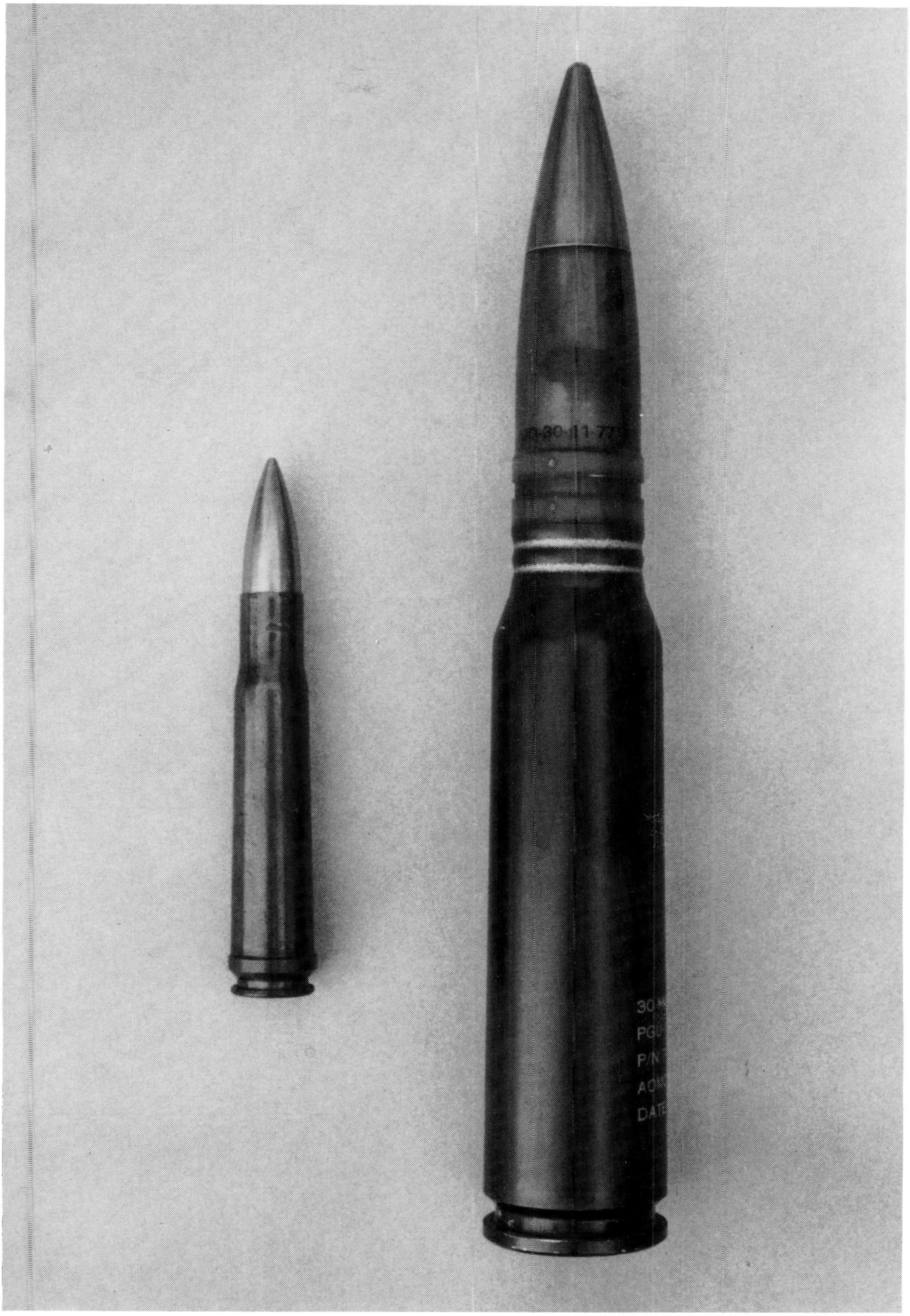

Yesterday and Today: The ·55 Boys Anti-tank rifle cartridge of the 1930s is dwarfed by the awsome 30 mm GAU-8 Anti-tank shell, used exclusively by the American Fairchild A-10 "Tankbuster".
The A-10's seven barrelled rotary cannon can deliver seventy of these high-velocity shells to its target in a single, one second burst!